ELECTRIC METERS

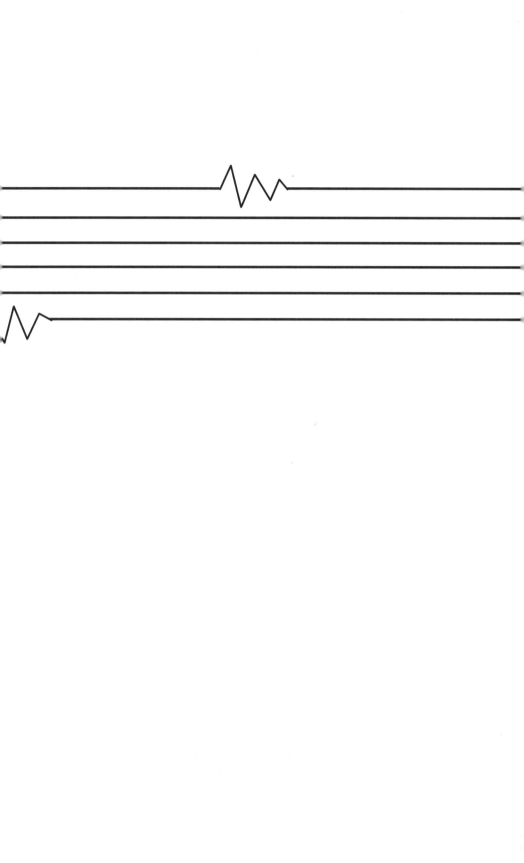

ELECTRIC

VICTORIAN
PHYSIOLOGICAL
POETICS

METERS

JASON R. RUDY

Ohio University Press • Athens

Ohio University Press, Athens, Ohio 45701
www.ohioswallow.com
© 2009 by Ohio University Press
All rights reserved

Printed in the United States of America
Ohio University Press books are printed on acid-free paper ⊗ ™

16 15 14 13 12 11 10 09   5 4 3 2 1

Library of Congress Cataloging-in-Publication Data

Rudy, Jason R., 1975–
  Electric meters : Victorian physiological poetics / Jason R. Rudy.
      p. cm.
  Includes bibliographical references and index.
  ISBN 978-0-8214-1882-6 (hc : alk. paper)
 1. English poetry—19th century—History and criticism. 2. Literature and
science—Great Britain—History—19th century. I. Title.
  PR595.S33R83 2009
  821'.80936—dc22

                                                          2009000019

For the women in my life, and most especially

Carolyn Williams
Emma Mason
Marilee Lindemann
Martha Nell Smith

and my mother,
Patricia Ann Rudy

You could see that the poems themselves, committed long ago to the Nile's papyruses, transmitted the Apollonian inspiration and breathed the music of the celestial lyre; indeed a sacred contagion excites the throng of readers with a like enthusiasm and the same ardor passes from one poet to engender inspiration in the heart of others, like the iron ring lifted up by the hidden force of a Magnesian stone that attaches to itself a long chain in a pendant bond and fastens them together with invisible hooks.

—Angelo Poliziano, "Nutricia" (1486)

A poem is energy transferred from where the poet got it . . . by way of the poem itself to, all the way over to, the reader. . . . [T]he poem itself must, at all points, be a high energy-construct and, at all points, an energy-discharge.

—Charles Olsen, "Projective Verse" (1950)

CONTENTS

ACKNOWLEDGMENTS

This project began at Rutgers University with the support and guidance of several dedicated friends. I thank first and foremost Carolyn Williams, long an inspiration in realms academic and beyond, and an ongoing source of wisdom, strength, and good fun. Barry V. Qualls, Jonah Siegel, Virginia Jackson, and Yopie Prins were among my first readers, and their insights and skepticism have made this a far better book. Kate Flint read an early version of my project and, at just the right moment, encouraged me to leave much of it behind and start afresh; I heartily thank her for that. Of the many other friends from Rutgers who remain important to me, I would like to acknowledge Tanya Agathacleous, Vincent Lankewish, and Rick Lee.

I am grateful for my colleagues in the English Department at the University of Maryland, College Park. Marilee Lindemann and Martha Nell Smith invited me into their lives, offering me a place to stay while I commuted for a year, and nothing has been the same since. To have such friends who also happen to be one's colleagues is a rare pleasure indeed. Other colleagues have been instrumental in the crafting of this book. I thank most especially Bill Cohen, my fellow Victorianist, who read the manuscript in toto and commented with wit and fine judgment on nearly every page. For reading individual chapters and pointing me in new and important directions, I thank Jonathan Auerbach, Tita Chico, Gerard Passannante, and Josh Weiner.

Many other friends have influenced this project and have made the writing of it a more joyful process. Charles LaPorte and Emma Mason shaped my thinking at every step, and continue to support me with their good humor and enthusiasm. Kirstie Blair, Linda K. Hughes, Meredith Martin, Ana Pareja-Vadillo, Natalie Phillips, Beverly Taylor, and Marion Thain each brought careful scrutiny to reading pieces of the project. For support more nebulous but equally important, I thank Margaret Carr, Amanda Claybaugh,

Rex Hatfield, Michael Olmert, Patrick O'Malley, Fred Roden, and Geoffrey Schramm. I am grateful for having met Nicholas Syrett, who no doubt will find these acknowledgments egregiously brief but will understand that they are deeply felt.

I would like to thank the General Research Board at the University of Maryland at College Park for providing a stipend for summer research in 2005 and the English Department at the University of Maryland for supporting a semester's leave in the fall of 2006, while I completed this book. I thank Grace Timmins at the Tennyson Research Centre for her careful assistance and for making the Tennyson archive a welcoming space to work. I thank the staffs at the British Library, Oxford University's Bodleian Library, the National Library of Scotland, and Princeton University's Firestone Library for facilitating my research. Rex Hatfield and John Logan at Princeton University generously helped with the book's images. I thank David Sanders at Ohio University Press for his enthusiasm and confidence; two anonymous readers for the press provided important guidance in the final stages of writing, and I am grateful for that.

Two pieces of chapter 3 were originally published in the journal *Victorian Poetry:* the first as "Rhythmic Intimacy, Spasmodic Epistemology" (volume 42, Winter 2004: 451–72); the second as "On Cultural Neoformalism, Spasmodic Poetry, and the Victorian Ballad" (volume 41, Winter 2003: 590–96). They are reprinted here in expanded form with permission from West Virginia University Press. The second half of chapter 5 appeared originally in *Victorian Literature and Culture* as "Rapturous Forms: Mathilde Blind's Darwinian Poetics" (volume 34, Fall 2006: 443–59) and is reprinted here with permission from Cambridge University Press. I am grateful to the editors of both presses for their permission to reprint.

To my family I owe more than I could ever say, having received from them the gifts of confidence and great love. I happily acknowledge here a lifetime of support from my parents, Patricia Ann Rudy and Glenn R. Rudy, and from my siblings, Michael and Elizabeth. I thank especially my mother, for reading to me every day as a child and teaching me to see the world as a place of beauty and pleasure. My love for great literature and the arts was in large part inspired by my grandmother, Gloria Rudy, who did not live to see me become a professor but would have been proud. My son, Aaron Minh Beer-Rudy, brightens most every day and teaches me about what is important in life.

ABBREVIATIONS

ACS	Swinburne, *The Complete Works of Algernon Charles Swinburne*, "Bonchurch Edition," ed. Sir Edmund Gosse and Thomas James Wise
ALT	Tennyson, *The Poems of Tennyson*, ed. Christopher Ricks
BA	*The British Album*
BCB	Blind, *Commonplace Book*
BPW	Blind, *The Poetical Works of Mathilde Blind*, ed. Arthur Symons
DPW	Dobell, *The Poetical Works of Sydney Dobell*
EBB	Barrett Browning, *The Complete Works of Elizabeth Barrett Browning*
GMH	Hopkins, *The Poetical Works of Gerard Manley Hopkins*, ed. Norman H. Mackenzie
OED	*Oxford English Dictionary*
PCP	Patmore, *The Poems of Coventry Patmore*, ed. Frederick Page
PE	Patmore, *Essay on English Metrical Law*
RSP	Robinson, *Selected Poems*, ed. Judith Pascoe
SDB	Dobell, *Balder*
SL	Swinburne, *The Swinburne Letters*, ed. Cecil Y. Lang
TL	Tennyson, *The Letters of Alfred, Lord Tennyson*, ed. Cecil Y. Lang and Edgar F. Shannon

Physiological Poetics

O for a Life of Sensations rather than of Thoughts!

—John Keats, letter to Benjamin Bailey (1817)

Man acts by electricity.

—Alfred Smee, *Instinct and Reason: Deduced from Electro-biology* (1850)

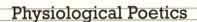EARLY FIVE HUNDRED YEARS SEPARATE THE FLORENTINE poet Angelo Poliziano from the American Charles Olsen, but the two agree in their understanding of poetry as a dynamic, charged mode of communication. Echoing Plato, Poliziano describes poetry as working like a magnetic stone, exerting its "hidden force" on readers; for Olsen, poetry "is energy transferred from where the poet got it . . . by way of the poem itself to, all the way over to, the reader" (see epigraphs to this book; Poliziano, 125; Olsen, 240).[1] The discerning reader confronts in both Poliziano and Olsen two possible—and somewhat contradictory—directives for poetic experience. The first treats literature figuratively and understands poetry to be *like* a magnet, *like* the transfer of energy. The experience of reading poetry in this model remains primarily an intellectual endeavor; the

individual who picks up Tennyson's *In Memoriam*, for example, feels the tug
of strong emotion because she has thought strongly about Tennyson's words
and the ideas and feelings they represent. The energy transferred from poem
to reader occurs here through the medium of the thinking brain. Not so for
the second model of poetic experience, which erases the distance between
the poem and the reader and understands poetry quite literally *as* magnetic,
a direct transfer of energy. In this instance, the reader of *In Memoriam* feels
Tennyson's charge of thought/feeling as it moves—magnetically, electri-
cally—from page to body. The reader remains mostly unconscious of the
transference of energy; she experiences the poem viscerally, intimately,
bodily. This second model of poetic experience, which locates the body as
central to the individual's encounter with a poem, rests at the heart of *Elec-
tric Meters*. This book tells the history of physiological poetics in the British
nineteenth century, focusing on the period between 1832 and 1872 as the
height of Britain's poetic engagement with bodily modes of experience.

Indeed, the history of Victorian poetry is in no small part a history of
the human body. Whether we look to Alfred Tennyson's "poetics of sensa-
tion," the midcentury "Spasmodic" phenomenon, or the so-called fleshly
school of the 1870s, Victorian poetry demands to be read as physiologically
inspired: rhythms that pulse in the body, a rhetoric of sensation that readers
might feel compelled to experience. Like Poliziano and Olsen, Victorian poets
turned to various manifestations of electricity—lightning strikes, electric
shocks, nerve impulses, telegraph signals—to articulate the work of physio-
logical poetics. The electrical sciences and bodily poetics, I argue, cannot
be separated, and they came together with especial force in the years be-
tween the 1830s, which witnessed the invention of the electric telegraph,
and the 1870s, when James Clerk Maxwell's electric field theory transformed
the study of electrodynamics. Because much of nineteenth-century electri-
cal theory had to do with human bodies, and specifically with the ways that
individual human bodies might be connected to one another, electricity of-
fered Victorian poets a figure for thinking through the effects of poetry on
communities of readers. Electricity, in other words, serves in the nineteenth
century as a tool for exploring poetry's political consequences. Scholars
have long identified the political work of Victorian poetry, just as they have
recognized the astonishing physicality of Victorian poetics.[2] *Electric Meters*
insists that these phenomena be understood as two sides of the same coin,

and it uses electricity as a model for reading that aesthetic and physiological conjunction.

More specifically, I argue that Victorian readers understood the connections between bodily and poetic experience in ways that took more seriously the unself-conscious effects of poetic form. "Physiological poetics" thus refers to the metrical, rhythmic, and sonic effects that, along with other formal poetic features, were increasingly imagined as carrying physiological truths. Whereas the predominant eighteenth-century model of poetic transmission privileged the mind's interpretive role (the brain acting as mediator between the poem and the individual), nineteenth-century readers gave credit to the body as an arbiter of poetic truths. Whether one ought to read Poliziano and Olsen figuratively or literally, then, depends on the period in which one encounters their texts. Readers prior to the physiological trends of the Victorian period were more likely to opt for figuration, to understand a poem's semantic presence but not its mimetic facility. In contrast, the Victorian poets and critics at the center of this study err on the side of the literal: the poem is itself a magnetic force, "a high energy-construct" (Olsen, 240).

POETRY AND ELECTRICITY

Through the 1860s and '70s, while devising equations to describe the physical relations among electricity, magnetism, and light—the consequences of which formed an important cornerstone for Einstein's theory of relativity—James Clerk Maxwell also found an occasional spare moment to compose poetry.[3] His verses are neither entirely serious nor of the sort that rewards extended reflection, but they remain suggestive of the curious, persistent interplay through the nineteenth century between poetry and electricity. Maxwell composed the following riff on Tennyson's "The Splendour Falls," one of the great lyrics from *The Princess*, in 1874:

> The lamp-light falls on blackened walls,
>   And streams through narrow perforations,
> The long beam trails o'er pasteboard scales,
>   With slow-decaying oscillations.
> Flow, current, flow, set the quick light-spot flying,
> Flow, current, answer light-spot, flashing, quivering, dying.
>   (quoted in Campbell and Garnett, 409)

Maxwell refers here to the mirror galvanometer developed in the 1850s by William Thomson (later Lord Kelvin), a device used to measure the flow of electric current through submarine telegraph cables. The galvanometer was crucial for transatlantic telegraphy, as it enabled the reading of very weak electric currents.[4] The sonic resonances of Tennyson's bugle song, "Blow, bugle, blow, set the wild echoes flying," thus become in Maxwell's hands the flow of electricity through a cable, which is then made visible by the "oscillations" of a "lamp-light . . . on blackened walls." Maxwell does not mean for us to take his verse too seriously; entitled "Lectures to Women on Physical Science" (part I), the poem is at least as concerned with the erotics of instruction as it is with physics ("O love!" the speaker apostrophizes in the third stanza, "you fail to read the scale / Correct to tenths of a division" [410]).[5] But if Maxwell turns to poetry to interject some play into the laboratory—"A little literature helps to chase away mathematics from the mind," he writes in November 1863 (quoted in Campbell and Garnett, 253)—many of his less scientific contemporaries did the reverse, turning to electricity and the physical sciences to inspire new ways of thinking about poetry. This book will show, among other things, why in the nineteenth century Tennyson's echoing bugle song might so seamlessly have been aligned with the pulses of an electric telegraph. More broadly, I demonstrate how the electrical sciences came to offer the Victorians a valuable framework for reading and understanding poetry.

Electricity has long been a privileged figure for those describing the ineffable qualities that make poetry *poetic*. Percy Shelley tells us that poetry "startle[s]" with "the electric life which burns within . . . words," and this electric life is precisely what enables poetry, in Shelley's view, to rejuvenate language and thought (Shelley, 7:140). This figurative yoking of electricity and poetry articulates some of the most pressing concerns of nineteenth-century poetic theory. Newly harnessed as a tool of industry, science, and communication (the electric telegraph being the most important of electricity's new uses), electricity serves as a touchstone for nineteenth-century poets reflecting on the complex interactions of thought, emotion, and physiological experience. From the earliest electrical experiments, electricity has been depicted as having physiological and noncognitive effects on those who encounter it (the shock of an electric current, say), and poets throughout history have turned to the same language of bodily shock in describing "lyrical" experience. "[L]ike a lightning flash," writes Longinus, "[the sublime] reveals, at a stroke and in its entirety, the power of the orator"; Longinus's primary example of such sublime power is the poetry of Sappho, which "gather[s] soul and body into one, hearing and tongue, eyes and complexion; all dispersed and strangers before" (Longinus, 23–24). Through the "shock" of a felicitously placed word, a compelling linguistic friction, or a moving rhythmic pressure, poetry transmits, lightning-like, new truths to its readers.

The following chapters will demonstrate that in different ways, Mary Robinson, Felicia Hemans, Alfred Tennyson, Elizabeth Barrett Browning, Gerard Manley Hopkins, Algernon Swinburne, and Mathilde Blind look to electricity to make sense of poetry's effects on the human body, distinguishing themselves from their predecessors in their overriding concern with physicality, with the material human body through which we experience poetry. Yet this physicality must be read within a larger political framework for nineteenth-century poetry and poetic theory. Whitman's "body electric" is only the most familiar of nineteenth-century poetic elisions between physiology and electricity, elisions that ask us to think about affinities between bodily affect and poetic communication, between physiological shock and intellectual absorption, and between individual experience and communal consciousness. In Maxwell's rewriting of Tennyson, for example, the telegraph's pulsing electric current represents a mode of communication already implicit in the original poem. Tennyson's "The Splendour Falls" transforms into poetic language, rhythm, and sound the echoing of a bugle song Tennyson heard over a lake in Killarney, Ireland, during an 1848 visit (H. Tennyson, 1:291–93): "Blow, bugle, blow, set the wild echoes flying, / Blow, bugle; answer, echoes, dying, dying, dying" (ALT, 2:231). This work of transformation—a transcription of sonic waves into written form—becomes in Maxwell's poem the translation of an oscillating light into a telegraphic message (the telegrapher "reads" letters from the to-and-fro swaying of the lamplight). Both poems explore the intersection of poetry with sensory experience and different modes of communication. The following chapters foreground such intersections of poetry, physiology, and the electrical sciences, suggesting how "physiological poetics" both depend on and enhance the phenomenon I call "electric meters," the complex interplay of poetic form and electrical epistemologies (ideas or structures of thought inspired by the work of electricity).

In focusing on the interplay of physiology and electricity, I remain true to scientific history. The human body is very much at the heart of the earliest electrical experiments, and it was often by means of their own bodies that scientists, from roughly the 1740s on, came to understand the nature of electric charges (Delbourgo, 25–30). I want to emphasize from the outset the distance in these experimental moments between bodily feeling (experiencing the electric shock) and thoughtful engagement with scientific ideas (thinking through electrical theories, hypotheses, and physical laws). Electricity becomes a compelling literary figure in part due to the gap between physiological experience and mental cognition. Consider, for example, the language Benjamin Franklin uses to describe an electrical shock, an accident that occurred during an experiment in 1750: "It seem'd an universal Blow from head to foot throughout the Body, and followed by a violent quick Trembling in the Trunk, which went gradually off in a few seconds. It was some Minutes before I could collect my Thoughts so as to know what was the Matter. . . . My Arms and Back of my Neck felt somewhat numb the remainder of the Evening, and my Breast-bone was sore for a Week after, as if it had been bruised" (letter to William Watson, 4 February 1750; quoted in Cohen, 94). Franklin does not lose consciousness from the shock, but at the moment of electrification his physical body takes center stage, fully pushing his active mind to the wings. Only after "some Minutes" can Franklin "collect [his] Thoughts" as he gradually awakens from his stupor, the point at which he becomes conscious of what happened. Franklin's physiological experience makes apparent the truth of electricity's vast power, yet only subsequently is Franklin's brain able to perceive the truth of his experience; the electric shock imposes a temporal gap between experience and cognition.

Franklin's mishap was accidental, but attempts to make sense of electrical shocks and their noncognitive effects on the human body were surprisingly common in the mid-1700s. Perhaps the most infamous of these experiments transpired in 1746, when Jean-Antoine Nollet, a French scientist who was soon to become the foremost European expert on electricity, amassed a circle of nearly two hundred Carthusian monks, each linked to his neighbors by a twenty-five-foot line of iron wire. When Nollet connected the ends of the wires to a rudimentary electric battery, a great communal spasm among the monks offered spectators one of the most important scenes in eighteenth-century science. "It is singular," wrote Nollet after the experiment, "to see the multitude of different gestures, and to hear the instantaneous exclamation of those surprised by the shock" (quoted in Heilbron, 312).[6] Like the temporal lapse between Franklin's physiological experience of the electric shock and his conscious realization of what had happened, Nollet here achieves knowledge only subsequent to and at a distance from the violent, noncognitive physiological experiences of the Carthusian monks. Nollet's experiment both demonstrates the communicative potential in electricity (the circuit of electrified monks might be thought of as leading ultimately to the development of the electric telegraph in the 1830s) and suggests the necessarily physiological nature of such communication.

Nollet's and Franklin's experiments also resonate with a mounting interest in the physiology of poetic experience. Writing in 1757, Edmund Burke frames his discussion of *Paradise Lost* with language that echoes, and seems to make use of, contemporary electrical science: "The mind" of Milton's reader "is hurried out of itself, by a cro[w]d of great and confused images" (Burke 1968, 62). Poetry communicates not by conscious thought but "by the contagion of our passions" (175). Those genuinely affected by poetry experience emotional shocks that, in their disjunction from conscious thought, seem not unlike the electric pulses enjoyed by Nollet's monks. "If the affection be well conveyed," Burke concludes, "it will work its effect without any clear idea; often without any idea at all of the thing which has originally given rise to it" (176). Burke's language looks forward to the poetics of sensibility that soon would dominate eighteenth-century aesthetics, imagining poetry as affective experience transmitted, via spoken language, from composing poet to reading individual. My point here is not to suggest that eighteenth-century science makes the physiology of poetic experience suddenly visible. Poetry has always, in various ways, been associated with bodily experience, from Longinus's exhortations on Sappho's sublimity, to Poliziano's magnetic attachments, to the "heavenly harmony" celebrated in Dryden's 1687 "Song for St. Cecilia's Day." But there can be little doubt that the poetics of sensibility push physiology to the foreground of poetic theory in new and increasingly demonstrative ways, setting the scene for the Victorians' all-out engagement with a poetics of the body. We witness this attention to physiology in reading John Stuart Mill's 1833 assertion that poetry represents "thoughts and words in which emotion spontaneously embodies itself"; poets, he concludes, are "[t]hose who are so constituted, that emotions are links of association by which their ideas, both sensuous and spiritual, are connected together" (Mill, 1:356). Across the nineteenth century, poets and literary critics grappled with this notion of embodied lyricism, from Arthur Hallam's poetics of sensation in 1831 to Robert Buchanan's 1871 critique of the "fleshly" school of poetry. In the many permutations of these thoughts, poetry remains a bodily experience, felt like an electric shock through and through.

It is as physiological experience that poetry facilitates the "association"—in Mill's words, which intentionally reference the associationist tradition of Locke, Hume, Hartley, and others—of "ideas . . . sensuous and spiritual." The very qualities of associationist philosophy that made Coleridge wince—that is, its privileging of the "primary sensations" and its skepticism of "an infinite spirit . . . an intelligent and holy will" (Coleridge, 75)—were for Mill and many of his Victorian peers fundamental to poetic practice in its ideal form.[7] This ideal remains in circulation today: for example, with Barbara Hardy's suggestion that lyric poetry "does not provide an explanation, judgment or narrative; what it does provide is feeling, alone and without histories or characters" (Hardy 1977, 1), and Susan Stewart's description of lyric creation as "the transformation of sense experience into words" (Stewart, 26). The continuity among these writers rests in their understanding of poetry as physiological and essentially noncognitive. Within this mode of poetic interpretation, a mode that came to dominate poetic practice in the nineteenth century, electricity most powerfully stands as a figure for poetic experience. But electricity is not simply a trope used to describe or to elaborate a poetic function. In the nineteenth century, electricity was the most prominent figure for a more widespread and pervasive interest in communication, from William Cooke and Charles Wheatstone's invention of the electric telegraph to Alexander Bain's analysis of nerve impulses in the human body. The nineteenth century, as John Durham Peters has argued, "saw unprecedented transformations in the conditions of human contact," which played out through new technologies for transmitting and recording information (Peters, 138). Recent work by Paul Gilmore, Richard Menke, Laura Otis, and Katherine Stubbs has suggested how profoundly and variously these electrical technologies, and the electric telegraph in particular, altered the Victorian literary landscape.[8] But this literary history has almost exclusively focused on prose fiction as the object of analysis.[9] It was inevitable that poets, too, would take an interest in these advances, and that they would come to think differently about their work as a result. Jay Clayton's recent insight into the intensely physical nature of telegraphic communication—a physicality that Friedrich Kittler, among others, overlooks—suggests in part why poets would have had an especial investment in this new technology; much as "the telegraph links hand, ear, and letter with remarkable power" (Clayton, 68), this book shows how Victorian poets ultimately came to see their work as physiologically based, as connecting intimately and instantaneously word, mind, and body.[10]

The Victorians' physiological approach to poetry manifests both thematically and, more important, as a part of poetry's formal structure. Rhythm in particular becomes a key element for poetic communication, suggesting through its stress and release a physiological give and take that, like a telegraphic transmission, connects individuals via bodily sensation. In this approach to Victorian poetics, I build on the work of critics who in the past decade have reinvigorated the study of poetic form, and drawn attention to the necessary interactions between form and the human body. Matthew Campbell's *Rhythm and Will in Victorian Poetry* (1999), for example, encourages readers to experience rhythm as "more than just a sound," to understand poetic impulses as permitting "the speaker to express an experience of the activity of the body". (Campbell, 18). Kirstie Blair's *Victorian Poetry and the Culture of the Heart* (2006) situates such bodily rhythmic experiences within the Victorian physiological sciences. Blair shows how rhythm pervades Victorian scientific discourse and comes to be understood "as an organic force, related to bodily movements and hence able to influence the breath or heartbeat of both poet and reader" (Blair 2006b, 17). Yopie Prins's work on meter has pushed our understanding of form in new and important directions, most especially by way of her notion of a "linguistic materialism" that allows voice to "materialize" in Victorian poetry "through the counting of metrical marks" (Prins 2000, 92).[11] These studies suggest that nineteenth-century advances in the physiological sciences had a particular influence on poets, who understood their work to be connected necessarily to the human body and its functions. Yet with few exceptions, poetry has remained peripheral to the recent surge of interest in literature and physiology. In Anne Stiles's fine collection of essays, *Neurology and Literature, 1860–1920*, for example, "literature" means almost exclusively prose, and the novel in particular.

Nicholas Dames's provocative inquiry into what he calls "physiological novel theory," though important as a focused reading of Dames's genre of choice, has implications beyond the study of the novel. In fact, the three Victorian theorists whom Dames identifies as central to physiological novel theory—Alexander Bain, George Henry Lewes, and E. S. Dallas (Dames, 9)—all made important contributions to the theorization of poetics.[12] Even when writing about essays explicitly on the nature of poetry—Paul Valéry's lecture "Propos sur la poésie" and George Eliot's "Notes on Form in Art"—Dames resists acknowledging that it was often to poetry that nineteenth-century thinkers turned when considering the connections between literature and physiological affect (Dames, 26–27, 49). In a way unprecedented in the Western tradition, nineteenth-century poets understood what Derek Attridge calls "the psychological and physiological reality" that poetic rhythm conveys to "reader[s] and listener[s] alike" (Attridge 1990, 1016). Recent studies in the field of cognitive poetics by Reuven Tsur and Andrew Elfenbein articulate in modern terms ideas that surfaced first among Victorian thinkers such as Bain, Lewes, and Dallas, among many others.[13]

The physiological thrust of Victorian poetics develops in tandem with, and in necessary relation to, a series of formal poetic innovations. Bridging the genteel refinements of neoclassicism and the radical austerity of modernism, the nineteenth century was a period of audacious poetic experiment, much of which has been glossed over and dismissed as either aesthetically deficient or atypical of the period. While critics have long recognized the importance of the dramatic monologue as a Victorian invention, comparatively little attention has been given to the period's metrical and rhythmic innovations. Those formal innovations that *do* get attention—Whitman's early nod toward free verse, for example, and Hopkins's invention of "sprung rhythm"—are most often identified as not belonging to the arc of nineteenth-century poetics (Hopkins especially has long been read as a "modern" poet, an anomaly of the Victorian period).[14] This blindness to the diversity of Victorian prosody has resulted in a proliferation of critical misreadings: a long-standing refusal, for example, to take seriously the contributions of the Spasmodic poets; an insistence that poets such as Hopkins and Swinburne somehow stood outside the general trends of British poetics; a resistance to perceiving the crucial role of Romantic women poets in Victorian reading practices.[15] From the metrical novelty of Coleridge's "Christabel" (1816) to

Coventry Patmore's midcentury attempts to bring classical quantitative verse into English, nineteenth-century prosody surprises with its creativity and its willingness to break with the often rigid formality of earlier periods.[16] The Victorians' formal dexterity must be read within the context of the period's engagement with both physiology and the electrical sciences. Within this broader historical and cultural context, the century's more outlandish experiments (Sydney Dobell's "Spasmodic" poetics and Patmore's quantitative verse) seem somewhat less outlandish, whereas a number of more familiar works (Tennyson's *Princess* and Barrett Browning's *Aurora Leigh*) emerge as more extraordinary than might once have been thought.

Electric Meters thus enters the ongoing conversation around physiology and literature to help make sense of the enormous shifts in British poetics that occur across the nineteenth century, and to explicate more specifically the cultural and political nature of these changes. It has often been suggested that Victorian poetry can be distinguished from that of earlier periods by poets' attempts to communicate differently, for example, via the dramatic monologue or the prose poem. More broadly, according to Isobel Armstrong, "The effort to renegotiate a content to every relationship between self and the world is the Victorian poet's project" (Armstrong 1993, 7). In the nineteenth century, there can be no greater figure for interpersonal communication—the negotiation of self and world—than electricity, and no greater manifestation of this phenomenon in literary form than poetic rhythm. Accordingly, the chapters that follow track the shifts in poetic theory, from the Romantic poetess tradition through to late-Victorian figures such as Hopkins and Swinburne, that engage both philosophically and formally with the electrical sciences and technologies. In positioning their work within scientific discourses, Victorian poets and poetic theorists negotiate the cultural and political dynamics inherent in artistic, and specifically poetic, transmission.

ELECTRIC METERS

The story I tell begins in the eighteenth century, with the "philosophical nightmare of muddled ideas, weak logic and bad writing" that has been called the literature of sensibility (Ellis, 7). Victorian readers looking to understand poetry's physiological effects often started in the late eighteenth century, when poets such as the Della Cruscans brought the human body—its sighs and tears and passionate thrills—to the fore of poetic composition. Sensibility has its origins in the body, as John Mullan has argued: "'Sensibility' was a word that began by referring to specifically bodily sensitivities, and only in the mid-eighteenth century began commonly to denote an emotional, and even moral, faculty: 'Sensibility' with a capital 'S'" (Mullan 1997, 427).[17] My first chapter, "The Electric Poetess," uses the trope of electric charge to read the poetry of Mary Robinson, who wrote at the peak of eighteenth-century sensibility and participated in the Della Cruscan movement, and Felicia Hemans, a late-Romantic contributor to the poetics of sensibility. The electric connections within and among individuals as they are imagined by these women poets take up in diverse and productive ways the "language of feeling" heralded by Hume, Richardson, and others. Unlike Wordsworth, whose directive to "recollect[]" passionate feeling "in tranquility" (Wordsworth, 460) points to a necessary distance between the feeling body and the thinking poet, Robinson and Hemans suggest a less comfortable balancing between physiological intimacy and thoughtful communication. This uneasy balancing would come to haunt poets in the later nineteenth century. Robinson and Hemans are also necessary figures insofar as their works make explicit the political consequences of physiological poetics. In different ways, Robinson and Hemans consider how poetry might function as a model for democratic citizenship: how the experience of reading a poem might allow an individual to connect intellectually and emotionally to other individuals who share in that poetic experience. Electricity offers both poets a figure for the sort of connection poetry might provide: an intellectual shock of recognition, the sudden realization of communal sympathy.

The remaining four chapters concentrate primarily on the forty-year period separating Alfred Tennyson's "sensational" poetics of the 1830s and the uproar in the 1870s over Dante Gabriel Rossetti, Algernon Swinburne, and the "fleshly" school of poetry. Much as Arthur Hallam, following in the empiricist tradition of Locke, Hartley, and Hume, had argued in 1831 that "sound conveys . . . meaning where words would not," Robert Buchanan opens his 1871 screed against Rossetti deploring those who value "poetic expression" over "poetic thought" (Hallam, 96; Buchanan, 335). Both critics address essentially the same point, though from opposite argumentative positions; that is, reading poetry in the mid-Victorian period seems no longer an intellectual endeavor, but a full-bodied, physiological experience.

In this period, electricity advances from being primarily a trope, as it is in the main for Robinson and Hemans, to representing a new, physiological mode of poetic transmission. And whereas Robinson and Hemans each understand the political implications of electrical poetics, only in the early Victorian period—in the years following the 1832 Reform Bill and the advent, via Chartism, of a strong and vocal working class—do poets realize the full political potential of poetic form. My work here builds on Isobel Armstrong's study of the politicization of poetic sensibility in the 1830s, as well as Matthew Reynolds's more recent account of political consciousness in Victorian poetics (Armstrong 1993, 25–111; Reynolds). I argue especially for the importance of human physiology within this political and aesthetic dynamic. With increasing enthusiasm, Victorian poets came to understand the necessary connections between bodily sensation and poetic experience. Tennyson's poetry of sensation evolves naturally into the Spasmodic poetics of the 1850s—the subject of chapter 3—which in turn inspire the intensely physiological experiments of Hopkins and Swinburne in the 1860s and '70s discussed in chapters 4 and 5.

Chapter 2, "Tennyson's Telegraphic Poetics," situates the poet's 1847 "medley" *The Princess* within this highly politicized poetic discourse, showing how the poem's hesitant engagement with both the new electrical sciences and the poetics of physiological sensation reflects a similarly hesitant approach to working-class culture following the uprisings of the 1830s and '40s. I argue that Tennyson models the poem's structure—a succession of male storytellers, each of whom takes a turn contributing to the tale—on a circle of girls who electrify themselves, much like Nollet's monks, in the poem's opening pages. The figure of a human electric circuit inspires Tennyson to meditate on the relation between physical bodies and aesthetic form, while the political dynamics of the poem's narrative connect that physiological structure to some of the most important social questions of the day, including the Victorian struggles for and against class and gender equality. The chapter puts Tennyson in dialogue with his contemporary, Thomas Hood, as well as with some popular writers on the telegraph, to develop more fully the interplay of class and sensation suggested in my reading of *The Princess*.

The central chapter of the book, "Rhythms of Spasm," concentrates on a little-known group of working-class poets who came to prominence at the midpoint between Tennyson's sensationalism and Rossetti's so-called flesh-liness. Labeled the "Spasmodic" school by their detractors, Sydney Dobell and Alexander Smith conducted important experiments through the 1850s on the communicative potential of poetic rhythm. Their poetry and poetic theories, largely overlooked in the present day, were immensely popular and influential in the 1850s. I argue that Dobell's 1853 epic poem *Balder* couples a theory of bodily sensation, inspired by the electrical and physio-logical sciences, with a formal model of poetic composition. Rhythm for Dobell expresses metonymically the physiological conditions of the human body—its pulses either harmonize with or strain against the throbbing of our physical beings—and poets communicate most readily through a reader's sympathetic and unmediated experience of these rhythmic im-pulses. Only with the Spasmodic poets does the physiological shock of elec-tricity approach literal enactment in poetic form. Like the sensation fiction that followed closely on the heels of spasmody, Dobell's poetry is meant to be felt like a literal, bodily shock. Precisely because of the intimacy imag-ined between the working-class poet and the bourgeois reader, Spasmodic poetry was seen to threaten Victorian middle-class cultural values. In the second half of the chapter, I examine the conservative turn against Spas-modic poetics, a response manifested formally in renewed attention to met-rical structure. Tennyson's *Maud* occupies a middle ground in this debate, both incorporating elements of the Spasmodic style and suggesting, through the insanity of the poem's speaker, the ultimate failure of unfettered physio-logical poetics.

The post-Spasmodic period witnessed a surge of interest in prosody, a widespread effort to understand in objective terms how poetry works; the later decades of the century were influenced as well by the new "dominance of the nerves" in popular scientific discourse (Blair 2006b, 227), which grounded the physiological effects of poetry in tangible, scientific evidence. Chapter 4, "Patmore, Hopkins, and the Uncertain Body of Victorian Po-etry," focuses on two of the more extreme experimenters in this period: Coventry Patmore and Gerard Manley Hopkins. The study of Patmore's poetry and poetic theory has been for the most part occluded by what read-ers know of his most popular work, *The Angel in the House* (1854 and 1856). But Patmore's 1857 *Essay on English Metrical Law* and his 1877 volume of odes, *The Unknown Eros*, show Patmore to be more innovative, and more interesting, than most critics have allowed. His work is especially important as a tonic to the physiological extremes of his contemporaries, as Patmore strove to maintain an intellectual reserve against the bodily pull of poetic rhythm. The chapter closes with a reading of Hopkins's "Wreck of the Deutschland" (1876), situating Hopkins's "sprung rhythm" as an elegant refinement, unrecognized by modern critics, of Spasmodic poetics. Hopkins works to abstract or spiritualize the intensity of bodily shock, making electricity a figure for religious transcendence as well as aesthetic transmission.

The fifth and final chapter, "Rapture and the Flesh, Swinburne to Blind," examines the work of two late-Victorian poets—Algernon Swinburne and Mathilde Blind—and what I call the poetics of rapture. "Rapture and the Flesh" continues the work of chapter 4 in thinking through post-Spasmodic physiological poetics, here with attention to an understanding of rhythm as unifying not only individuals, but also the living world in its entirety. Inspired by the electric field theory developed at midcentury by Michael Faraday and James Clerk Maxwell, as well as by Darwin's insights into the place of rhythm in the evolution of species, British poets reconsidered the place of individual physiological experience within their communities and, widening the view, within the universe as a whole. I read Swinburne's "By the North Sea" (1880) and "The Lake of Gaube" (1899), and Blind's *Ascent of Man* (1889), among other poems, as meditations on the possibility for "rapture"—that is, physiological, emotional, and spiritual connection—in the modern, post-Darwinian, post-Maxwellian world. In the aftermath of spasmody, these poets depict electricity and poetic rhythm as unruly entities that often keep individuals apart from one another, failing to act—as Tennyson and Dobell, for example, had imagined—as intimate, connective tissue among human individuals.

Electric Meters concludes with an examination of spiritualist poetics, a phenomenon that stretches across the nineteenth century but peaks, along with spasmody, in the 1850s. Electricity and rhythmic experience took on entirely new and fantastic meanings as a result of the spiritualist movement. Several poets at midcentury claimed the ability to communicate with the dead through rhythmic patterning, a formal elaboration of what was popularly called "spirit-tapping." In the preface to her 1864 *Poems from the Inner Life*, for example, Lizzie Doten describes how she would "catch the thrill of the innumerable voices resounding through the universe, and translate their message into human language" (Doten, viii). Spiritualist poetry especially exemplifies the Victorian desire for connectedness, the seeming need to communicate, as Tennyson put it, beyond "[v]ague words" and in a language understood universally, in the human body (*In Memoriam* XCV; ALT, 2:413). In canonical poetry, too, most notably in the work of Elizabeth Barrett Browning, we can see the spiritualist ideal playing out as a fantasy of connectedness that moves beyond individual bodies (as in the Spasmodic model), beyond the living world (as in Swinburne's and Blind's poems), and encompassing the vastness of all things physical and metaphysical. As the flip side of the scientific culture to which most of this book makes reference, spiritualism offers a fitting afterthought to the preceding chapters, a way of reframing electric models of poetic communication.

Like nerve impulses that seem universal in their experience, the rhythmic pulsing of electric meters inspired poets to consider how, or whether, language might be reconfigured to vibrate in tune with all human individuals. Nineteenth-century poets looked to electricity in anticipation of a language that might render indistinct the boundaries between sound and sense, between emotion and thought, and—perhaps—between individuals isolated in the modern world. Keats's early call for "a Life of Sensations rather than of Thoughts!" echoes throughout the century as a fantasy of interpersonal connection and communication. *Electric Meters* examines the enthusiasms and, ultimately, the frustrations inspired by this utopian project.

The Electric Poetess

ROBINSON, HEMANS, AND THE CHARGE OF ROMANTICISM

Striking the electric chain wherewith we are darkly bound[.]

—Byron, *Childe Harold* (1818)

I T WAS ELECTRICITY'S SEEMING UNIVERSALITY OF EXPERIENCE that, from the beginning, most inspired eighteenth-century thinkers. Electrical shocks affected everyone, regardless of age, sex, race, or class. In sentiments echoed by many of his contemporaries, for example, Joseph Priestley writes in his *History and Present State of Electricity* (first edition, 1767) that "the electric fluid is no local, or occasional agent in the theatre of the world. Late discoveries show that its presence and effects are every where, and that it acts a principal part in the grandest and most interesting scenes of nature. It is not, like magnetism, confined to one kind of bodies, but every thing we know is a conductor or non-conductor of electricity" (Priestley, 1:xiv). Richard Lovett makes a similar claim in his 1774 *Electric Philosopher*: "The electric fluid . . . appears to be a universal agent in the strictest sense, so

as to occupy and fill all space, not only all free and open spaces, but the minut-
est vacuities and interstices or powers of the most compact and solid bodies"
(quoted in Ritterbush, 18). Historians of science have shown how Enlighten-
ment thinkers turned to electricity to support universalizing ideals in every-
thing from metaphysical philosophy to political theory. Benjamin Franklin's
electric experiments, for example, were linked in Britain and France to his
democratic politics and the founding of the United States (Riskin, 134–36;
Fulford, Lee, and Kitson, 179–97).[1] Thomas Simmons Mackintosh's *"Electri-
cal Theory" of the Universe*, a faux-scientific treatise from 1838, represents the
general opinion among the British public, consistent into the early Victorian
period, in its endorsement of "ONE UNIVERSAL LAW, that shall comprehend
every action and re-action, both physical and moral" (Mackintosh, 5). Em-
ploying a language of vibration dating back to David Hartley's 1749 *Observa-
tions on Man*, Mackintosh proposes electricity as the governing force behind
practically everything in the universe:

> The unity of this universal science will be rendered still more evi-
> dent if we further consider, that the motion of all inanimate matter,
> of atoms, worlds, and systems of worlds, is due to the action and
> re-action of the ultimate forces of attraction and repulsion, and
> that the motions or actions of all animated beings, of individuals,
> families, communities and nations, in short, *all animated nature*, is
> due to the action and reaction of the same ultimate and universal
> forces, through the sensations, a force of moral attraction being
> manifested towards such objects as give pleasure, and the moral
> repulsion towards such as give pain. (53; emphasis mine)

Electricity for Mackintosh links the moral to the physiological. In this
utopian vision, electricity reveals the interconnectedness of all human beings,
thereby supporting not only a hackneyed version of Romantic principles
but also, as Iwan Rhys Morus has suggested, the socialist ideals that Mack-
intosh and others connected to the nascent Chartist movement of the 1830s
(Morus, 135–38).

Whether poetic impulses could have a similarly universal effect remained
a question, however. That is, could words rhythmically arranged on a page
communicate with electrical universality? In her preface to *Sappho and Phaon*,
her 1796 sonnet sequence, Mary Robinson—actress, novelist, poet, and

sometime consort to the Prince of Wales—suggests that "different minds are variously affected by the infinite diversity of harmonious effusions." Nonetheless, Robinson continues, "there are, I believe, very few that are wholly insensible to the powers of poetic composition" (RSP, 147). Like the simultaneous shock felt by the monks connected in Nollet's circuit (see introduction to the present volume), poetry is seen as forming communities through affective experience (Nollet had wondered at "the multitude of different gestures" taken on by his electrified monks but also "the instantaneous exclamation of those surprised" [quoted in Heilbron, 312]). Though distinct in their responses, both the monks and Robinson's readers share a simultaneity of experience that links them in a network of feeling, a kind of "sociability," as John Mullan puts it, "which is dependent upon the communication of passions and sentiments," and which literary critics have long identified as characteristic of eighteenth-century writing (Mullan 1988, 2).[2]

Whereas Robinson emphasizes the potential in verse for communal experience, her contemporary Hannah More takes a more circumspect approach. More had at one time tutored the young Robinson, but as an advocate for political and cultural conservatism she came ultimately to "resent[] her connection with her old pupil," the sensational and politically radical "Perdita," as Robinson was called (Byrne, 8). In her 1786 poem "The Bas Blue," More points to the limits of communal understanding while describing the "circulation" of "Conversation" among sympathetic thinkers within her intellectual set:

> In taste, in learning, wit, or science,
> Still kindred souls demand alliance:
> Each in the other joys to find
> The image answering to his mind.
> But sparks electric only strike
> On souls electrical alike;
> The flash of intellect expires,
> Unless it meet congenial fires.
>
> (More, 1:17)

Like the electricity that darts from hand to hand in Nollet's circle, a "flash of intellect" connects the thinkers in More's salon as ideas pass from one to

another. But More suggests a limited, less universal experience of her intel-
lectual "sparks." Whereas everyone experiences Nollet's electric shock, only
"kindred souls" will enjoy the sympathetic "alliance[s]" of More's clique. More
here aligns herself with the culturally conservative strain of eighteenth-
century sensibility, those who believed, as G. J. Barker-Benfield observes,
that "[d]egrees of sensibility . . . betokened both social and moral status"—
that, for example, a man of high social standing would by nature exhibit a
more powerful response to a scene of pain than an uneducated worker
(Barker-Benfield, 9).

It is no coincidence that the poetics of sensibility emerged at roughly
the same time scientists such as Nollet were publicizing their electrical ex-
periments on the human body. Inspired by the influence of Locke and
like-minded empiricists, both poets and scientists turned to sensory experi-
ence as the most reliable source of knowledge. Hume writes in his *Enquiry
Concerning Human Understanding* (1748) that only through "feeling and
sensation" can "an idea can have access to the mind" (Hume, 98). Poets and
scientists of the late eighteenth century took this maxim to heart, engineer-
ing both literary works and scientific experiments that isolated the human
body and its myriad feelings and sensations. But as the above passages from
Robinson and More suggest, the question remained whether electrical and
poetic effects would always act on individuals in the same way. Like any
language, the effectiveness of poetry as a mode of communication depends
at some level on the universality of its experience. Susan Stewart has written
that, "[a]s metered language, language that retains and projects the force of
individual sense experience and yet reaches toward intersubjective meaning,
poetry sustains and transforms the threshold between individual and social
existence" (Stewart, 2). In this chapter, I historicize the "threshold," as Stew-
art describes it, "between individual and social existence" as it manifests in
the decades leading up to the 1830s and the years of Victoria's reign, using
electricity as a figure through which to understand these interpersonal and
aesthetic relations. After establishing a more concrete sense of electricity as
it was understood at the turn of the nineteenth century, I will make two ar-
guments about the nature of Romantic sensibility and its electric disposi-
tions. First, using Mary Robinson as a model, I will suggest that British
poetry at the turn of the nineteenth century offers readers dramatic por-
trayals of bodily feeling but not mimetic embodiments of physiological

experience. The accoutrements of sensibility—pulses, heartbeats, tears—figure prominently in Robinson's poetry, but we are meant to use our thinking minds (as opposed to our feeling bodies) to sympathize with her various passionate tableaux. The second point concerns the role played by the electrical and physiological sciences in the Romantic distancing of "feeling" (understood as an abstract emotional state) from "sensation" (bodily experience). Felicia Hemans serves as a touchstone for this move away from the physiological, in which electricity becomes a figure for a kind of imaginative feeling that might supercede bodily sensation. For all their talk of bodily sensation, then, the practitioners of Romantic sensibility keep physiological experience firmly at the level of the discursive; only in subsequent years would poets embrace the affective potential in poetic form, and in rhythm specifically. Victorian poetry's turn to the body, the subject of the chapters that follow, will be all the more palpable after examining the Romantics' surprising resistance to a poetics of felt experience.

ROMANTIC ELECTRICITY

Scientific experiments seemed consistently to challenge a hierarchical view of sensibility, the belief that some are more affected by sensation than others. One especially provocative scene in the history of the electrical sciences, an experiment that might be seen as contesting the idea of nervous "refinement," took place at the University of Glasgow on 4 November 1818, roughly six months after the publication of Mary Shelley's *Frankenstein*. Dr. Andrew Ure later delivered an account of the proceedings to the Glasgow Literary Society on 10 December 1818; his lecture was published the following year in the *Quarterly Journal of Science, Literature and the Arts*. As Ure recounts the event, the body of an executed murderer, having been "suspended from the gallows nearly an hour," was brought to the "anatomical theatre" at the university, where Dr. Jeffray, "distinguished Professor of Anatomy," was to perform a series of groundbreaking "galvanic experiments" (Ure, 288). A voltaic battery was charged in the theatre as the audience awaited the corpse. Upon its arrival, two incisions were made in the dead body: one at the nape of the neck, revealing the "spinal marrow"; another at the hip, accessing the sciatic nerve. Into each opening, Dr. Jeffray placed a "pointed rod" connected to one end of the charged battery, at which point "every muscle of the [dead man's] body was immediately agitated with convulsive movements, resembling a violent shuddering from cold." Variations of the experiment proceeded: "On moving the second rod from the hip to the heel, the knee being previously bent, the leg was thrown out with such violence, as nearly to overturn one of the assistants, who in vain attempted to prevent its extension" (289).

The results of these first experiments would have been fairly predictable, following from the work of Luigi Galvani, who in 1791 had shown how electricity inspired muscular contractions in disembodied frog legs, and Alessandro Volta, who one year later had used whole frogs, both dead and alive, to show that electricity excites nerves, which subsequently provoke convulsions in muscles.[3] Jeffray's experiment also comes at the peak of what Sharon Ruston has called "the vitality debate," stretching from 1814 to 1819, in which physicians such as John Abernethy speculated that electricity was the source of all life (Ruston, 43).[4] Previous experiments, such as those performed by John Aldini on an executed criminal in 1803, had established that a dead human body would jerk spasmodically in response to electrical currents. Aldini was able to inspire movement that "almost . . . [gave] an appearance of re-animation" (Aldini, 9). But Jeffray's work in 1818 was to move into frightening new territory. An electrical current applied to the left phrenic nerve (which, as Ure explains, connects to the diaphragm) inspired the contraction of the respiratory muscles, simulating breathing in the dead body: "Full, nay, laborious breathing, instantly commenced. The chest heaved, and fell; the belly was protruded, and again collapsed, with the relaxing and retiring diaphragm" (Ure, 290). Finally, an incision was made in the forehead, revealing the "supra-orbital nerve" and thereby facilitating the most striking experiment of the day: "The one conducting rod being applied to [the supra-orbital nerve], and the other to the heel, most extraordinary grimaces were exhibited every time that the electric discharges were made. . . . [T]hus fifty shocks, each greater than the preceding one, were given in two seconds: every muscle in his countenance was simultaneously thrown into fearful action; rage, horror, despair, anguish, and ghastly smiles, united their hideous expression in the murderer's face, surpassing far the wildest representations of a Fuseli or a Kean" (290). Audience members were shocked by this progression of apparent emotional states through the body of a dead man: "At this period several of the spectators were forced to leave the apartment from terror or sickness, and one gentleman fainted" (290). Shortly after, the charge was applied to the man's forefinger and the corpse "seemed to point to the different spectators, some of whom thought he had come to life" (291).

Ure's narrative, and especially the disgusted responses he recounts, reveals a handful of thoughts that make it a helpful anecdote. Dr. Jeffray's experiments point to a certain ambivalence that accompanies early nineteenth-century ideas of electricity, an ambivalence that becomes especially clear when electricity and physiology (nerves, muscles) cross into the space of human feeling and sensibility. The ambivalence manifests specifically, in this example, when electricity inspires in the dead man what seem to be a variety of emotional states, including "rage, horror, despair, [and] anguish." It is one thing to consider the mechanism of our muscular contractions and to understand that such mechanisms rely on electrical nerve impulses. It is quite another matter to think of human emotion itself as mechanical in nature. If a dead man may express horror or anguish in the same manner as a living human being, then what is to be thought of those feelings and sentiments we like to imagine as making us most human? Jeffray's experiment hints that such feelings and sentiments may not be nearly as unique as they once might have seemed; flip the "anguish" switch through the supraorbital nerve, and a seemingly genuine display of anguish crosses the visage of the dead criminal. But the experiment is at least as provocative as it is horrifying. If the dead criminal might respond to electrical impulses, then perhaps thought, feeling, and emotion are simply hardwired into our own all-too-human (that is, mechanical) bodies. It may very well be that we are all, in various ways, merely conduits for electrical impulses.

Provocative, horrifying, or both, Dr. Jeffray's experiments return us to the universality that Mackintosh and others located in electrical experience. Any one of us, were we so unfortunate as to be put in Dr. Jeffray's anatomical theater, would respond similarly to his electric shocks—respond not only with muscular spasms, but also with expressions of great passion. That these signs of feeling are only an outward demonstration, a muscular response to electricity rather than an indication of genuine feeling, hardly matters to Jeffray's audience. Ure compares the dead man's passionate expressions to those presented by the painter Henry Fuseli and the actor Edmund Kean, with the passions inspired by electricity far exceeding anything invented by either artist or performer. That is to say, the dead man's passions seem more real, more genuine, than anything that could be achieved via aesthetic representation, even though we know that the apparent emotions of the criminal are purely physiological and bear no relation to anything the dead man may once have felt or thought. Electricity in Dr. Jeffray's laboratory thus seems to function as a vehicle for feeling itself, not simply the muscular representation of feeling. This understanding of electricity-as-vehicle is what Percy Shelley had in mind when referring in 1821 to "the electric life which burns within [the] words" of the "more celebrated writers of the present day"; it is the "electric" quality of poetry that converts mere language into something greater, the compositions that make poets unacknowledged legislators of the world (Shelley, 7:140). Whereas Hannah More insists that "sparks electric only strike / On souls electrical alike," Dr. Jeffray's experiment indicates that this simply is not true. At issue with the dead criminal is not the "soul" or the intellect, but the physical body: nerves and muscle tissue, components common to all human beings.

In its play on the physical human body, Jeffray's electricity functions outside the realm of intellect. When one moves from the scientist's corpse to living human beings, the Romantic electric shock works primarily as extralingual affect, comprehended—like the shocks of Nollet's monks—through sensory experience ("sensation"), which is then translated, unconsciously, into emotion ("feeling"). Byron suggests something of the nature of this progress while meditating on the process of grief in *Childe Harold's Pilgrimage* (Canto IV, published in 1818):

23.
But ever and anon of griefs subdued
There comes a token like a scorpion's sting,
Scarce seen, but with fresh bitterness imbued;
And slight withal may be the things which bring
Back on the heart the weight which it would fling
Aside for ever: it may be a sound—
A tone of music,—summer's eve—or spring—
A flower—the wind—the ocean—which shall wound,
Striking the electric chain wherewith we are darkly bound;

24.
And how and why we know not, nor can trace
Home to its cloud this lightning of the mind,

But feel the shock renew'd, nor can efface
The blight and blackening which it leaves behind,
Which out of things familiar, undesign'd,
When least we deem of such, calls up to view
The spectres whom no exorcism can bind,
The cold—the changed—perchance the dead—anew,
The mourn'd, the loved, the lost—too many!—yet how few!

(Byron, 2:132, lines 199–216)

According to Byron, we know not what will trigger the "sting" of grief, but it is most often inspired by sensory experience: the sound of music, the feel of wind, the sight or smell of a flower. Whatever it is connects us instantaneously, through the "electric chain wherewith we are darkly bound," back to the original experience of loss. This chain is simultaneously a link between each individual and sensory experience, and a link among all human individuals: we all experience music, summer's eve, and the wind, and are thereby "bound" together, even if consciously "we know not" the details of this fundamental connectivity. Byron suggests subtly, through the off-rhyme of "sound," "wound," "bound," that there may be an imperfect connection between sensory experience and emotional affect. But there can be no question that our emotional feelings are "bound" necessarily to our physiological experiences, just as human individuals are connected with one another, imperfectly or not.

Sensibility is the term that, from the mid-1700s through the early nineteenth century, best articulates the physiological and affective experiences described above as "electric." But within this electric sensibility rests a contradiction, or at least a tension, between the bodily and the semantic. Although Byron, for example, writes compellingly of the "electric chain" through which our sympathies might resonate, the actual stanzas of *Childe Harold* depend on language and conscious thought for the transmission of meaning. We understand Byron to possess sensibility, but our perception of that sensibility comes by means of our intellectual engagement, not by a "natural" resonance with the poet's language or the particular form his words take on the page. This is, in part, the point of Wordsworth's insistence on recollection in tranquility, which removes the poet from overwhelming sensibility and enables what Coleridge calls "manly reflection" (Coleridge, 53). Mary Robinson and Felicia Hemans demonstrate a keen awareness of

this paradox at the heart of sensibility. Each poet turns to electricity in nego-
tiating the immediate physicality of poetic experience, the bodily "sensation"
that Wordsworth, Coleridge, and even Byron generally keep at a thought-
ful, reflective distance.

MARY ROBINSON'S ELECTRIC UNIVERSE

Mary Darby Robinson was a genuine celebrity, capturing the imagination
of the British public during the last three decades of the eighteenth century.
Not only a famous Shakespearean actor and a "fashion icon," as Paula Byrne
shows, with various articles of clothing named in her honor—the "Robinson
Vest," the "Robinson Hat" (Byrne, 193)—she was also viewed by her contem-
poraries as "arguably *the* poet of sensibility" and "the poster girl for unfettered
female passion" (RSP, 48, 42). She was known to have spent an evening on
the "Celestial or Magnetico-electrico bed" in Dr. James Graham's "Temple
of Health and Hymen," where wealthy patrons of the 1780s went "to cure
impotence and infertility by channeling the 'electric fluid'" (Fulford, 25).
And through the so-called Della Cruscan movement of the 1780s and '90s,
Robinson and her fellow Della Cruscans strikingly elaborated the connec-
tions among poetry, sensibility, and electricity. Consisting of Robert Merry
("Della Crusca"), Hannah Cowley ("Anna Matilda"), and, somewhat pe-
ripherally, Robinson ("Laura"), the Della Cruscans exchanged poetry of ex-
aggerated feeling via publications in *The World*, a journal of polite society
first printed in 1787. British readers followed the amorous exchanges with
voyeuristic glee, as first Anna Matilda and Della Crusca fell in epistolary
love, and then Robinson—seeing an opportunity for more celebrity—butted
her way into Della Crusca's heart, much to Anna Matilda's rage and agony.

For my argument, the narrative of these exchanges matters less than the
Della Cruscan style, with its constant reference to the thrilling, pulsing ef-
fects of (poetic) love. Note throughout what follows how Della Cruscan
feeling remains at the descriptive level. Poetry for these writers is meant to
play upon and inspire the human body, but it does so through suggestion,
not direct stimulation. For example, in the first of what would be a nearly
two-year series of poetic exchanges with Della Crusca, Anna Matilda urges
her fellow poet, "SEIZE again thy golden quill, / And with its point my
bosom thrill" (*BA*, 3; 10 July 1787).[5] Della Crusca replies in kind: "The
quick'ning sense, the throb d'vine, / Fancy, and feeling, all are thine" (*BA*,

11; 21 August 1787). Anna Matilda's "bosom" responds to the figurative press of Della Crusca's quill, just as Della Crusca's senses quicken while he reads Anna Matilda's poetic missives. To read Anna Matilda's descriptions of throbbing hearts is thus, theoretically, to feel one's own heart throb in sympathy. One need not touch a physical body to inspire the sensation of physical touching; words and a properly active and sympathetic imagination will more than suffice. Yet there is little more than suggestion to inspire such an emotive response, and the unsympathetic reader will find—as generations of subsequent readers have found—mere sentiment in the Della Cruscan style.[6]

Critics have thus often noted what Jerome McGann calls the "consciously artificial" world of Della Cruscan poetry (McGann 1996, 86). There can be little doubt that Anna Matilda's "quick'ning sense" and "throb d'vine," for example, seem removed from anything resembling genuine expression (does anyone, ever, really talk like that?). But an artificial or poorly articulated vehicle need not diminish the truth of a metaphor's tenor. Behind Anna Matilda's overwrought figuration, one might still discern feelings— love, loss, anger, jealousy—with which most adult readers might readily identify. Indeed, in many ways, the Della Cruscans foreground their artificiality so as to interrogate the process by which thought and feeling might be communicated in measured language. Much as Hannah More wonders at how "intellect" might be transmitted via electrical shocks of sensibility, Anna Matilda and Della Crusca address through their poetry the conflict between unselfconscious, passionate feeling and reasoned thought. In her "Ode: To Indifference," Anna Matilda positions sensibility as the antagonist to an imprisoned "Reason":

> Oh SENSIBILITY! thy scepter sad
> Points, where the *frantic glance* proclaims THEE MAD!
> Strain'd to excess, Reason is chain'd thy slave,
> Or the poor victim shuns thee in the grave;
> To thee each crime, each evil owes its birth,
> That in gigantic horror treads the earth!
>
> SAVAGE UNTAM'D! she smiles to drink our tears,
> And where's no *solid ill*, she wounds with *fears;*

Riots in sighs, is sooth'd when most we smart—
Now, while she guides my pen, her FANG's within my heart.
(*BA*, 70; 16 January 1788)

These verses are meant to show the formal "[s]train[s of] excess" that come, according to the poem, from a too-active sensibility; though the lines are roughly iambic, one stumbles over the intentionally awkward rhythmic inversions ("*Strain'd* to ex*cess, rea*son is *chain'd* thy *slave*"). On the surface, intellect would seem to have nary a place in Anna Matilda's poetics; one finds here little of the "[r]eason" that sensibility seems to have imprisoned. But Anna Matilda's "consciously artificial" style bespeaks a sort of reason, discernable beneath the passage's inflated rhetoric and halting rhythm. One must process intellectually the "horror" that Anna Matilda wishes her readers to experience; those who want to engage with the Della Cruscans must find a corresponding mental picture—"gigantic horror . . . !" "Savage untam'd!"—for each image offered up in the poetry. Like the body in Jeffray's experiment, the reader of these verses is meant to respond, here to the charge of affect rather than electricity itself. But the reader of Della Cruscan poetry must engage his brain, at least in part, and not rely simply on physiological charges.

The Della Cruscans became a literary phenomenon at a time when, according to Janet Todd, sensibility in Britain was on the decline, seen as self-centered and corrupt (Todd, 62). Their popularity came in part because their turn from "reason" offered British readers a welcome distraction from domestic and international unease (Pascoe, 87). Mary Robinson, ever perceptive of the shifting fashions, eagerly joined in the epistolary fray. She writes as "Laura," playing the part of a reader moved to passion by Della Crusca's verses:

Since his lov'd voice first caught my ear,
    Oft have I tried to calm my woe,
Oft have I brush'd away the tear—
    The tear his numbers taught to flow.
I seize the Lyre, to sooth my grief,
Court mazy Science for relief;—
Vain is the effort, 'tis in vain—

The fierce vibration fills my brain,
Burns thro' each aching nerve with poignant smart,
And riots cureless in my bleeding heart.

(*BA*, 301; 1 March 1789)

Robinson here is interestingly conflicted in pinpointing the source of her passion. First attracted to Della Crusca's "voice," she then takes instruction from "his numbers" (the formal metrical effects of his verse), which teach her tears "to flow." The "numbers" seem to win out, echoed in Robinson's "fierce vibration" and, we are meant to imagine, in the rhythmic play of her verses. Robinson has apparently caught the "epidemic malady" of the Della Cruscans, as her contemporary William Gifford put it, which spread like an infectious disease "from fool to fool" (Gifford, xii). Or, one might say, like an electric shock. By the poets' definition, Della Cruscan experience is instantaneous and universal, like the experience of electricity. Though the poetry requires a degree of mental processing, the assumption implicit in the Della Cruscan style is that the poetry will be experienced in the same way by all readers; each individual will respond similarly to the idea of "horror" or "savagery," for example, because such concepts and feelings are universal.

Robinson's contributions to the Della Cruscan phenomenon consistently turn to the language of shock to convey ideas and sensations understood as universal; indeed, throughout her writing career, Robinson employed the trope of electricity to describe the sudden apprehension of thoughts or feelings. In her *Memoirs*, for example, the suggestion that the young Mary Robinson should take to the stage "rushed like electricity through [her] brain"; at one of her first performances, Robinson's curtsy "seemed to electrify the whole house"; and encountering an old acquaintance resulted in a startled tremor, "as if he had received a shock of electricity" (Robinson 1895, 125, 132, 108). Electricity starts out in these examples simply as a figure for physiological shock, but at key points in her poetry, electricity stands as a model for egalitarian human relations, a kind of democratic ideal of shared experience. One such example from Robinson's Della Cruscan period is her 1790 poem "Ainsi va le Monde," a response to the French Revolution that she inscribed to Della Crusca. It concludes by triangulating the powers of poetry, "Freedom," and "Promethean fire":

Apollo strikes his lyre's rebounding strings,
Responsive notes divine Cecilia sings,
The tuneful sisters prompt the heavenly choir,
Thy temple glitters with Promethean fire.
The sacred Priestess in the center stands,
She strews the sapphire floor with flow-ry bands.
See! from her shrine electric incense rise;
Hark! "Freedom" echoes thro' the vaulted skies.
The Goddess speaks! O mark the blest decree,
TYRANTS SHALL FALL—TRIUMPHANT MAN BE FREE!

(RSP, 113–14, lines 331–40)

In this poetic fantasy, Apollo's musical playing sets off a chain reaction by which the French people, inspired by a kind of celestial resonance, achieve political liberty. Robinson begins with an ethereal, noncorporeal god, but her image of "rebounding strings" takes readers ultimately to physiological, bodily experience. Freedom for Robinson—a political ideal—depends on individuals coming alive to bodily experience and recognizing the shared, human nature of that experience. "The rapt'rous energies of social love" that had long been "wasted" and "numb'd" will now come to life, inspired by the ideals of freedom (RSP, 111, lines 256–60):

Thro' all the scenes of Nature's varying plan,
Celestial Freedom warms the breast of man;
Led by her daring hand, what pow'r can bind
The boundless efforts of the lab'ring mind.
The god-like fervour, thrilling thro' the heart,
Gives new creation to each vital part;
Throbs rapture thro' each palpitating vein,
Wings the rapt thought, and warms the fertile brain;
To her the noblest attributes of Heav'n
Ambition, valour, eloquence, are giv'n.

(RSP, 108, lines 157–66)

Robinson here anatomizes the effects of freedom on the human body—its "heart," "each vital part," "each palpitating vein," "the fertile brain"—using end-stopped rhymes to emphasize her physiological attention. These are not individual hearts, veins, and brains, but universal body parts; in our shared physiology, we likewise share the thrilling fervor of celestial freedom. This, in effect, is the foundation of the Della Cruscan style: the belief that bodily experience—anything from the fluttering of a lover's heart to the fervor of a French revolutionary—might be communicated universally through poetry, through the arrangement of images, thoughts, and feelings in measured language.

Robinson also follows the lead of her Della Cruscan peers in calling attention to her poetry *as poetry*, as an aesthetic creation. If Robinson's verse "thrill[s] thro' the heart," it does so because Robinson informs us that freedom, and by extension her poem on the subject, has this effect on those who truly experience it. The effect is not unlike the laugh-tracks that accompany television sitcoms, instructing viewers to find a particular scene funny, to laugh along with the crowd. So, too, Robinson never hesitates to broadcast her self-consciousness as a poet writing to an audience, coaching her readers throughout on the appropriate response to her verses: *now*, she seems to say, "throb rapturously."[7] In this way, Robinson creates the "parallel universe" that Stuart Curran describes as characteristic of her later poems; like Coleridge, who took her lead, Robinson "attempt[s] through poetic effect to create a parallel universe that seems to be akin to ours but to operate by laws to which our norms are alien" (Curran, 20). Curran identifies Robinson as a precursor to such Victorian creations as Tennyson's "Mariana" and her isolated grange, poetically fabricated but entirely visceral in a reader's experience.[8] Robinson's Della Cruscan world is importantly distinct from Tennyson's—Robinson creates not universes of sonic effects, as Tennyson does, but communities that arise through imagined affective experience—but Curran is right to see her style as a precursor to early Victorian poetic experiments. Like Tennyson, Robinson asks her readers to leap headfirst and without deliberation into the space of her poem. If "consciously artificial" in its style, Della Cruscan poetry aims for the genuine in its effects. Robinson's poetic ideal resembles what Robert Langbaum has called the poetry of experience, poetry in which "the imaginative apprehension gained through immediate experience is primary and certain, whereas the analytic reflection that follows is secondary and problematical" (Langbaum, 35). For Langbaum, such poetry signals Romanticism's turn

Spell-bound by sorrow! What were her pursuits?
Fasting and pray'r; long nights of meditation;
And days consum'd in tears. The matin song,
By repetition dull, familiar grown,
Pass'd o'er her lip mechanically cold,
And little mark'd devotion.

(305)

Through a kind of theatrical visuality (one imagines a curtain rising to re-
veal the scene of the dim cloister), Robinson attacks the "[p]repost'rous
sacrifice" of the young woman, "[c]ondemn'd" like the monk "to waste [her]
bloom in one dull speck / Of freezing solitude" (307). As much a call to
communitarian sensibility as anything else, Robinson's poem demands that
her reader enter the imaginative space of the wasting vestal. Like the poet
George Dyer, who in 1802 argued that lyric poetry is particularly adapted
"to enliven[ing] the social and tender affections" (Dyer, 1:lxxii), Robinson
here anticipates the work of later poets, many from the working classes,
who would, as Anne Janowitz has shown, insist on a "collective, embedded
experience" as central to the work of lyric poetry (Janowitz, 7).

Yet the great perversity of Robinson's verse, and perhaps what helps to
make her style difficult for modern readers to appreciate, is how aloof it
seems—on a formal level—from the electrical sensibility it so insistently de-
scribes. Robinson regularly gestures to affective experience, what she calls
in "The Cell of the Atheist," a poem of 1799, "the thrill / Of Heav'n-born
POESY" that "[d]art[s] the electric fire" "thro' every vein" (RSP, 312). But her
poems fail to demonstrate, except through the imagination, the actual physio-
logical power of such electric life. Later poets such as Tennyson, Hopkins,
and the so-called Spasmodic writers of the 1850s (discussed in subsequent
chapters) turned to poetic form—to rhythm, meter, rhyme, and various
sonic effects—to induce in their readers "the thrill / Of Heav'n-born
POESY." But such practices are not part of Robinson's repertoire. This is not
to say that Robinson was uninterested or unaccomplished in formal tech-
nique. But Robinson's oeuvre avoids the physicality of sensation one finds
in the works of later Victorian poets, who not only describe feeling but also
use poetic form to compel the *experience* of that feeling.[10] In this, Robinson
was at one with her peers at the turn of the nineteenth century. Robinson
gestures to the manifestation of sensation in the physical body, but sympa-

thetic identification remains throughout her poetry at the level of imagination: a scene playing out that readers witness from afar, as in a drama, rather than participate in actively. If one feels an electrical thrill in identifying with the isolated monk or the devout vestal, the spark comes entirely of one's own powers of identification and imagination. Robinson urges us toward this work of identification, but the structure of her poetry does not in itself compel a reader to feel, literally, the "[d]art" of "electric fire."

HEMANS'S ELECTRIC TOUCH

Robinson's form may not compel physiological sensation, but her poetry makes constant reference to the physical body; she is a poet entirely comfortable describing her throbbing, pulsing heart and limbs, especially while in her Della Cruscan mode. Felicia Hemans, who emerged as Britain's foremost female poet in the 1820s, explicitly distances herself from such engagement with the body, removing sensation instead to a more theoretical space of reflection. I have suggested elsewhere that Hemans stood as the early Victorians' most beloved poet in large part because she restrained the passionate gush or overflow common in her Romantic predecessors.[11] According to her sister Harriet Hughes, Hemans never practiced "such strain of hyperbole as used to prevail in the Della Cruscan coteries" (quoted in Mason 2006, 34). Francis Jeffrey's important *Edinburgh Review* essay of 1829 might stand as representative of public opinion. Hemans's verses, he writes, are "singularly sweet, elegant, and tender—touching, perhaps, and contemplative, rather than vehement and overpowering; and not only finished throughout with an exquisite delicacy, and even severity of execution, but informed with a purity and loftiness of feeling, and a certain sober and humble tone of indulgence and piety, which must satisfy all judgments, and allay the apprehensions of those who are most afraid of the passionate exaggerations of poetry" (Jeffrey, 34). Hemans took to heart the Wordsworthian injunction to recollect in tranquility her spontaneous overflow of powerful feeling, and so her poetry focuses less on the physical body's passionate experiences than it does on the mind's subsequent analyses of those moments. Even moments that move toward literalized touching maintain a conscientious distance from the purely physiological. In "Properzia Rossi" (1828), for example, the sculptor Rossi addresses her work of art, a version of Ariadne:

Forsaken Ariadne! thou shalt wear
My form, my lineaments; but oh! more fair,
Touched into lovelier being by the glow
      Which in me dwells[.]

(Hemans, 2:99)

Hemans plays here with "touch" in both its emotional and its physical senses. But clearly more important than the literal touch with which Rossi creates her sculpture is the touching "glow" of Rossi's sentiment, which brings real life to the figure. Hemans always defers to the experience of internalized affect rather than the kind of palpitating, rapturous language of Mary Robinson and her Della Cruscan peers.

That said, when electricity enters Hemans's writing, the poet's distance from physiological affect frequently becomes a subject for concern. Even as she celebrates the emotional connections that an electric-like lyric sensibility facilitates, Hemans wishes for a more physiologically grounded poetic style. For example, in a poem from 1830, "The Lyre's Lament," the lament of the lyre is precisely that it is *not* being touched by human hands. It hangs from a rock by the sea, "murmuring" as the wind passes over its strings. "O melancholy wind," sighs the lyre,

Thou canst not wake the spirit
      That in me slumbering lies,
Thou strikest not forth th' electric fire
      Of buried melodies.

(2:259)

"Where," asks the lyre in conclusion, "Where is the touch to give me life?" (2:260). The wind produces in Hemans's lyre music of a sort, as with an aeolian harp, but it needs an actual hand's touch to achieve "life." Without such a touch, the lyre fails to make audible "the spell—the gift—the lightning— / Within [its] frame concealed" (2:259). Poetry, in other words, requires inspiration (the breath of wind), but it falls short of ideal if it is not also grounded in the experiences of the human body. Electricity here—both the "electric fire / Of buried melodies" and "the lightning— / Within my frame concealed"—is an internal phenomenon, a vital quality located within the speaker's physical body, struggling to make itself known. He-mans thus shifts uncomfortably between two aesthetic poles; she main-tains, on the one hand, the quiet and dignified reserve celebrated by Jeffrey and many others, while on the other hand she longs for something of the passionate, physiological expression that we see regularly in the work of Mary Robinson.[12]

With her conflicted approach to physiological poetics, electricity stands throughout Hemans's writing career as a figure for an ideal organic sensi-bility, a touch that, like that of Properzia Rossi, works to both physical and emotional effect. Hemans was also clearly inspired by the idea of electricity as a unifying force of nature, located both within the human body and out-side, in the natural world. Her 1816 work, *The Restoration of the Works of Art to Italy*, recounts a singing voice whose "energies resound, / With power electric, through the realms around" (Hemans, 1:127). And in a poem published in 1834, a year before her death, Hemans describes a hymn that "[o]'erflows [the] dim recesses" of a cathedral,

> leaving not
> One tomb unthrill'd by the strong sympathy
> Answering the electric notes.
>
> ("Cathedral Hymn"; 2:451)

Hemans here imagines a kind of dispersed lyric subjectivity, a lyric that speaks through, among, around—but not necessarily *to*—others. As music, "electric notes," the hymn inspires a kind of sympathetic resonance. The hymn passes by, that is, and the individual bodies (here corpses) experience the thrill of its passing. The process is not didactic or directed, but rather—as Mill judged it in the year prior to this poem's composition—overheard.[13] More accurately, it is over*felt*. A captive audience, the dead bodies form a kind of ideal community, a reflection of the church-going congregation in which they had once participated:

> And lo! the throng of beating human hearts,
> With all their secret scrolls of buried grief,
> All their full treasures of immortal hope,
> Gather'd before their God! Hark! how the flood

Of the rich organ harmony bears up
Their voice on its high waves!—a mighty burst!

(2:451)

This is the sort of passionate experience Hemans can sanction without hesitation. Passion in the space of the cathedral or the graveyard is, as Hemans represents it, entirely unself-conscious—grounded not in the individual's personal thoughts, concerns, and desires, but in reverence for the Christian divinity. The "harmony" of the organ's music suggests for Hemans a universalized sensibility arising from transcendent, spiritual experience as opposed to the bodily sensuousness of Robinson's Della Cruscan epistles. One might well connect Hemans's ideal of poetic transcendence to E. T. A. Hoffmann's nearly contemporaneous assertion that music—specifically, Beethoven's Fifth Symphony—"leads the listener imperturbably forward in a climax that climbs up and up into the spirit world of the infinite" (Hoffmann, 85). Like Hoffmann, Hemans urges her readers away from a materialist or physiological experience of the artwork and toward an ideal or transcendent, spiritual engagement.[14] But unlike Hoffmann, whose sights are set distinctly on the infinite, Hemans's ultimate goal remains the communal good. In pushing readers toward transcendence, Hemans highlights—in Emma Mason's words—the "radically pedagogic" function of poetry: "moralizing, christianizing and rendering [readers] emotive and thoughtful" (Mason 2006, 34). That Hemans accomplishes such grand effects among a community of the dead should not obstruct the ideal of her vision, though it may suggest the difficulty of its enactment. "Join, join, my soul!" she writes, "In thine own lowly, trembling consciousness, / And thine own solitude, the glorious hymn" (2:451).

Hemans's dispersed and undirected lyric sensibility follows in a tradition of Romantic women poets who, as critics have recently argued, seemed self-consciously to evacuate a strong sense of selfhood from their verses.[15] In working with familiar tropes, these women poets privilege the generic over the individual, promoting a more universal experience of their verses. Hemans—like Robinson in *The Progress of Liberty*—thereby imagines a shared lyric sensibility as a model for a better sort of British community. But electricity also enables Hemans to enact a form of lyric sensibility that evades the purely physiological, and to "touch," figuratively, what she saw as spiritual, internal, and more profoundly universal than sensory experience alone ever could be. We might imagine Hemans here writing against the ideas suggested by Dr. Jeffray, whose electrical experiments elicited from a corpse displays of "rage, horror, despair, anguish, and ghastly smiles." Like Jeffray, Hemans also touches dead bodies with electrical shocks, but Hemans's shocks are always figurative, and are meant to strike the body not with physical force but with what she took to be a kind of transcendent spirit. Hemans writes specifically against the materialist tradition that would locate human life in the body. In so doing, she transforms electricity from a literal shock to a figurative impulse: an impulse to inspire a communal conscience. Poetry for Hemans thereby enacts a transition from body to spirit, from individual to community, and electricity offers an ideal figure for this movement.

Hemans uses such a figure for transcendence, Byron's image of "the electric chain wherewith we are darkly bound" (discussed above), as an epigraph for three poems published in 1828 and 1829. In each instance, Hemans's reading of Byron encompasses both the figurative and the literal. The original quotation, of course, refers to the process of grieving—specifically, the phenomenon of being reminded, as by a shock, of a weighted sadness. This is the subject as well of Hemans's three poems. In "The Voice of Music," published first in *The Winter's Wreath* of 1829, one of the many literary annuals to which she contributed, Hemans again finds in music the power to connect with a greater force, spiritual in nature:

> Something of mystery there surely dwells,
> Waiting thy touch, in our bosom-cells;
> Something that finds not its answer here—
> A chain to be clasp'd in another sphere.
>
> (Hemans, 2:297)

In the conclusion to the present volume, I return to this image of an electrical chain stretching into "another sphere," a vision of spiritual communication that was hugely popular in the mid-Victorian period. Poets later in the century imagined poetry, and specifically poetic rhythm, as a potential vehicle for transmission between the living and the dead. Hemans here imagines music as a less-literal mode of communication; she hears music that "wake[s], by one gentle breath, / Passionate visions of love and death!" (2:297). Like

Robinson, who understands affect to be universal and, as a result, ideally suited as a grounding for democratic citizenship, Hemans writes of the emotional pull of music that was not written with her specific emotions in mind. How, she asks, can the music speak so distinctly to her as an individual? "What is thy power, from the soul's deep spring / In sudden gushes the tears to bring?" (2:297). The answer is that all humans experience such feeling; music "touch[es]" those feelings inherent to human nature. Hemans sees this universality as proof of something greater than existence in this life, greater than any individual human life: "[T]hou tellest my soul that its birth / Links it with regions more bright than earth" (2:298).

The Byronic epigraph appears again in "The Spirit's Mysteries," published as part of the 1828 *Records of Woman*. The speaker in this poem finds "in sweet sounds" feelings that she never experienced but recognizes as common to human nature:

> The power that dwelleth in sweet sounds to waken
>   Vague yearnings, like the sailor's for the shore,
> And dim remembrances, whose hue seems taken
>   From some bright former state, our own no more;
> Is not this a mystery?—Who shall say
> Whence are those thoughts, and whither tends their way?
>
>   (2:168)

Oscar Wilde expresses a similar sentiment in "The Critic as Artist" (1891) when he writes that playing Chopin always makes him "feel as if [he] had been weeping over sins that [he] had never committed, and mourning over tragedies that were not [his] own. Music . . . creates for one a past of which one has been ignorant, and fills one with a sense of sorrows that have been hidden from one's tears" (Wilde, 1011). Hemans marvels over the "[v]ague yearnings" that music stirs, the mystery that sound inspires such powerful emotions. This phenomenon, according to Hemans, functions very much like an electric shock, the images "flash[ing]" over our minds (2:168).

Byron's phrase the "lightning of the mind" (*Childe Harold* IV, stanza 24) seems echoed in the third poem of Hemans to have the "electric chain" epigraph, "The Haunted Ground," published in the *New Monthly Magazine* of January 1828. Hemans writes of "a thrill on the chords of the stricken mind" that, wandering in a cemetery, finds itself weighted by "[t]he chain by those spirits brought back from the past" (1:654–65). The speaker of Hemans's poem reflects on the feelings and experiences of the dead around her:

> Song hath been here—with its flow of thought,
> Love—with its passionate visions fraught;
> Death—breathing stillness and sadness round—
> And is it not—is it not haunted ground?
>
> (1:654)

In passages such as this, Hemans positions herself directly on the "threshold," as Susan Stewart calls it, "between individual and social experience." Hemans uses the lyric precisely as a meditation on this porous boundary, moving imaginatively through the passionate experiences of those long dead and buried. The ground is "haunted" because Hemans and others like her exert their powers of imagination to reflect on those whose lives have passed. In this way, the poem implicitly acknowledges the generic nature of feeling; only because human experience is common—shared, familiar—can Hemans imagine feelings that had once been experienced by others. Dr. Jeffray's experiments also point to the generic nature of human feeling, but the scientific laboratory leaves room only for a mechanical, materialist understanding of the human body and its experiences. Hemans works through sympathetic identification to breathe a different kind of life into her dead bodies. Poetry is a vehicle for feeling, encouraging readers to imagine sympathetically the experiences of others, experiences that are universal to human life.[16] Like Jeffray's corpse, then, both Hemans (as she strolls through the graveyard) and her readers (as they read her poems) experience electric-like shocks. But this is less a cause for alarm—recall the horrified, sickened witnesses in Jeffray's theatre—than it is an occasion to celebrate the deep-rooted feelings that connect us as human beings: an echo, no doubt, of what Wordsworth called our "primal sympathy."

This sympathy of thought and experience is what Hemans's contemporaries most praised when reviewing her poems. She works, according to the *Edinburgh Monthly Review*, "by a fine tact of sympathy, a vivacity and fertility of imagination. . . . She excites emotion which endures, and which gives fresh delight on repetition, by expressing natural feeling, in a sweet flow of tenderness, or a sustained and deep tone of pathos" (Review of *Tales and Historic Scenes*, 207). Hemans's "natural feeling" strikes a noticeably different tone than Robinson's verses, which were consistently attacked as sentimental and, in many ways, false.[17] Yet both Robinson and Hemans ostensibly set out to encourage the kind of social bonds seemingly idealized in the passage of electricity through communities of human bodies. The freedom that for Robinson was inspired by the French Revolution and explored in "Ainsi va le Monde" is for Hemans a more abstract belief in personal sovereignty, and both women see poetry as central to the achievement of these political goals.[18] The difference lies primarily in their approach to emotional affect. Whereas Robinson directs her readers through the experience of each passion—anatomizing the effects of love, for example, on each body part—Hemans avoids the language of pure physiology, insisting instead on a thoughtful, even intellectual experience of emotion. Yes, Hemans seems to say, the physical body is important, but there can be nothing of value to a muscular spasm if it does not reflect or inspire in some way a more deeply rooted feeling. Poetry, for Hemans, must work against the mechanized view of sentimental literature, the belief that, like the pseudo-emotions of Dr. Jeffray's corpse, the emotions inspired by novels and poems are by nature prefabricated and mechanical. According to Hemans, the poetics of sensibility need not function in such a manner. As much as Jeffray's corpse writhes, its contortions mean little next to the genuine feelings of the living and to the real power of sympathetic identification embodied in Hemans's verses.

The work of poetic embodiment, and the particular difficulties in navigating between false and genuine affect, remained central to poetic theory well into the Victorian period. It was an especially vexing concern for the young Alfred Tennyson, who grew up listening to his mother read Hemans aloud (C. Tennyson, 14). Tennyson's early "poetics of sensation," as Arthur Hallam called it, develops and pushes in new directions Hemans's abstract language of electric sensibility. Like Hemans and Robinson before her, Tennyson imagines poetry as a force for communal ties and democratic citizenship, but Tennyson's commitment to such ideals was made increasingly difficult by the 1832 Reform Bill and the movement toward universal manhood suffrage. Tennyson struggles both to deploy and to contain the language of sensibility, but he ultimately proves more comfortable than either Robinson or Hemans with a poetics of the body. The political challenges inherent in the move toward a truly physiological poetic form, and Tennyson's central role in these developments, are the subjects of the chapter that follows.

Tennyson's Telegraphic Poetics

Yes, this electric chain from East to West
  More than mere metal, more than Mammon can
Bind us together, kinsmen, in the best
    As most affectionate and frankest bond,
    Brethren at one,—and, looking far beyond,
The World in an electric Union blest.

> —Martin Farquhar Tupper, "Morse's Telegraph" (1860)

T HE FOURTH OF JUNE IN 1832 MARKED NOT ONLY THE passing of the great Reform Bill, the event that many take to have inaugurated the Victorian era, but also the opening of the Adelaide Gallery of Practical Science, another sort of introduction to the period that would follow.[1] The Adelaide Gallery, as described by an article in the *Penny Magazine of the Society for the Diffusion of Useful Knowledge*, was popular for its fanciful mixing of amusement and instruction by means of heterogeneous displays ranging from "powerful electro-magnets . . . which communicate such a rapid succession of electric shocks, that few persons can withstand them above a few seconds," to a steam gun that "discharges a number of bullets (said to be seventy in four seconds) against an iron target placed at the end of the room." At the center of the gallery was a seventy-foot-long, six-thousand-gallon canal "for the exhibition of models of steamboats, which traverse it" ("Adelaide Gallery," 417–18). Whereas subscriptions to elite scientific organizations such as the Royal Institution had been prohibitively expensive for the middle and working classes, everyone flocked to the Adelaide Gallery and its myriad exhibitions, all for the price of a mere shilling. The *Times* of London noted in an approving, if irrepressibly snide, response that "there is no fact more remarkable than the various degrees of earnestness with which the different classes of the community demand knowledge":

> The higher class of mechanics spare from their hard-earned wages considerable sums in order to procure in their institutes the best scientific instructors. Those immediately above them, comprising clerks in offices, smaller tradesmen, and others, have also their reading-rooms and lectures. Several of these institutions have lately arisen in the metropolis, in which amusement is wisely combined with science. The middle and some of the upper classes have long had their Royal and London Institutions, and these are now much better attended than formerly. But the mere fact, that the scientific exhibitions at the Adelaide Gallery, at the Museum of National Manufactures in Leicester-square, at the chymical exhibition in Regent-street . . . are each of them successfully taken up as mercantile speculations, prove most indisputably the demand for scientific knowledge. (*Times*, 22 May 1834, 3)

Seen as populist at heart, though also "mercantile" in practice, the Adelaide Gallery offers a suggestive model for the interplay of science and class around the time of the great Reform. The Adelaide was one of several institutions founded in the early 1830s that worked to encourage solidarity across class lines. Even before the Reform Bill, the *Times* had pointed to organizations such as the Society for the Diffusion of Useful Knowledge in hopes that they might "render [the 'humbler' classes] more docile and manageable in the affairs of life, and more obedient to the voice of reason" (*Times*, 22 March 1827, 2).

Within a year of the Adelaide's opening, the young Alfred Tennyson and his friend Arthur Henry Hallam twice visited the new gallery. In April 1833, Hallam wrote to his fiancée, Tennyson's sister Emily, of "that fairy palace, the Gallery of Practical Science, [where Alfred and I] saw the wonderful

Magnets, and heard the Steam Gun" (TL, 1:91). Three months later, Tenny-
son returned to Cambridge, where he had until recently been a student, to at-
tend the third annual meeting of the British Association for the Advancement
of Science. The British Association was a diverse group whose "particular ge-
nius," according to two recent historians, "lay in its ability to serve as an in-
strument of public order and social cohesion" (Morrell and Thackray, 22).[2] As
with the Adelaide Gallery and the Society for the Diffusion of Useful Knowl-
edge, at least part of the inspiration for the British Association was the desire
to mediate the political turmoil of the day. That Tennyson attended the Cam-
bridge meeting should come as no surprise: his interest in the scientific devel-
opments of his age has been well documented; his Cambridge tutor, William
Whewell, played host to the meeting; and Tennyson's political views meshed
perfectly with the "meliorist, centrist, reforming political attitude" that
marked the association's early years (Morrell and Thackray, 25).[3] Tennyson's
attendance at the British Association meeting and his earlier visits to the Ade-
laide Gallery comprise two important elements of the scene I want to paint as
a context for this chapter, the trajectory of which leads from Tennyson's "sen-
sational" poetics of the 1830s to a trio of poems—one each by Tennyson,
Thomas Hood, and the American "G. W. Russell"—that together map out a
new direction for poetry in the Victorian age. Of particular significance is
Tennyson's "medley" of 1847, *The Princess*, a poem that uses an electric tele-
graph to reflect on the convergence of physiological sensation, poetic affect,
and political consciousness. Unlike the poems of Mary Robinson and Felicia
Hemans, which insistently keep physiological experience at the level of figu-
ration, Tennyson's poetry takes steps toward embodied poetic form, a poetic
practice in which bodily experience is not simply referenced but enacted. The
intimacies between text and body encompass both aesthetic and political goals
that were central to Tennyson's work from his first full volume, the *Poems,
Chiefly Lyrical* of 1830, through to *Maud* (1855), the latter of which is exam-
ined in chapter 3. The challenges of yoking physiological affect to poetic
form, and the political implications of these convergences, occupy the center
of Tennyson's concerns through the first several decades of his career.

SENSATIONAL POLITICS, CIRCA 1832

Tennyson's poetry was read as politically inflected and physiologically mov-
ing from the very beginning. One could not hope for a clearer example of this

than William Johnson Fox's 1831 review of *Poems, Chiefly Lyrical*, which uses Tennyson's volume as grounds from which to dilate on radical political philosophy. Fox, identified by an early biographer as a "Unitarian minister, popular lecturer, Radical journalist, Anti–Corn Law League orator, M.P. for Oldham, and educationalist" (Garnett, viii), opens his review insisting that all individuals, regardless of class or education, have the ability to appreciate poetry: "The elements of poetry are universal."[4] He continues, with reference to physiology and the electrical sciences, "The exercise of the organs of sight and sense stimulates man to some degree of descriptive poetry; wherever there is passion, there is dramatic poetry; wherever enthusiasm, there is lyric poetry; wherever reflection, there is metaphysical poetry. It is as widely diffused as the electric fluid. It may be seen flashing out by fits and starts all the world over. The most ignorant talk poetry when they are in a state of excitement, the firmly-organized think and feel poetry with every breeze of sensation that sweeps over their well-tuned nerves" (Fox, 211). The connections here among poetry, politics, and the science of "electrical fluid" are far from casual. Fox finds in the sensational experience of poetry—"senses, feelings, nerves, and brain"—a model for social progress, and he sees electrical communication as a figurative model for achieving this progress (216). True change, Fox imagines, will take place when the passions and enthusiasms of poetry are dispersed to the world at large, bearing with them the radical social and political sentiments central to Fox's project.[5] Like Mary Robinson and Felicia Hemans (whose views of the egalitarian potential within poetic affect are discussed in chapter 1), Fox believes wholeheartedly in the poet's duties toward the communal good. Fox's radical politics, however, push Robinson's and Hemans's ideals to an extreme. "A genuine poet," Fox concludes, "has deep responsibilities to his country and the world" (223); as a communicator, the poet stands at the nexus of an electric-like network, radiating out thoughts and sentiments to readers nationwide. True poets thus "can influence the associations of unnumbered minds; they can command the sympathies of unnumbered hearts; they can disseminate principles; they can give those principles power over men's imaginations; they can excite in a good cause the sustained enthusiasm that is sure to conquer; they can blast the laurels of the tyrants, and hallow the memories of the martyrs of patriotism; they can act with a force, the extent of which it is difficult to estimate, upon national feelings and character, and consequently upon national happiness" (224).

One may wonder at first glance what Fox sees in *Poems, Chiefly Lyrical* that might lead to these remarkable events. Poems such as "Claribel," "Lilian," and "Isabel"—the volume's opening ditties—hardly call to mind working-class insurrection or the struggle for universal manhood suffrage (though admittedly "The Kraken" offers something for the insurrectionist at heart). Fox's point is not so much that reading these poems will inspire one to "blast the laurels of the tyrants," but rather that democratic sentiment would be strengthened were readers of Tennyson's poetry to identify with one another as parts of an affective, political community. As the "sensation[s]" of a poem "sweep . . . over [our] well-tuned nerves," we understand our interconnectedness much as the electric shock led Nollet's monks—and those watching the spectacle—to understand their own necessary physiological and affective relations.

Fox was also correct in identifying Tennyson as sympathetic to this political/aesthetic fantasy. From his earliest writings, Tennyson highlights moments of intense physiological experience. "Armageddon," for example, composed when the poet was around fifteen, concludes with a vision of all creation resonating with a rhythmic pulse:

> There was a beating in the atmosphere,
> An indefinable pulsation
> Inaudible to outward sense, but felt
> Through the deep heart of every living thing,
> As if the great soul of the Universe
> Heaved with tumultuous throbbings on the vast
> Suspense of some grand issue.
>
> (ALT, 1:85, IV, lines 28–34)

This universal beating, what Herbert Tucker calls an "ontological throb," returns throughout the poet's long career as an ideal of interpersonal experience (Tucker 1988, 48). But Tennyson never again imagines quite such a totality of influence—"*every* living thing"—or such an optimistic conclusion. When Tennyson came to revise "Armageddon" into the prize-winning "Timbuctoo" (1829), he eliminated this passage, drawing attention instead to the human mind's active engagement with sensation:

A maze of piercing, trackless, thrilling thoughts,
Involving and embracing each with each,
Rapid as fire, inextricably linked,
Expanding momently with every sight
And sound which struck the palpitating sense,
The issue of strong impulse, hurried through
The riven rapt brain[.]

(ALT, 1:194, lines 113–19)

The human body here seems at first simply a passive vessel for synaesthetic physiological experience; the mind is overwhelmed by sensation. Even the speaker's "thrilling thoughts" distinguish themselves by the force of their impression, not the brilliance of their insight. Whereas Fox writes of poetry as an "electric fluid . . . flashing out by fits and starts all the world over," Tennyson imagines thoughts that, "[r]apid as fire," beget a brain both "riven"— that is, split or torn apart—and "rapt": called to attention through the process of its physical reconfiguration. One comes by the "ontological throb" of "Armageddon" not by choice but by necessity—it pulls us in with a universal heave and tug, subjecting both mind and body to its rhythmic sway. But there remains a necessarily active element within the Tennysonian brain of "Timbuctoo," in the "thrilling thoughts" that "[i]nvolv[e]" and "embrac[e]" one another, even if only a thin line distinguishes active mental control from passive physiological response.

Tennyson's careful balancing in "Timbuctoo" between the active process of thought and the passive experience of sensation parallels, and may be indebted to, the philosophical work of his Cambridge tutor, Whewell, who through the 1820s and '30s was concerned with negotiating this very same divide. The key issue for Whewell was the degree to which an active mind, a mind fully engaged in critical thinking, might mould raw sensory data. Following Kant's subjective approach to knowledge, Whewell believed the mind to be always an active participant in perception (Levine, 24; Yeo, 12–13).[6] Whewell makes this clear in the introduction to his *History of the Inductive Sciences:* "[T]o the formation of science, two things are requisite;— Facts and Ideas; observation of Things without, and an inward effort of Thought; or, in other words, Sense and Reason" (Whewell, 1:43).[7] One passage from "Timbuctoo" draws especial attention to the poet's newfound ambivalence between sensation and thought:

> I know not if I shape
> These things with accurate similitude
> From visible objects, for but dimly now,
> Less vivid than a half-forgotten dream,
> The memory of that mental excellence
> Comes o'er me, and it may be I entwine
> The indecision of my present mind
> With its past clearness, yet it seems to me
> As even then the torrent of quick thought
> Absorbed me from the nature of itself
> With its own fleetness.
>
> (ALT, 1:195, lines 130–40)

Tennyson's speaker is conscious of how his brain may filter and revise the data it absorbs from sensory experience. All the indecision of the passage—"I know not," "it may be," "it seems to me"—highlights the poet's awareness of subjectivity in human perception. The earlier Tennyson of "Armageddon" boasted of perceiving with "God's omniscience" (ALT, 1:81, II, line 27); not so the Tennyson of 1829, whose "human brain" at one point "[s]tagger[s] beneath the vision" (ALT, 1:196, lines 181–82), profoundly lacking the omniscience of his youth.[8]

By the time Fox wrote his 1831 review of Tennyson, then, the poet had already outgrown the sort of naïve sensationalism celebrated in Fox's essay. It is perhaps true, according to Tennyson's early poetry, that a poet—in Fox's words—"can influence the associations of unnumbered minds" and "can command the sympathies of unnumbered hearts." But Tennyson seems skeptical of relying on such a simple model of dissemination; the human mind gets in the way of pure sensory experience, actively interpreting and thereby altering a one-to-one relation between poem and poetic experience. Arthur Hallam's "On Some of the Characteristics of Modern Poetry," published seven months after Fox's review, approaches Tennyson's poetry from a perspective seemingly more in line with the poet's own views of sensation and thought. Donald S. Hair has shown the extent to which Hallam borrows in his essay from the associationist tradition of Locke, Berkeley, Hume, and Hartley, concentrating on interconnections in the poetry between physiological experience and thought (Hair, 41–56). In much the same way as Fox writes of the "senses, feelings, nerves, and brain" that come together in making poetry a radical political tool, Hallam identifies the political strength to be found in the "fine organs" of the very best poets that "tremble . . . into emotion at colours, and sounds, and movements, unperceived or unregarded by duller temperaments" (Hallam, 87).[9] But whereas Fox trumpets the potential for all individuals to share in the poet's experiences, Hallam suggests that individuals will respond variously to the poet's language of sensibility: "For since the emotions of the poet, during composition, follow a regular law of association, it follows that to accompany their progress up to the harmonious prospect of the whole, and to perceive the proper dependence of every step on that which preceded, it is absolutely necessary *to start from the same point*" (89). Because each of us necessarily starts from a different point and because these differences are exacerbated by class and educational background, among other distinctions, it seems unlikely from Hallam's perspective that one might achieve Fox's model of universal poetic synthesis. At least, this is so for the poet's intellectual engagements and the author's *"moral . . . point of vision"* (89). It is not so, however, with respect to physiology, "because nature has placed in every man the simple elements, of which art is the sublimation" (89). Hallam may thereby question the ability of the poet, as Fox puts it, to "disseminate principles" and to "give those principles power over men's imaginations," but he leaves room for Tennyson's early fantasy of an "indefinable pulsation" that might be "felt / Through the deep heart of every living thing." The very greatest poets—Shakespeare, Dante, Homer—"keep no aristocratic state, apart from the sentiments of society at large; they speak to the hearts of all, and by the magnetic force of their conceptions elevate inferior intellects into a higher and purer atmosphere" (90);[10] the aesthetic sphere as Hallam sees it relies not on class structure but on universal, physiological sensation.

The responses of Hallam and Fox to Tennyson's 1830 volume coincide with, and in some ways motivate, renewed efforts to demonize the poetry of sensation on the part of both the conservative press and a new generation of anti-Romantic poets. For these writers and thinkers, the conjunction of physiological affect with poetic form loomed as a threat warranting firm censure. Isobel Armstrong has shown the extent to which Hallam's sensational poetics were read as having radical political implications. Sensation as Hallam presented it was taken to be an "ideological solvent" that defamiliarized "habitual forms of thought by exploring disruptive conditions of perception which will ultimately reconfigure consciousness" and, in the end, might enable the "regeneration of society" (Armstrong 1993, 32, 34).[11] John Wilson, a.k.a. Christopher North, the high-Tory literary critic for *Blackwood's*, led the attack against the poetics of sensation in a May 1832 essay on Tennyson. Wilson quotes at length from Fox's *Westminster* review of *Poems, Chiefly Lyrical*—he calls Fox "the quack in the Westminster"—and then launches into a frenetic assault on Fox's idea of poetry in general and Fox's review of Tennyson in particular: "It is a perfect specimen of the super-hyperbolical ultra-extravagance of outrageous Cockney eulogistic foolishness, with which not even a quantity of common sense less than nothing has been suffered, for an indivisible moment of time, to mingle; the purest mere matter of moonshine ever mouthed by an idiot-lunatic, slavering in the palsied dotage of the extremest superannuation ever inflicted on a being, long ago, perhaps, in some slight respects and low degrees human, but now sensibly and audibly reduced below the level of the Pongos" (728–29). One suspects that Wilson's anger here was inspired less by Fox's praise of a little-known poet still in his early twenties than by the political implications of Fox's poetic theory. Wilson opens his review insisting that "every thing is poetry which is *not* mere sensation" (721; emphasis mine), overturning at once Fox's elevation of feelings that might "command the sympathies of unnumbered hearts." If literature is to inspire the masses, then it must for Wilson focus on ideals, not physiological sensations: "the transcendant and eternal grandeur of commonplace and all-time truths" (725). Literature must, in other words, accommodate itself to certain accepted standards: culturally accepted and historically established "truths," as opposed to the arbitrary thoughts and feelings of any one individual poet.

Wilson's ideas here have much in common with William Whewell's insistence that knowledge must be based not exclusively on experience (the data we each take in and process through our senses) but on a priori, universal truths that structure our sensory experiences. Both may be seen as reacting to the extremes of Lockean empiricism, which had been criticized since its earliest days as relying too unconditionally, and too uncritically, on idio-syncratic personal impressions. As Anthony Ashley Cooper, the Third Earl of Shaftesbury, mockingly put it in the early eighteenth century, according to Locke "neither right nor wrong, virtue nor vice, are any thing in them-selves; nor is there any trace or idea of them naturally imprinted on human minds" (Shaftesbury, 346).[12] Lockean empiricism, that is to say, leads one straight down the path of moral relativism. For Whewell, however, the issue has less to do with virtue or vice than it does with scientific method. He writes to John Herschel in 1841 that his "argument is all in a single sen-tence. You *must* adopt such a view of the nature of scientific truth as makes universal and necessary propositions possible; for it appears that there are such, not only in arithmetic and geometry, but in mechanics, physics and other things. I know no solution of this difficulty except by assuming *a priori* grounds" (quoted in Snyder, 43). Antiprogressive critics such as John Wil-son understood how such a belief in a priori fact—"the transcendant and eternal grandeur of commonplace and all-time truths"—might be put to culturally conservative uses. Wilson values the sort of circular logic that tells us something is true because it has always been so, that there is no need to look beyond the immediacy of what we know by familiarity to be true. Laura J. Snyder points out that this was John Stuart Mill's most salient point of conflict in his protracted dispute with Whewell: "Mill noted that the intuitionists [those who, like Whewell, believed that truth could be ar-rived at through intuition] claimed the criterion of a necessary truth was that its contrary was 'inconceivable'; he feared that this standard could be used to argue that any innovations which seemed inconceivable to the ruling classes of society must be rejected as contrary to the way things necessarily must be" (Snyder, 96). Such logic would suggest, for example, that voting rights for women and for the working classes should be withheld if those in power cannot conceive of a society functioning under genuinely democratic prin-ciples. The negotiation of active thought and passive sensational experience thus plays out as a political confrontation, the antisensationalist position being that individuals cannot possibly maintain order if the final arbiter of truth is to be the human body itself.

Wilson's Tory conservatism found an able poetic mouthpiece in the fig-ure of Henry Taylor, author of the closet drama *Philip van Artevelde* (1834). Equally formalist screed and political manifesto, Taylor uses the preface of his poem to mock those poets to whom "[a] feeling came more easily . . . than a reflection." Taylor was perhaps the leading anti-Romantic of his generation, and *Philip* gained a notable following. His preface suggests that poets who feel rather than reflect are egregiously out of touch with actual life and the lived experiences of human individuals:

> Either they did not look upon mankind with observant eyes, or they did not feel it to be any part of their vocation to turn what they saw to account. It did not belong to poetry, in their apprehension, to thread the mazes of life in all its classes and under all its circumstances, common as well as romantic, and, seeing all things, to infer and to instruct: on the contrary, it was to stand aloof from every thing that is plain and true; to have little concern with what is rational or wise; it was to be, like music, a moving and enchanting art, acting upon the fancy, the affections, the passions, but scarcely connected with the exercise of the intellectual faculties. (Taylor, 1:xii)

What Taylor calls "the affections" and "the passions" are necessarily individual and idiosyncratic, and thereby have nothing constructive to say to the community at large. Such poetry is "enchanting" and fanciful, but "scarcely . . . intellectual." Hence Byron, the specific object of Taylor's attack, was immensely popular, but his poetry offers little beyond indulgence in "selfish passions" (xviii). Byron alienates reason from his verses, claims Taylor, opening the doors to "anarchy and abstraction" and a state "where imagination exercises the shadow of an authority, over a people of phantoms, in a land of dreams" (xxvi). What is needed is a return to reason, to feeling governed by active thought, and to a form of poetry—that is, diction, rhythm, and rhyme—reflective of emotional containment. Taylor offers as an example of reasoned containment his own *Philip van Artevelde*, a poem painfully regular in both formal design and thematic development. That readers of the time by and large responded favorably to Taylor's work says a great deal about the political climate of the 1830s and the understood connections between politics and poetic form. Writing in the *Edinburgh Review*, Thomas Henry Lister calls the poem "a remedy for that over-excited and unhealthy tone of feeling" that inspired the period's "marked indifference to poetical productions" (Lister, 1). In the *Quarterly Review*, J. G. Lockhart compares *Philip van Artevelde* to other poems of the day—poems by "vain, narrow, and barbarous men"—and is reminded of a "tall massive tower rising into the clear air above a wilderness of black roofs and quaint gables" (Lockhart, 369), an overwhelming phallus bringing order and control to the populace.[13]

Even Tennyson, the poet of sensation himself, attests to his appreciation of Taylor's poetic style, though he resists the extremities of Taylor's position: "I think [Philip van Artevelde] a noble fellow. I close with him in most that he says of modern poetry though it may be that he does not take sufficiently into consideration the *peculiar* strength evolved by such writers as Byron and Shelley which however mistaken they may be did yet give the world another heart and new pulses—and so are we kept going" (TL, 1:120). As is so often the case, Tennyson charts out a middle ground between Taylor and the Romantic poets Taylor loathes, acknowledging the "*peculiar* strength" of sensibility, even if he resists, as critics such as Herbert Tucker have shown, the pull of Romanticism's more extreme practices.[14] By some accounts, it was nothing new to idealize a balance between reflection and sensation; poetic sensibility had always grounded itself in what Jerome McGann calls "the radical involvement of mind and body" (McGann 1996, 127), and we have seen already how Felicia Hemans balanced carefully between intellectual engagement and the language of physiological affect. But the various antagonisms among Fox, Taylor, Tennyson, Mill, and Whewell constitute a more politically engaged interrogation into the specific nature of this "involvement" between thought and feeling, mind and body. John Keble, then professor of poetry at Oxford, summarized the conservative aesthetic view in his "Inaugural Oration" of 1832, an address delivered just months after the passage of the great Reform Bill: "[T]he glorious art of Poetry [is] a kind of medicine divinely bestowed upon man: which gives healing relief to secret mental emotion, yet without detriment to modest reserve: and, while giving scope to enthusiasm, yet rules it with *order* and due *control*" (Keble, 1:22; emphasis mine). Keble here references what would come be known as the Tractarian doctrine of reserve, the regulation of religious zeal or "enthusiasm" associated from the seventeenth century with religious prophesying and ecstatic experience.[15] Keble firmly links this kind of aesthetic and religious restraint to political stability: "[T]he functions of noble poetry and good citizenship [are] . . . closely intertwined" (1:17, 14).

Keble's views here reflect a broader, conservative engagement with poetry's political implications, suggesting in part why Tennyson's earliest volumes were subject to such intense scrutiny and debate.

Before turning more fully to Tennyson's poetry, we should consider one final voice in the 1830s debate on sensibility. John Stuart Mill's 1835 review of Tennyson's poetry, and Mill's 1833 essays on poetry, "What Is Poetry?" and "The Two Kinds of Poetry," seem in many ways indebted to Hallam's 1831 review. The ultimate goals of poetry are much the same for both Hallam and Mill; each views poetry as a vehicle for sympathy that might support social cohesion. Mill writes that "the noblest end of poetry as an intellectual pursuit" is to "act[] upon the desires and characters of mankind *through their emotions*, to raise them towards the perfection of their nature" (Mill, 1:414; emphasis mine). In his essay on Tennyson, Hallam presents sympathy as the binding force of community, community that arises (as it does in Fox's essay) through the passionate experience of poetry: "[T]he true poet addresses himself, in all his conceptions, to the common nature of us all"; "There are innumerable shades of fine emotion in the human heart. . . . [A]nd in music they find a medium through which they pass from heart to heart" (Hallam, 89, 96–97). Mill and Hallam also distinguish between "reflective" poets such as Wordsworth and "poets of sensation" such as Keats and Shelley (Hallam, 85, 87). For Mill, Wordsworth represents "the poetry of culture" (Mill, 1:361), the complete submission of feeling to conscious thought. According to Mill, Wordsworth "never seems *possessed* by any feeling; no emotion seems ever so strong as to have entire sway, for the time being, over the current of his thoughts" (1:359); Hallam judges "much [that] has been said" by Wordsworth to be "good as philosophy, powerful as rhetoric, but false as poetry" (Hallam, 86).

For all their similarities, however, Mill departs from Hallam in elaborating a poetics of sensation that maintains a firm connection to active thought. Mill argues, famously, that poetry is made up of "the thoughts and words in which emotion *spontaneously* embodies itself," but he also insists that poets "are so constituted, that emotions are links of association by which their ideas, both sensuous and spiritual, are connected together" (Mill, 1:356; emphasis mine). For Mill, feeling works as a "spontaneous" unifying principle for the mental processes, "ideas, both sensuous and spiritual."[16] The greatest of poets—Mill uses Shelley as his example—write "under the overruling influence of some one state of feeling" so that their feelings might "harmoniz[e]" the disparate thoughts and images of their work (1:360). In his essay on Tennyson, Mill strengthens this insistence on the intellectual component of poetic composition:

> Every great poet, every poet who has extensively or permanently influenced mankind, has been a great thinker;—has had a philosophy, though perhaps he did not call it by that name;—has had his mind full of thoughts, derived not merely from passive sensibility, but from trains of reflection, from observation, analysis, and generalization. . . . [T]he poet's success . . . will be in proportion to the intrinsic value of his thoughts, and to the command which he has acquired over the materials of his imagination, for placing those thoughts in a strong light before the intellect, and impressing them on the feelings. (1:413–14)

This is where Mill and Hallam most clearly part ways, and where Mill, contradictory and ambiguous though much of his writing on poetry is, more accurately anticipates Tennyson's mature work. Whereas for Hallam the body of the poet "tremble[s] into emotion at colours, and sounds, and movements" such that bodily sensation leads to poetic insight (Hallam, 87), for Mill the process works in exactly the opposite manner; the poet's active work of "observation, analysis, and generalization" results in thoughts that are "impress[ed] . . . on the feelings." Though the result for each is the same—readers being moved to poetic feeling—the process of reaching that conclusion differs importantly. Mill seemingly short-circuits sensory experience, such that the active human brain remains always in control of sensory data. Before a vision, a smell, a taste, or a touch might trigger an emotional response, the brain first filters the raw sensory data and, in a sense, frames that data by way of "analysis and generalization." Sensibility is thereby dependent, as it seems in so much of Tennyson's poetry, on the active human brain. Whewell, too, believed the brain to be necessary in filtering sensory experience, but for Whewell the brain's part was to impose what he called "Fundamental Ideas"—"*Ideas*, as being something not derived from sensation, but governing sensation, and consequently giving form to our experience" (quoted in Snyder, 41)—whereas for Mill the ideas come through

the process of analysis itself. Whewell, that is, approaches sensory experi-
ence with a preconceived understanding of what he might reasonably ex-
pect to see; Mill lets his brain actively interpret sensory data as he goes
along, resisting the pull of thoughts already in place. Hallam emerges as a
radical figure in light of both Mill and Whewell, allowing the brain to take a
passive role while sensory experience plays out howsoever it may in the
human body.

There is thus little agreement among thinkers of the 1830s when it
comes to questions of sensation and empiricism. Tennyson's first two volumes
of poetry become the locus of much debate on these topics because he frames
questions of thought and feeling with genuine ambivalence. We might see
this ambivalence as a careful navigation of what had become a highly charged
discourse around physiological sensation, a discourse made all the more rele-
vant by the unstable political dynamics of the early 1830s. What at first
seem insignificant differences among Mill, Whewell, Hallam, Taylor, Wil-
son, and Fox in fact represent importantly distinct models for poetic—and,
by extension, political—experience. We turn now to Tennyson's 1847 "med-
ley," *The Princess*, to examine more specifically the intersection of empiri-
cism and politics in Tennyson's work; the poem also allows us to return to
the matter of electricity, which turns out to be critical to understanding the
poem's engagement with sensational poetics.

TELEGRAPHING *THE PRINCESS*

The Princess fully engages with the questions of feeling and knowledge posed
in the reviews of Tennyson's earlier work. The poem opens upon the "broad
lawns" of Sir Walter Vivian's estate, where a local "Institute"—a working-
class organization—is holding a festival. Tennyson had witnessed a similar
event in July 1842, a day-long fair organized by the mechanics' institute near
Maidstone, just southeast of London (Killham, 61). The scene also reminds
one of the working-class crowd that Tennyson and Hallam must have ob-
served while touring the Adelaide Gallery of Practical Science in 1833. As
The Princess gets under way, Tennyson sketches for his readers the pleasures
of the institute's festival, where "sport / Went hand in hand with Science"
(ALT, 2:190–91, Prologue, lines 79–80): a man shoots a cannon, a hot-air
balloon rises and a parachute falls, a "petty railway" circles nearby (190, line
74). More remarkable, though often overlooked, one also discovers at the

fair a cluster of young women eager to experience the pleasures of a power-
ful electric shock:

> a group of girls
> In circle waited, whom the electric shock
> Dislinked with shrieks and laughter[.]
>
> (190, lines 68–70)

The light tone of this passage, aided by its comic enjambments, suggests
that Tennyson was not as surprised as one might imagine by the scene of
electrification. Such experiments—circles of hand-holding individuals through
which electric currents passed—were a common form of Victorian entertain-
ment, inspired even at the distance of a century by Nollet's experiment of
1746 (see introduction to this volume). Tennyson's girls form a circle through
which a strong electric charge is passed, inducing spasmodic writhing and
the breaking apart of the circuit: "the electric shock / Dislinked." *The
Princess* thus offers in its introductory pages an electric logic that structures
both the form and the content of the poem that follows.

Readers familiar with *The Princess* will recall that the narrative is told by
a succession of male storytellers lounging in a circle. Between the narrative
segments, women sing lyrical interludes to give "breathing-space" to the
men (ALT, 2:189, Prologue, line 35). Tennyson's tale is thus passed from
hand to hand, a "scattered scheme of seven" that admits to achieving only
an approximation of unity (ALT, 2:293, Conclusion, line 8). The poem's in-
congruous narrative, what one critic calls "a gangly, disjointed communal
myth" (Albright, 214), centers on a women's university from which men are
prohibited on pain of death. The princess who runs the university has been
promised in marriage to a neighboring prince, who infiltrates the university,
dressed as a woman, to win the young woman's affections. As the poem pro-
gresses, as the story passes from one speaker to the next, the narrative takes
a variety of increasingly improbable turns, in addition to alternating back
and forth generically between narrative and lyric forms: the prince and the
friends who accompanied him are discovered; a war ensues between the
kingdoms of the prince and the princess; the women's university is con-
verted to a war hospital; the prince, wounded in battle, is nursed back to
health by the princess, who at long last falls in love with him. The point of

FIGURE 2.1. "A Deep, Dire, Dreadful Tragedy, In Four Acts" (Act 4: "Rushed!"), by R. A. Empey. Assaulted by telegraphic impulses. (In W. J. Johnston, ed., *Lightning Flashes and Electric Dashes*, first published 1877.)

"[t]he physical impact of sound" (Clayton, 52), as well as with the physiological effects of electricity.[20] Workers had to be trained to "read" patterns of pulsing sound, to make sense of what at first could be understood only as bodily sensation, as stressed and unstressed, long and short, rhythmic impulses. The experiences of the telegraph clerks in both the short story and the cartoon draw our attention to the intense, bodily experience of "reading" and then transmitting a language experienced first as physical stress.

So too in *The Princess*, readers are asked to imagine communication as physiologically felt. With the circle of electrified girls and the neighboring model telegraph as structural models for the poem, Tennyson offers as intimate connective tissue the lyric poems that interrupt the narrative passages. Like the prince's seizures, Tennyson added these lyric interludes subsequent to the poem's original publication: the lyrics in 1850, the seizures in 1851. Both lyrics and seizures articulate a formal structure that Tennyson clearly saw as lacking in the original work.[21] As brief flashes of lyric inti-macy—"Sweet and low," "The splendour falls," "Home they brought her warrior dead," and so forth—the poems coincide with the touching of one hand to another, or the passing of the narrative tale from one male speaker to the next (an affective model positioning the poem's women, as Eve Kosofsky Sedgwick notes, between the poem's storytelling men [Sedgwick, 127]). It has been suggested that Tennyson subordinates the women of *The Princess* "to the lowly status of intermittent lyrical 'punctuations' of the men's narrative" (Eagleton, 102). But Tennyson insists in a variety of ways on the necessary work these lyrical moments perform. Not merely a sign of "the beautiful artistry of which women . . . were truly capable" (Clapp-Itnyre, 242), these lyrics emphasize the necessary affective and physiological processes of communication on which the entire poem hinges. Like the relay points of an intricate telegraph network or the nodes of an individual's nervous system, *The Princess* passes its story onward, slightly altered with each generic shift and narrative exchange, yet coherent as a network of ideas and sensations. The poem's coherence, to the extent that it is coherent, comes about largely by way of the affective model enabled through the lyric interludes, the songs performed by the women.

If these songs function like electric shocks passed from hand to hand, they also look back to Tennyson's fantasy in "Armageddon" of an "indefin-able pulsation / Inaudible to outward sense, but felt / Through the deep heart of every living thing." We have seen how Tennyson turned away from this original, purely affective model of experience, seemingly skeptical of its achievement. In "Timbuctoo," Tennyson interjects physiological affect with intellectual rigor, roughly following Whewell's balancing of sensation and reason. The electrified girls stand out for Tennyson as an inspiration for *The Princess* precisely because they offer a reconciliation of physiological sensa-tion and active thought that was not available to the poet in the late 1820s. The electric telegraph seems in fact the ideal model for Tennyson's poetry, the perfect juxtaposing of feeling and thought, body and mind, that might allow the poet to have his cake and eat it, too, assuming that a poem could ever truly resemble a telegraphic impulse. Neither dangerously unruly nor exclusively intellectual, telegraphic poetics mediate in a flash the most con-tradictory poetic theories of the 1830s, offering an ideal—if abstract—struc-ture for poetic transmission. The encounter with Tennyson's poem, then, would go something like this: the reader absorbs and processes intellectually the narrative from, for example, part three, which details some of the prince's stay in the women's university; one of the women then sings "The Splendour Falls," a lyric whose thematic and formal attention to sonic effect—"Blow, bugle, blow, set the wild echoes flying"—conjures in the reader an emotional response; this feeling cements in place and broadens the reader's response to the original narrative, adding depth of feeling and insight; the lyrical affect then smoothes over the disjunctions between parts three and four (narrative installments told by distinct individuals), facilitating the continuation of the narrative, the passing of the story from hand to hand. In the space between parts five and six, the lyric "Home they brought her warrior dead" similarly bridges the emotional and sequential gaps between the prince's fall in battle and his convalescence in the women's university, now a war hospital. The lyric prepares the reader for the princess's abrupt change of heart, uncovering a layer of emotional complexity otherwise obscured by the forward push of narrative.

Tennyson's "telegraphic poetics," then, arise not from the presence of an actual electric shock in *The Princess* (though the poet's inclusion of the electrified girls remains important), but from formal maneuvers that mimic the work of an electrified circuit. Like Benjamin Franklin, whose experience of an electric shock I discuss in the introduction, readers of *The Princess* move between raw sensation and active interpretation ("It was some Minutes before I could recollect my Thoughts so as to know what was the Matter," writes Franklin). Tennyson distinguishes these categories in part by gender (the women sing the lyrics, the men compose the narrative) and in part by genre. But any reader of the poem encounters both, resulting in the sometimes jarring oscillation between narrative and lyric modes. This reading of a formal telegraphic presence in *The Princess*, a presence literally embodied in the men and women who perform the poem's different movements, works against the oft repeated suggestion that telegraphy was understood in the 1840s and '50s as somehow bodiless, existing in a spiritual or intellectual realm distinct from human corporeality.[22] While telegraphic thinking often ran parallel to, and intermingled with, thinking about spiritualism—the subject of the conclusion to this book—it was also understood to function primarily through the human bodies that sent and received electric signals (hence the cartoon of the electrified telegrapher). In devising a poetic structure that echoes the telegraphic process, Tennyson attempts to reconcile the extremes of early Victorian poetic theory: Hallam's poetics of sensation, Mill's plea for "observation, analysis, and generalization," and Henry Taylor's conservative insistence on "the intellectual faculties." In its way, *The Princess* accomplishes all these things, jumping from one generic frame to another with a facility that continues to bewilder critics, even as it surprised Tennyson's contemporaries.

Perhaps most important, however, the poem's telegraphic model of communication works to highlight and connect thematically the poem's two key political concerns: the "Woman Question" and, less explicitly, Chartism. One must not forget that the girls playing with electricity at the poem's opening are working-class girls. The aristocrats who eventually narrate the story of *The Princess* pass by and observe "the multitude, a thousand heads" (190, Prologue, line 57)—that is, the working-class crowd—on their way to the ruined abbey where they repose and invent their tale. Until the poem's conclusion, little more is mentioned of the crowd, but it remains a presence through the poem, most notably when a blush of the princess is compared to a scene of working-class revolt:

> over brow
> And cheek and bosom brake the wrathful bloom
> As of some fire against a stormy cloud,
> When the wild peasant rights himself, the rick
> Flames, and his anger reddens in the heavens.
>
> (243, IV, lines 363–67)

Tennyson had participated in efforts to extinguish fires set by disgruntled peasants while still a student at Cambridge (C. Tennyson, 100). Though Tennyson supported the reform movements of the early 1830s and "largely sympathized with the labourers in their demands," he rejected as unnecessary the violence that often accompanied radical political movements (H. Tennyson, 1:41). Herbert Tucker is thus no doubt correct in suggesting that the rick-burning metaphor positions Ida as "a type of the recanting radical, the once wild peasant who now 'rights himself' by abandoning the error of his ways and falling back into line with public rectitude" (Tucker 1988, 359). The revolting peasants, conjured figuratively via the anger of the princess, function as an alternative vision to the peaceful, fun-loving workers of the Prologue. Class conflict is not quite "omitted from Tennyson's England," as Sedgwick suggests (Sedgwick, 126)—the reference to Chartist unrest is unmistakable—but the violence is certainly repressed, sidelined figuratively into an expression of anger.[23] The working-class crowd is thereby "[d]is-linked" from the narrative of *The Princess*, even as it hovers on the peripheries of the poem with an ominous and unavoidable presence.

Chartist unrest makes its most legible appearance in *The Princess* through affective, bodily experience. The "wrathful bloom" of the princess's anger plays out, not only through its gesture to working-class rioters, but also with a near-complete loss of physiological control:

> her breast,
> Beaten with some great passion at her heart,
> Palpitated, her hand shook[.]
>
> (243, IV, lines 368–70)

Sensibility, gender, and Chartist politics here converge in the palpitating, passionate body of the princess. The formal vision of the poem as a whole insists on such interweaving as it moves from the circle of electrified girls in the Prologue through to the poem's juxtaposing of lyrical song, working-class violence, and feminist politics. But the particular fear of *The Princess*, implicit in this juxtaposing, remains the specter of a working-class crowd united through physiological experience. It is a fear common to British literature of the period, even among writers sympathetic to working-class causes. Tennyson may have had in mind a handful of texts that link together class violence, electric physiology, and progressive politics, including—as just one of many possible examples—Robert Southey's closet drama *Wat Tyler* (composed 1794; published 1817); a sympathetic portrayal of the early British revolutionary. Toward the end of Southey's drama, after the working-class Tyler has been killed for challenging the king's authority to levy burdensome taxes on the poor, one of Tyler's compatriots looks forward to a time when it is recognized that all men are equal:

> And there will be a time when this great truth
> Shall be confess'd—be felt by all mankind.

The electric truth shall run from man to man,
And the blood-cemented pyramid of greatness
Shall fall before the flash.
                    (Southey, 97, act 3, scene 2, lines 65–69)

Tennyson's poem never reaches such a degree of idealism—or radicalism—
but *The Princess* draws our attention in a similar manner to the physiologi-
cal nature of "truth" as it moves through crowds of individuals. The
Conclusion of *The Princess* finds the workers from the Prologue "swarming
now, / To take their leave" (ALT, 2:294, Conclusion, lines 37–38) from the
nobleman's estate. In lines Tennyson added in 1850, one of the aristocratic
storytellers—"The Tory member's elder son"—anxiously remarks on the
continental upheavals of 1848:

God bless the narrow sea which keeps her off,
And keeps our Britain, whole within herself,
A nation yet, the rulers and the ruled—
Some sense of duty, something of a faith,
Some reverence for the laws ourselves have made,
Some patient force to change them when we will,
Some civic manhood firm against the crowd—
But yonder, whiff! there comes a sudden heat,
The gravest citizen seems to lose his head,
The king is scared, the soldier will not fight,
The little boys begin to shoot and stab,
A kingdom topples over with a shriek
Like an old woman, and down rolls the world
In mock heroics stranger than our own;
Revolts, republics, revolutions, most
No graver than a schoolboys' barring out;
Too comic for the solemn things they are,
Too solemn for the comic touches in them,
Like our wild Princess with as wise a dream
As some of theirs—God bless the narrow seas!
I wish they were a whole Atlantic broad.
                    (295, Conclusion, lines 51–71)

The speaker of the frame-narrative immediately moves to quiet these concerns, pointing to "the genial day, the happy crowd, / The sport half-science" (295, Conclusion, lines 75–76). But the image of French insurrection, and the suggestion that such violence festers in the hearts and minds of the British working classes, remains.

Tennyson's somewhat ambivalent engagement with the working-class crowd, equally affirmative and apprehensive, parallels his uneasy depiction of the fictional community of women whose all-female university occupies the center of the tale. The women who run the university, including the princess, disavow the kind of sensibility that Victorians typically ascribed to women; they insist instead on a stoical, and even utilitarian, adherence to truth, fact, and emotional containment. Thus, when one of the women sings the song "Tears, Idle Tears," the princess responds "with some disdain" that "thine are fancies hatched / In silken-folded idleness" (233–34, IV, lines 43, 48–49); that is, any song about tears "from the depth of some divine despair, / Ris[ing] in the heart, and gather[ing] to the eyes" (232, IV, lines 22–23) is too redolent of sensibility for this new community of women. Yet the end of Tennyson's poem finds the princess falling in love with the prince, and reentering the world of men, through a sympathy that manifests first as a physiological spasm: as she "shuddered, a twitch of pain / Tortured her mouth" (270, VI, lines 89–90). The bodily experience of sensibility is what breaks the princess's "iron will": "Her noble heart was molten in her breast" (271, VI, lines 102–3).[24] Ida thereby acquiesces to a style of feeling she had previously censured, allowing the community of women to rejoin the community of humankind through affective experience, by giving in to sympathetic feeling. Ida's love for the prince has long disappointed those who admire her resistance to Victorian patriarchy, but her love also serves to complicate our reading of the working-class crowd on Sir Walter Vivian's estate. Emotive experience seems necessary, to a point, to hold together communities of individuals (the women would not rejoin the men without it). But like the flash of electricity that simultaneously connects and disconnects the individuals in the circle, affect too strong works against the kind of social conjunctions it means to inspire. Indeed, overpowering affect seems most readily to lead to the rick-burning, nation-threatening violence that Tennyson locates in Chartism and, more generally, working-class culture. Strong feeling thereby looms as a threat against entrenched power while simultaneously underpinning the very idea of community.

Such conflicts within affective experience are not unique to *The Princess*, but are symptomatic of a recurring problem in nineteenth-century British poetry. How does one keep the electric thrill enclosed within the safe confines of aesthetic experience? How can a poet ensure that his pulsing sensibility (necessary for the composition of great works) will not leak out to inspire readers to acts of passionate revolt? In 1757, Burke wrote glowingly of "the contagion of our passions" inspired by Milton's *Paradise Lost:* "[W]e catch a fire already kindled in another" (Burke 1968, 175). But this reading would have been impossible for the Tory critic after the fall of Versailles; in the *Reflections on the Revolution in France*, Burke writes famously of his "love" for "a manly, moral, regulated liberty" at odds with his earlier "fire" (Burke 1986, 90). If *The Princess* is, as Charles Kingsley suggested in 1850, a "mirror of the nineteenth century, possessed of its own new art and science, its own new temptations and aspirations" (Kingsley 1850, 250), then the electric-like negotiations of class, gender, and poetic form are what make it so. The poem demonstrates an uncanny balancing of the political and aesthetic concerns articulated in the 1830s by Mill, Hallam, Taylor, and Wilson. Poetry in *The Princess* works by telegraphing thoughts and feeling via formal maneuvers and emotional shocks. In so doing, it aligns and brings into focus a constellation of cultural, political, and aesthetic concerns, in particular the gendered dynamics of sensibility and bourgeois perceptions of the working classes. To understand poetic transmission as electric in nature is to foreground one's bodily relationship to aesthetic production, and—by extension—the relationship of one's body to others. The work of the Victorian poet is to find such spaces for poetry in a political environment hostile to affect (indeed, hostile to noncognitive communication of any sort). Tennyson's tentative rapprochement in *The Princess*, a careful balancing of aesthetic, cultural, and political anxieties, will stand as an especially fine example of the poetic strategies examined throughout the present book. It also suggests a framework for reading a body of poems somewhat more explicitly political in nature, poems to which we now turn.

RADICAL SENSIBILITY

Thomas Hood's 1843 "The Song of the Shirt" was a "national sensation" (Hill, 153), calling attention to the horrid conditions under which many working-class individuals labored. Hood's poem describes British workers variously as slaves and as prisoners, toiling in monotonous, ceaseless labor. The central figure of the poem is a seamstress:

> With fingers weary and worn,
>   With eyelids heavy and red,
> A woman sat, in unwomanly rags,
>   Plying her needle and thread—
>   Stitch! stitch! stitch!
>   In poverty, hunger, and dirt,
> And still with a voice of dolorous pitch
> She sang the "Song of the Shirt!"
>
> (Hood, 625)

Hood's poem resonated with the British public, dramatically increasing the circulation of *Punch*, the journal in which it was first published.[25] Three decades later, the poem retained enough of a presence to serve as the basis for a parody by "G. W. Russell" entitled "The Song of the Plug" (1877). Published in *Lightning Flashes and Electric Dashes*, an American collection of writings on the electric telegraph, the poem is a ballad on the toils of an electric telegraph clerk:

> With thumb and fore-finger worn,
>   With expression of infernal glee,
> A country plug sat in his place of toil
>   Plying his dare deviltry.
> Break! break! break!
>   As contented as cats on the rug.
> And, still on a key of excellent make,
>   He warbled the song of the plug.
>
> (Russell, 28)

Russell's parody connects the seamstress's weary fingers to those of the electric telegrapher, linking the rise of a telegraphic community to the empowering of Hood's working-class community. From his isolated "place of toil," the telegraph clerk imagines a community of telegraphers united "this vast country o'er"—united through their patterns of rhythmic breaking. Slowly but surely, the clerk insists, this community "will live and thrive and grow" until the world "shall have no peace" (28).

Alongside the mock-revolutionary humor of Russell's poem and the earnest concern of Hood's, one also hears echoes of Tennyson's 1842 lyric, "Break, Break, Break." Like "The Song of the Shirt" and "The Song of the Plug," Tennyson's poem is primarily about the work of communication, the process of sharing thoughts and feelings with other individuals. Though "Break, Break, Break" is most often described as a lyric expression of Tennyson's personal grief for Arthur Hallam, who had died unexpectedly in 1833, the poem is less about Hallam than it is about Tennyson's failure to vocalize his loss; the subject of "Break, Break, Break" is the failure of poetry to express the "thoughts" of the suffering poet.[26] The poem, quoted below in full, explicitly hypothesizes a personal, internal lyric that will never be written or spoken directly:

Break, break, break,
    On thy cold gray stones, O Sea!
And I would that my tongue could utter
    The thoughts that arise in me.

O well for the fisherman's boy,
    That he shouts with his sister at play!
O well for the sailor lad,
    That he sings in his boat on the bay!

And the stately ships go on
    To their haven under the hill;
But O for the touch of a vanished hand,
    And the sound of a voice that is still!

Break, break, break,
    At the foot of thy crags, O Sea!
But the tender grace of a day that is dead
    Will never come back to me.

                       (ALT, 2:24)

The highest level of lyric expression is here inexpressible, a body of thoughts the tongue can *not* utter. Rather than articulating an overflow of human feeling, the poem projects feeling into the waves that break on the seashore. In the sound of inexorable breaking, as in the shouting and singing of the fisherman's boy and the sailor lad, we encounter unself-conscious, personal expression. But this is a kind of personal overflow that the speaker of the poem specifically avoids. Though "thoughts . . . arise" in the speaker as resolutely as the waves break on the shore, he resists the expression of those thoughts in the form of language. In the end, little can be said of the poem's speaker, except that he cannot speak what he would like, an ambiguity reinforced by the rhythmic superfluity of the opening stanza's "I": "And I would that my tongue could utter / The thoughts that arise in me." Most of what we seem to know about this rhythmically elided speaker comes from imagining thoughts that have been left unuttered.

The poem remains ambiguous about expression even in the third stanza, when the speaker seems more clearly to express his anguish: "But O for the touch of a vanished hand, / And the sound of a voice that is still!" Here at least one editor makes a confident biographical connection to Hallam; "a vanished hand" becomes, without doubt, Hallam's hand.[27] Like the poem's nostalgia, however, which seems as much a longing for lyric expressiveness as it is a longing for Hallam, the hand and the voice of the third stanza work well in at least two readings. Tennyson gestures here not only to Hallam's silent voice, but also to his own unsung feeling; he refers not only to the hand of his dead friend, but also to his own writing hand, the absent touch of pen on paper that would have recorded his deepest thoughts and passions. What appear at first to be moments of personal revelation remain intimations of a voice, a story, a lyricism that this poem will never realize.

In place of written or spoken verbal expression, "Break, Break, Break" offers sound, specifically the breaking of waves on stones. Tennyson calls our attention to this peculiar kind of sonic production insofar as the sea is linked metonymically to its own expression; the water itself creates its own breaking sound, breaking apart as it does so. Tennyson seems to wish for a similarly unrestrained form of self-expression, even as the poem as a whole reinforces emotional restraint. Uninhibited and driven by its own forward momentum, the sound of the sea's breaking comes entirely from its own internal composition and subsequent de-composition. Though the speaker mourns the distance between his own feeling and spoken language—"And I would that my tongue could utter / The thoughts that arise in me"—he resists the vocalization that would put thoughts into words and, in so doing, violate his own sense of self-coherence. Fully inhabiting the emotional space of the poem, that is, would be akin to breaking, like the water, on "cold gray stones": vocalization by way of bodily disintegration. Not until the following decade, the 1850s, would the Spasmodic poets (the subject of chapter 3) experiment with such bodily modes of communication.

Hood's "Song of the Shirt" replaces the voluble breaking of Tennyson's sea with the nearly silent stitch-work of a poor seamstress: "Stitch! stitch! stitch!" As she stitches, the seamstress sings the song that makes up most of Hood's poem. Though Hood belonged very much within the middling classes, he borrows here from the style of working-class, and specifically Chartist, poetry of his time, endowing a solitary voice with the weight of the collective. Hood's seamstress, that is, speaks generically as a representative of her class, much as Chartist poets such as Ernest Jones "invigorate[d] the voice of the collective" by means of "the power of subjectivity and meditation" (Janowitz, 143). In Russell's "Song of the Plug," this figurative and abstract voice of the collective becomes a genuine community of voices united through telegraphic communication. Russell transforms Tennyson's lamenting "Break, break, break" into the celebration of the electrical breaking that enables plugs to understand one another; he thus revises the Tennysonian speaker who cannot speak into a telegrapher who cannot help but communicate:

> Break! break! break!
> When currents are weak and when strong,
> . . . .
> He merrily warbled his song.

Evoking the familiar works of both Tennyson and Hood, "The Song of the Plug" suggests that the reserved sensibility of Tennyson's poetry must be replaced with a more exuberant expression of thought and feeling. Victorian poems on the telegraph tended to celebrate in this way what one poet, the American Christopher Cranch, called the "[n]ew nerves, new pulse, new motion" made possible by the "swift electric speech" of the telegraph (Cranch,

145). But Russell's poem also makes explicit the class anxieties inherent in such a move. Tennyson's underlying fear in *The Princess* is precisely that a working-class crowd will experience the sort of communal language of telegraphy—simultaneously somatic and intellectual—that in Russell's poetry allows the playful, if faintly ominous, proliferation of disruptive "breaks." The lyrics of *The Princess*, if "telegraphic" in some respects, always also leave space for interpretation (Tennyson never tells us explicitly what to make of lyrics such as "The Splendour Falls" or "Sweet and Low"), and this allows for a community of individuals who will each find his or her own meaning in the affective experience of the poems. Russell's plug, in contrast, sends clear and distinct messages via the telegraph; his long and short pulses radiate messages to his compatriots nationwide, with a clarity that Tennyson vigorously avoided. From "Timbuctoo" on, Tennyson insisted on the active interpretive work of the human mind, much as Whewell saw individuals self-consciously shaping sensory data. This is as much a political insistence as it is aesthetic; those who think for themselves are by definition not part of the mob, that unruly entity that so haunts the Victorian imagination and whose presence clearly shapes a poem such as *The Princess*.[28] We can thus see Tennyson's poetic style, carefully developed through the 1830s and '40s, alongside contemporary institutions such as the Adelaide Gallery of Practical Science and the Society for the Diffusion of Useful Knowledge, as functioning in various ways to "render . . . more docile and manageable" the working classes, as the *Times* put it, by encouraging active thought and discriminating reason.

Arthur Hallam's poet of sensation, then, was in fact a poet of great reserve—so much so that many of Tennyson's contemporaries wished the poet to express himself more forthrightly. John Sterling, one of Tennyson's college friends, complained in 1842 that "[e]*motion* . . . is restrained in all [of Tennyson's] writings" (Sterling, 415), and Elizabeth Barrett Browning likewise objected in R. H. Horne's *New Spirit of the Age* (1844) that Tennyson "refuses to be expansive to his public, opening his heart on the hinges of music, as other poets do" (Horne, 2:30). Alexander Smith, perhaps the most talented of the Spasmodic poets, wrote in 1868 that Tennyson "holds the mirror up to the time, but it is an enchanted one, and reflects but noble faces. People will weary of his finish as they weary of pictures executed on ivory; and he will be succeeded by some far stormier and less perfectly balanced spirit" (Smith 1868, 174). Tennyson was no doubt aware of such criticism. The man who was soon to become Britain's poet laureate looks with fond eyes on the electrified girls of *The Princess*, but for reasons both political and aesthetic, in his writing he knowingly resists the extremes of such physiological and noncognitive work. We turn now to the work of the Spasmodic poets, who in many ways represent the most complete realization of Arthur Hallam's poetics of sensation. Through their language and rhythm, the Spasmodic poets attempt to re-create physiological and passionate experience in a style to which poets such as Mary Robinson, Felicia Hemans, and Alfred Tennyson could only gesture. Coming for the most part from the working classes, the Spasmodics composed the kind of passionate poetry that Tennyson seemed capable of writing yet was forever disavowing as too extreme, too extravagant, and ultimately, in a time of national unease, too dangerous.

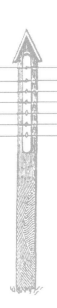

CHAPTER THREE

Rhythms of Spasm

DOBELL, AYTOUN, AND THE CRISIS OF FORM

> Maillard (for his drum still rolls) is, by heaven-rending acclamation,
> admitted General. Maillard hastens the languid march. Maillard,
> beating rhythmic, with sharp ran-tan, all along the Quais, leads
> forward, with difficulty his Menadic host.
>
> —Thomas Carlyle, *The French Revolution* (1837)

> I believe the vulgarest Cockney crowd, flung out million-fold on a
> Whit Sunday, with nothing but beer and dull folly to depend on
> for amusement, would at once kindle into something human, if
> you set them to do almost any regulated act in common. And would
> dismiss their beer and dull foolery, in the silent charm of rhythmic
> human companionship, in the practical feeling, probably new, that
> all of us are made on one pattern, and are, in an unfathomable way,
> brothers to one another.
>
> —Thomas Carlyle, "Shooting Niagara—And After?" (1867)

IN THESE TWO EPIGRAPHS, CARLYLE REFLECTS THE ANXIETIES of his day in considering the effect of rhythmic impulses on crowds of individuals. The first, from *The French Revolution*, pictures the ran-tan, rhythmic beating of a drum hastening the French crowd onward toward Versailles and regicide, just barely organizing "inarticulate frenzy" into the "loosest flowing order" (Carlyle, 2:255, 256). Later in *The French Revolution*, Carlyle returns to the language of rhythm in describing the conquering French soldiers, who "with rhythmic march-melody, waxing ever quicker, to double and to treble quick . . . rally . . . advance . . . rush, death-defying, man-devouring"; in the context of revolutionary France, "rhythmic" patterns organize the inarticulate and ineffective passions of crowds into violent and frightfully effective destructive forces (4:84).

In the second epigraph, Carlyle shifts the context for imagining the work of rhythm, looking instead to crowds in England just prior to the Reform Bill of 1867. "Shooting Niagara" has little positive to say about the fate of an England bent on achieving something like democracy, but toward the end of the essay Carlyle conceives of a successful British state organized around compulsory military service, a rhythmic organization of individuals through which "the entire Population could be thoroughly drilled into coöperative movement" (Carlyle, 30:40): "Discipline, in simultaneous movement and action . . . is one of the noblest capabilities of man (most sadly undervalued hitherto); and one he takes the greatest pleasure in exercising and unfolding, not to mention at all the invaluable benefit it would afford him if unfolded. From correct marching in line, to rhythmic dancing in cotillon or minuet . . . there is a natural charm in it; the fulfilment of a deep-seated, universal desire, to all rhythmic social creatures!" (30:42). The path from the marching French rebels to the English "Cockney crowd" that might, as Carlyle puts it, "dismiss their beer and dull foolery, in the silent charm of rhythmic human companionship" (30:43) is not so terribly indirect. More significantly, the path more easily proceeds from the rhythmic Cockney crowd to the marching French rebels. Rhythmic organization doused with a heavy measure of passionate feeling advances with equal facility toward, on the one hand, delight in communal experience and, on the other, anarchy and terror. And this, of course, is the point of Carlyle's 1867 essay; if working-class crowds are to be organized and set to action, better that they follow the drilling of a sergeant's whistle than the revolutionary beating of a ran-tan drum. Better, that is, to use rhythm to discipline communal passion than to set passion loose on an ordered state.

Carlyle's invocations of rhythm in 1837 and 1867 encircle the years of the Spasmodic literary crisis, and help to make sense of why, among the many reasons critics in the 1850s condemned what was called the Spasmodic style, none appears to have perplexed and frustrated readers so much as the poets' seemingly irregular use of rhythm. In response to Sydney Dobell's 1856 volume *England in Time of War,* a critic for the *Saturday Review* complains that the poet "neither sees, feels, nor thinks like ordinary men. . . . Before we are half through the book, we begin to distrust the evidence of our senses" (Review of *England in Time of War,* 304). A writer for the *National Review* similarly critiques the apparent disorder of Dobell's poetry:

"His thoughts and fancies flow like the sounds from an instrument of music, struck by the hand of a child,—a jumble of sweet and disconnected notes, without order or harmony" ("Sydney Dobell's Poems," 442). But Dobell and his Spasmodic compatriots were not alone in challenging the senses of their readers, and literary critics in the 1850s show increasing indignation and anxiety that any poet should, as Henry Chorley puts it, "rel[y] on the sympathy of the interpreter" to intuit a poem's intended rhythmic design (Chorley, 1327). Chorley protests in his review of Robert Browning's *Men and Women* that recent poets

> have expected [the reader] here to lean on a cadence,—there to
> lend accent to the rhyme, or motion to the languid phrase; in
> another place, to condense a multitude of syllables, so as to give an
> effect of concrete strength. . . . Our poets now speak in an unknown
> tongue,—wear whatever unpoetic garniture it pleases their conceit
> or their idleness to snatch up; and the end too often is, pain to those
> who love them best, and who most appreciate their high gifts and
> real nobleness,—and to the vast world, whom they might assist,
> they bring only a mystery and receive nothing but wonder and
> scorn. (1327)

Though concerned with more than formal irregularity, the reviewer identifies his contemporaries' rhythmic waywardness as part of their poems' "unpoetic garniture," their difficult language and, here in the case of Browning, the shocking images and figurative language. Many critics simply did not know how to read rhythmically irregular poetry, and they did not trust, or did not want to trust, to their intuition.[1]

The criticism perhaps would not have been as vehement had not Victorian readers associated the Spasmodics' unruly formal styles with Britain's fragmented and increasingly heterogeneous culture. When a writer for *Putnam's Monthly Magazine*, an American journal, called Alexander Smith "a child of the time," the point was clear enough ("Poems of Alexander Smith," 99). As various recent literary critics have demonstrated, the Spasmodic poets were linked by their antagonists to cultural crises in gender and sexuality, class and national identity, and religious practice.[2] But perhaps most threatening were not the particular cultural values Spasmodic poetry seemed to defy, but the formal methods poets such as Smith and Dobell used to propagate these challenges to British readers. According to Sydney Dobell, the most sophisticated theorist of Spasmodic poetics, the self-conscious work of poetic interpretation matters little next to the unself-conscious effects of rhythm on the physical bodies of readers. Dobell's poetic theory holds that poetry transmits knowledge and feeling primarily through rhythm, rather than through words or other formal structures. Spasmody as Dobell practices it moves the experience of poetic sensation from the semantic (as in the poems of Robinson and Hemans) and the structural (as in Tennyson's *Princess*) to actual, physical embodiment. Physiologically felt rhythm creates an intimacy between poet and reader such that the reader shares in the physical, and sometimes even mental, experiences of the poet. Hence, if Spasmodic poetry threatens Victorian cultural values by unseating conventional notions of gender, sexuality, class, nationality, and religion, Spasmodic *poetics*—and especially Dobell's notion of rhythm—threatens Victorian culture by promulgating these unconventional values, by offering a vehicle for the widespread dispersal of the eccentric. Indeed, for William Edmondstoune Aytoun, a firm Tory and the most vocal critic of the Spasmodic poets, metrical regularity enforces cultural stability as much as rhythmic spasms encourage much that is "wrong" with the times (which for Aytoun included new reform measures and the granting of rights to women).[3]

Dobell was well aware of this sort of critique, and in many ways his theory of poetry solicits such a response. Having been raised as part of the nonconformist "Church of God" (Jolly, 1:70), Dobell was comfortable challenging the status quo.[4] As a youth, he supported the "physical-force" Chartists (Jolly, 1:44–45), and his first full-length poem—*The Roman* (1850)—charts a monk's efforts to free Italy from the oppression of Austrian rule. Dobell's poetic theory channels his religious and political radicalism into an aesthetic program. Whereas Edmund Gosse would later dismiss Spasmodic poetry as "blustering blank verse," Dobell values bluster insofar as it enables poets to impress themselves more firmly upon readers' bodies and to forge intimate, affective links between poets and readers (Gosse 1877, 54). "Depend on it," Dobell writes to an aspiring poet, "whatever is to live on paper, must have lived in flesh and blood" (Jolly, 1:292). Physiological spasms reflect a "truth" of feeling: bodily feeling mimetically reproduced via poetic form. The poet then publicizes these feelings for others to experience:

"I have lived what I have sung," proclaims the poet Balder, "And it shall live" (SDB, 19, iii).[5] In a profoundly democratizing gesture, poetry in the spasmodic model seems no longer limited to an elite few but is directed instead to the human body and universal experiences—an attempt to realize in concrete terms Tennyson's earlier pulsation "felt / Through the deep heart of every living thing." This universality is exactly what Arthur Hugh Clough admired in the Spasmodic experiments, praising the "real flesh-and-blood heart and soul" of Spasmodic poetry insofar as it might speak to more than just those with "refined . . . and highly educated sensibilities." Matthew Arnold's poetry seems to Clough perhaps "too delicate . . . for common service," whereas Smith's *A Life-Drama* radiates outward with language and feelings intelligible to all its readers (Clough, 6, 12). George Henry Lewes exhibits similar enthusiasm in an 1853 *Westminster Review* essay on Alexander Smith, declaring that the young poet's "eager senses have embraced the world" with "sensuousness of imagery, and directness of fervid expression" (Lewes 1853, 523–24).

Dobell's poetic theory consistently presents such a universalized notion of feeling—a physiologically experienced feeling that embraces "the world." Woven through Dobell's speculations on poetic communication are references both to recent developments in the physiological sciences and to technological—and specifically electrical—innovations that had, in the early 1850s, only just made their way into popular service. We will look in the first part of the chapter to Dobell's poetic theories, then to the passionate rhythms of *Balder* (1853; dated 1854), and finally to Dobell's last volume of poems, *England in Time of War* (1856). Far from being an isolated and anomalous endeavor, Spasmodic poetry operated very much within the mainstream of mid-Victorian philosophy and social science. Dobell, in other words, had his finger on the pulse of Victorian thought in experimenting with what I call *rhythmic epistemology*, the communication of knowledge and feeling through physiological pulses. And the initial popularity of his work indicates that, while controversial, his poetry struck a nerve among readers of the mid-Victorian period.

We will turn in the second part of the chapter to examine the critical and poetic responses to Dobell's work, most notably W. E. Aytoun's brilliant parody *Firmilian* (1854). Aytoun dedicated much of his literary efforts in the 1850s to reining in the unbounded passions of Spasmodic formlessness, to refuting by means of poetic theory, as well as his own poetry, the empiricist notion that objective truth necessarily derives from subjective and physiological experience. His anxiety, and the Spasmodic theories against which he struggled, epitomize the divided literary scene of the 1850s, in which poets and critics responded variously to the political, social, and intellectual revolutions of the time: the Chartist uprisings of the 1840s, the violent revolutions of 1848, and the Crimean War, as well as scientific advances that would culminate with the 1859 publication of Darwin's *On the Origin of Species*. The Spasmodic controversy also brings to a head the poetic debates of the 1830s (discussed in the previous chapter), foregrounding in the clearest of terms the connections among poetry, bodily experience, and political thought.

THE BODY POETIC, CIRCA 1853

Consider the term Victorian critics used to isolate Dobell's poetic theory and to disparage its practice. The word *spasmodic* never had an especially positive connotation. The British witnessed in the 1830s an epidemic known as "spasmodic cholera"; the disease struck again in 1853–54, the period of the Spasmodic literary crisis, killing 26,000 (A. N. Wilson, 36). In 1847 Jane Eyre feels Rochester's "spasmodic movement of fury or despair" when Richard Mason interrupts their marriage ceremony (C. Brontë, 378). And Elizabeth Gaskell describes Ruth's "spasmodic effort" to tell the painful story of her son's illegitimate origins: "[S]he at length, holding him away from her, and nerving herself up to tell him all by one spasmodic effort" (Gaskell, 281). Kirstie Blair has traced the use of the word through nineteenth-century medical discourse, showing its association with weakness and effeminacy.[6] The *Oxford English Dictionary* defines *spasmodic* in terms roughly equivalent to those W. E. Aytoun used to characterize the Spasmodic poets: "Agitated, excited; emotional, high-strung; given to outbursts of excitement; characterized by a disjointed or unequal style of expression." But the *OED*'s definition of *spasm* emphasizes the uncontrollable nature to which the word refers, as it is used by Brontë and Gaskell: "Any sudden or convulsive movement of a violent character; a convulsion." This is also the sense of *spasmodic* as it is used by Darwin in *The Descent of Man* (1871): "Animals of all kinds which habitually use their voices utter various noises under any strong emotion, as when enraged and preparing to fight; but this may merely be the result of nervous excitement, which leads to the spasmodic contraction of almost all the muscles of the body, as when a man grinds his teeth and clenches his hands in rage or agony" (2:275).

When in 1854 W. E. Aytoun launched his attack on what he called, borrowing the term from Charles Kingsley, the "Spasmodic" school, he might have been surprised to know how accurately the term reflected Dobell's theory of poetry. To Dobell, poetry necessarily originates in spasmodic—that is to say, uncontrollable and unpremeditated—vibrations of the human body. Dobell suggests as much in an 1857 lecture, the "Nature of Poetry," that he gave in Edinburgh, wherein he argues that poetry "is actually in tune with our material flesh and blood," that it relies on "certain modes of verbal *motion* . . . certain *rhythms* and measures [that] are metaphors of ideas and feelings" (Dobell 1876, 22, 25). The most extreme examples of Spasmodic poetry seem to have been written with Dobell's theory in mind, as though conscious, formal analysis were to be cast aside in favor of one's own bodily response to poetry. It is in one's "material flesh and blood" that the reader will properly understand the Spasmodic poem, as the brain intuitively converts rhythmic impulses into knowledge, "ideas and feelings." It is through the spasmodic reaction of the human body to rhythm that the poetry will "live."

Dobell's understanding of rhythm develops in part from contemporary advances in the physiological sciences. In *The Senses and the Intellect* (1855), perhaps the most notable of the many physiological studies published in the decade, Alexander Bain argues for the dependence of thought on the physical experiences of the body. Bain, very much a part of the intellectual circle that included G. H. Lewes and Herbert Spencer, was among the first to insist that thought itself results from physical "currents" moving through the brain, a radical departure from the alternative theory of the time, which envisioned the brain as "a *sanctum sanctorum*, or inner chamber, where impressions are poured in and stored up" (Bain 1855, 61). In Bain's model, the human body becomes a living organism that derives knowledge through subjective, physiological experience, rather than an objective container in which knowledge from the surrounding world is "stored." Over several hundred pages, Bain catalogues each of the five senses, along with the processes by which encounters with the physical world inspire nerve transmissions, which ultimately constitute "the very essence of cerebral action" (62). Our knowledge of the world, in other words, comes from the brain's interpretation of nerve impulses, a transformation of physical rhythmic impulses into conscious thought. Bain compare the nervous system to the newly developed technology of the electric telegraph: "*The function of a nerve is to transmit impressions, influences, or stimuli, from one part of the system to another*. . . . Hence the term '*conductor*' applies to the lines of nerve passing to and fro throughout the body. These are in their essential function telegraph wires; for although the force conveyed by a nerve differs from the force conveyed by a telegraphic wire, there is an absolute sameness in this, that the influence is generated at one spot and transmitted to another through an intermediate substance, which substance acts the carrier part solely" (38). Bain in fact invented an early "printing telegraph," patented in 1846, that allowed incoming Morse code signals to be recorded on a paper ribbon (Beauchamp, 62); his figurative connection of the telegraph to nerve impulses is therefore not a casual gesture. Like a telegraph clerk who comes to understand a message through the experience of long and short electrical impulses, the human brain encounters and comes to understand the surrounding world through the rhythmic impress of sensation on the body. Sound waves, for example, "enter the passage of the outer ear, and strike the membrane of the tympanum" (Bain 1855, 199). The auditory nerve then "propagate[s] to the brain a different form of excitement according as the *beats* [received on the tympanum] are few or many" and according to "extremely minute differences of pitch [that] *impress themselves* discriminatively on the fibres" (206; emphasis mine). The brain at last interprets these rhythmic variations and determines the nature of the sound. Although this was not entirely a new concept—David Hartley had elaborated on "the vibrations which belong to ideas" as early as 1749—Bain yet establishes for his Victorian audience an epistemology of rhythm, a comprehensive physiology of the human body that locates in rhythmic—and, significantly, electric-like—experience the origin of all knowledge.[7] What for Tennyson had been a metaphor, a figure for understanding poetic form, becomes for Dobell a poetic practice: the figurative has evolved into the concrete.

Spasmodic poetics emerges out of this insistently physical and electrical understanding of the human body and its experience of the world, an understanding located not only in Bain's study but also in a wide-ranging mid-Victorian discourse on physiology.[8] In this discourse, Spasmodic poets find justification for understanding rhythm—and the human body's physical experience of rhythm—as a foundation for thought: rhythmically inflected sound waves strike the ear, causing vibrations, which the brain converts to forms of knowledge, much as workers at the telegraph convert electric impulses into intelligible language. Sydney Dobell makes these connections explicit in his 1857 lecture, in which he describes poetic rhythm as "vibrations . . . propagated through matter" and concludes that we must expect "a *general* submission" of the human body to these physical principles of sound (Dobell 1876, 23, 24). Dobell makes clear the origins of his rhythmic epistemology in referencing Sir Charles Wheatstone, co-inventor of the electric telegraph in Britain. Along with the German scientist Ernst Chladni and the French-born Felix Savart (both of whom conducted important experiments with sound waves in the early nineteenth century), Wheatstone had "shown to what a wonderful extent vibrations . . . when once set in motion are repeated by sympathetic and other action in innumerable reflexes, each bearing computable relations to the original impulse" (Dobell 1876, 24). Dobell connects Wheatstone's model for rhythmic communication with the work of Bain and other physiological scientists, describing the successive stages of an individual's sensory encounter with the world. In Bain's model, information progresses from the physiological experience of the body to the processes of the mind. So too, argues Dobell, poetry moves through paths of "*rhythmic succession*," such that the body experiences the "lower data" of poetic rhythm as a physical force, which is converted by the brain into "higher data," thoughts and ideas (25). The brain, in other words, converts the physical experience of rhythm into an intellectual construction of the poem and its meaning. In a powerfully assertive gesture of secularization, Dobell describes this process as "the word of Man made flesh and dwelling amongst us" (26). Thus, like the telegraph, which seems through patterns of electric impulses to cancel the effects of physical distance among individuals, poetic rhythm conveys across time and space the physical impress of a speaking poet on a community of readers. Poetry comes to "dwell[]" intimately in the bodies of its readers, individuals who vibrate to the rhythm of stressed and unstressed syllables and come to forms of knowledge through their rhythmic experiences. The profound differences between this mode of poetic experience and those that preceded it—between lived bodily experience and bodily affect understood as metaphor—cannot be overstated.

With mixed results, Dobell explores the communicative potential of poetry with physiologically inspired rhythms. Here is an "evensong" from *Balder* (1853; dated 1854), sung during one of the poem's few lighthearted moments, an idyllic interlude that interrupts what is otherwise an oppressive investigation into metaphysics and aesthetics. Balder sings, accompanying himself on a harp:

> The mavis sings upon the old oak tree
> Sweet and strong,
> Strong and sweet,
> Soft, sweet, and strong,
> And with his voice interpreteth the silence
> Of the dim vale when Philomel is mute!
> The dew lies like a light upon the grass,
> The cloud is as a swan upon the sky,
> The mist is as a brideweed on the moon.
> The shadows new and sweet
> Like maids unwonted in the dues of joy
> Play with the meadow flowers,
> And give with fearful fancies more and less,
> And come, and go, and flit
> A brief emotion in the moving air,
> And now are stirred to flight, and now are kind,
> Unset, uncertain, as the cheek of Love.
>
> (SDB, 123–24, xxiii)

Dobell's rhythm consistently surprises as it leaps among pentameter, dimeter, and trimeter lines. Echoing Tennyson's "Short swallow-flights of song, that dip / Their wings in tears, and skim away" (*In Memoriam* XLVIII; ALT, 2:366), Balder's song is meant to "come, and go, and flit / A brief emotion in the moving air." But unlike Tennyson's balanced tetrameter measures, Dobell's poem refuses a regular meter, relying for its effects on its irregularity. A Pindaric ode, perhaps, Balder's song may more appropriately be considered in light of Tennyson's nearly contemporaneous "Ode on the Death of the Duke of Wellington" (1852), which similarly abstains from strict metrical regularity. Like Dobell's *Balder*, Tennyson's Wellington ode was attacked by some as "[d]isdaining all rules of rhythm and meter" and judged "an intrin-sically poor performance" (quoted in Shannon, 155).[9] But as Dobell instructs us in his lecture, we are not meant to think consciously about such poems' formal designs, but rather to "submi[t]" to the spasms of the rhythmic "vi-brations" and trust that some form of knowledge will come as a result.

We can infer from Dobell's unpublished writings some of the poet's justification for believing so forcefully in rhythm. In "Origin of Rhythm, Sleep, &c.," Dobell emphasizes the centrality of rhythmic experience to human life. Life "is a systole and diastole"; be it waking and sleeping, inhal-ing and exhaling, or any number of other reflexive actions, rhythmic pat-terns govern the human body (Dobell 1876, 128). Dobell hypothesizes that our sense of rhythm, art, and even language originates in our bodies through the various processes of "systole and diastole," through patterned experience, in part because these processes are common to all human beings. Like Bain, whose physiological study implicitly argues for a fundamental universality in human experience (for example, that a pattern of "waxing and waning" sound "wakens up [in listening individuals] an intense current of emotion; in general . . . of a very solemnising kind" [Bain 1855, 207]), Dobell believes that all individuals respond in a like manner to patterned phenomena. Bain, we know, takes his inspiration for such thinking from the *System of Logic* (1840) of his friend John Stuart Mill, which surmises that the "thoughts, feelings, and actions of human beings" might eventually be understood within a system of "[g]eneral laws" from which "predictions [with respect to behavior and emotional response] may be founded"; Mill, that is, believes that scientists might in due time forecast—"though often not with complete accuracy"—the processes of human thought, feeling, and action (Mill, 8:846, 845).[10] If such predictions might be made by the scientist of human nature—or, to use Comte's neologism, by the sociologist—then the poet, in Dobell's view, might accurately predict how readers will respond to rhythmic patterns. Dobell writes in another unpublished essay, "Notes on the Relation of Language and Thought," that the poet uses sound to re-create "sense" by "producing the same state of mind as the thing repre-sented would produce—and this is done in various ways—by sounds that have essential connection with certain attitudes of mind, or by sounds that, by *suggesting certain acts of the organs of utterance*, influence the feelings, or by *rhythm* that, through various laws, affects the whole human system" (Dobell

1876, 138). The poet, then, is something of a scientist of human nature, crafting verses to elicit through physiological association patterns of universal thought and feeling. We as readers can only intuit the intended effect of Balder's evensong as we read the poem, experience its various rhythmic cadences, and note our unself-conscious passionate responses.

Curiously enough, however, the chief point of *Balder* seems to be less a matter of experimenting with rhythmic variation and physiological association than suggesting the potential dangers of such poetic handiwork. And though large passages of the poem engage with rhythmic experimentation, most of *Balder* progresses as lines of regular iambic pentameter. Rather than indulging uncritically in rhythmic hedonism, then, Dobell's poem speculates primarily on the hazards of rhythm understood as a physiological effect. Says Balder, meditating on a poem he hopes to compose,

> This hot breast
> Seems valley deep, and what the wind of Fate
> Strikes on that harp strung there to bursting, I,
> Descending, mean to catch as one unmoved
> In stern notation.
>
> (SDB, 70, xvii)

Balder here imagines himself an aeolian harp set to vibrate and transmit song originating in his "hot breast." Balder means to capture his passionate vibrations and to convert them into "stern notation" (that is, language and rhythm) so that he might broadcast them telegraphically to the world at large. In more ways than one, Balder's image of a harp string stretching across a "valley deep" resembles the telegraph lines newly traversing the British countryside. One telegraph anecdote, published in 1848, suggests that "[b]y placing . . . the ear to telegraph posts, when there is a sidewind, a low but constant musical sound is heard—the playing of the wind upon the wires." The writer goes on to imagine that if four or six telegraph wires were to be arranged "perpendicularly instead of, as now, horizontally . . . a grand Æolian telegraphic harp [could] be made, the winds composing their own music" (Archer, 19). Balder thus engages with a telegraphic fantasy, wishing to strike the telegraph-like harp strings of verse with the wind of his poetic inspiration. He later develops this grandiose notion of communication, referring to himself as the "[b]ard of the future! Master-Prophet! Man / Of Men, at whose strong girdle hang the keys / Of all things!" (SDB, 161, xxiv).

At first simply absurd, Balder's exaggerated Carlylean aspirations turn gruesome when one learns that Balder gives his speech immediately after having murdered his daughter, whom he kills specifically so that in "los[ing] / What nothing can restore" (66, xvi) he might be more intensely moved to feeling, and hence to compose poetry more intensely resonant with passion:

> I rise up childless, but no less
> Than I. There was one bolt in all the heavens
> Which falling on my head had with a touch
> Rent me in twain. This bursting water-spout
> Hath left me whole, but naked.
>
> (69, xvi)

Dobell was sympathetic to Balder's ideal of the poet as a telegraph-like aeolian harp, but his connection of this ideal to infanticide indicates no small degree of uncertainty in the telegraphic process.[11] *Balder* quickly degenerates into farce if one takes seriously, for example, the electric "bolt" meant to set the poet's composition flowing like a "bursting water-spout" (a parody, no doubt, of Wordsworthian spontaneous overflow). It is thus in the extremes of Balder's aspirations that we can read most clearly Dobell's critique of his own theory of poetry. Balder is self-absorbed, self-pitying, and immoral, and "Balderism," writes Dobell in a defensive preface to the poem's second edition, "is a predominant intellectual misfortune of our day" (DPW, 2:5).

Perhaps Balder does not represent the necessary result of rhythmic spasms, but his actions suggest at least one appalling misuse of Dobell's poetic theory. The challenge seems to be how to communicate spasmodic rhythm without degenerating into self-absorption and morbidity (terms Victorian critics commonly used to describe Dobell's poem). *Balder* returns consistently to this problem in an anxious inquiry into the physical nature of thought and feeling. Balder speaks for both Dobell and his age when remarking that

our heart-strings over-strung
Scare us with strange *involuntary* notes
Quivering and quaking[.]

(SDB, 61, xiv; emphasis mine)

Balder later performs such passionate overflow in a revelry at once ecstatic
and anxiety-ridden:

I know the wind!
The utter world doth touch me! I can grasp
The hands that stretch forth from the mystery
That passeth! I am crowded with my life!
It is too much! the vital march doth stop
To press about me!

(134, xxiv)

Near the end of the poem, as Balder considers murdering his wife (whose
grief for her murdered daughter and escalating madness distract Balder from
his composition), he laments,

The dark excess
That for so many days o'er-loaded all
My swollen veins, strangled each vital service,
And pressing hard the incommoded soul
In its unyielding tenement *convulsed*
The wholesome work of nature[.]

(255–56, xxxix; emphasis mine)

In each passage, Balder considers the dangers of sensory overload, the in-
tense impress of sensation on his physical and psychological being. He is
horrified at the "involuntary" nature of these impulses, feeling "crowded"
by sensation that ultimately "convulse[s]" from out of him, an uncontrolled—
that is to say, spasmodic—physiological excretion. Physical and metaphysi-
cal collapse upon one another in Balder's language, as the boundaries
between mind and body, "swollen vein" and "incommoded soul," seem less
and less distinct. Balder's whole being, an "unyielding tenement," writhes

to convulsions inspired by "dark excess," grief and self-loathing. Though these three passages maintain a fairly even iambic pentameter, they propose a rhythmic experience whereby one's "[q]uivering and quaking" heart-strings might overflow, seemingly, the boundaries of both poetic and physiological form. Here is feeling clearly not recollected in tranquility but convulsed from within onto the written page. This fantasy of rhythm, which even Balder seems not to achieve, imagines the metonymic extension of the tortured poet, whose body impresses itself into the poem at the moment of composition.

Fantasy or not, Balder achieves little objective distance from his passionate subjectivity. As in dramatic monologues such as "Porphyria's Lover" (1836), we intuit a critical attitude toward the poem's speaker mostly through the speaker's own excesses.[12] Yet there are, upon close examination, moments of critical self-reflection in *Balder*; moments when Balder seems to consider the ill effects of his poetic style. One of the most remarkable of these instances appears early in Balder's musings. He has been thinking in his study, as he is wont to do—indeed, almost the whole of the poem transpires in Balder's study—when a group of sailors pass by below his window, singing a "chant of Freedom" (46, ix). The song inspires Balder to reflect on what he considers freedom's opposite, tyranny. "Lo Tyranny!" he begins, and then envisages the progress of tyranny personified, a figure of excrement making his way across the landscape:

> thro' gurgling weight
> Of seething full corruption night and day
> His craving bowels, famished in his fill,
> Bellowed for more. Which, when the creature heard
> That bore him, dread, like a great shock of life,
> Convulsed it, and the myriad frantic hands,
> Sprang like the dances of a madman's dream.
> And so he came; and o'er his head a sweat
> Hung like a sulphurous vapour, and beneath
> Fetid and thunderous as from belching hell,
> The hot and hideous torrent of his dung
> Roared down explosive, and the earth, befouled
> And blackened by the stercorous pestilence,

Wasted below him, and where'er he passed
The people stank.

(47–48, ix)

Balder's idea of a tyranny that spews its infectious waste upon all those it passes seems in many ways a self-reflexive critique of his own Spasmodic style. Dobell—and Balder himself, apparently—would have agreed with W. E. Aytoun's comparison of his poem to "a beer-bottle voiding its cork, and spontaneously ejecting its contents right and left" (Aytoun 1854a, 534). Dobell's self-reflexivity seems especially apparent given the preceding sailors' song on freedom, a tale of naval victory told in a fairly regular metrical style:

"See yon ugly craft
  With the pennon at her main!
Hurrah, my merry boys,
  There goes the Betsy Jane!"

(SDB, 45, ix)

Freedom, associated here with the bravery of the British navy, is also a simple, balladlike narrative, a tale sung without internal reflection or metaphysical anxiety. Thus the "hot and hideous torrent" of tyranny's progress strikes an image "contrary" (46, ix) to freedom's song both thematically and formally. Tyranny as Balder imagines it convulses in a violently abject projection of rhythmic impulses, its impression heightened by twisted syntax, inflated diction, and the sonic effects of assonance and alliteration: "bowels . . . [b]ellowed," "famished . . . fill." Freedom, in contrast, performs a rhythmically predictable and syntactically regular chorus, a key perhaps to reading *Balder* as a critique of its own Spasmodic style. Dobell's point, of course, is not that Spasmodic rhythm necessarily resembles a "torrent of . . . dung," but rather that the possibility always exists, that the "corruption" of Spasmodic excess (which, ironically, much of *Balder* exemplifies) must be carefully avoided.

In direct contrast to tyranny's corrupting torrent, Dobell in a posthumously published essay on "Beauty, Love, Order, Unity" emphasizes the value of "the *harmony* of rhythmic *parts*." "Love," Dobell suggests, is a "passion toward unity," an effort to attain rhythmic harmony (Dobell 1876, 113). Tyranny, in contrast, might be construed as a passion toward disunity, the making of perpetual chaos. In *Balder*, then, freedom expresses itself with rhythmic predictability, as that which has already achieved formal harmony, whereas tyranny is a cacophony of sound. Dobell had meant *Balder* (subtitled "Part the First") to be a three-part progress "from Doubt to Faith, from Chaos to Order" (DPW, 2:3–4), but for reasons unknown, though probably connected with the critical sacking of the first part, Dobell never wrote the second two volumes of his poem. Within the overarching project of *Balder*, then, the second and third parts would have realized the order and unity that come of the poet's intense struggles. Balder's spasmodic bellowing would eventually have indicated his personal struggle against tyranny and toward freedom. The negative possibilities in physiological rhythm would have been overcome, and the poet would have reveled in Spasmodic impulses freed from the tyranny of introspection and morbidity.

This, of course, never happens in *Balder*, but it is one way of reading the trajectory of Dobell's post-*Balder* publications. Dobell published only two volumes of poetry after *Balder*. The first, *Sonnets on the War* (1855), was a collaboration with fellow Spasmodic poet Alexander Smith; the second, *England in Time of War* (1856), features Dobell's personal response to the Crimean struggle. The poems in the second volume indicate more clearly than his earlier efforts Dobell's program for embodying passionate thought and feeling in rhythmic impulses. The poems take the perspective of various individuals touched by the war: a woman awaiting the return of her son; an estranged lover; a sailor returning from battle. Periods of metrical regularity alternate with highly irregular passages that enlist repetition, assonance, and rhythmic stresses to produce in the reader a somatic response resonant with the scene described. In this, his final published volume of poetry, we see Dobell at last employing rhythm as a decisive vehicle for expression. For example, "An Evening Dream" recalls a British charge into battle:

> Clarion and clarion defying,
> Sounding, resounding, replying,
> Trumpets braying, pipers playing, chargers neighing,
> Near and far
> The to and fro storm of the never-done hurrahing,
> Thro' the bright weather banner and feather rising and falling,
> bugle and fife

Calling, recalling—for death or for life—
Our host moved on to the war,
While England, England, England, England, England!
Was blown from line to line near and far,
And like the morning sea, our bayonets you might see,
Come beaming, gleaming, streaming,
Streaming, gleaming, beaming,
Beaming, gleaming, streaming, to the war.

(DPW, 1:323)

The passage alternates in speed, from the light-footed "Trumpets braying, pipers playing, chargers neighing," to the ponderous repetitions of "England," which seem ultimately not indicative of patriotism but rather only a line of pressing trochees, a leaning in and a retreating "to and fro." We are, indeed, like the lines of British soldiers, "blown . . . near and far" by the poem's rhythmic cadences. We also find ourselves in the midst of a confusing melee of sounds, words difficult to distinguish from one another both in meaning and in sound: "Streaming, gleaming, beaming." We feel, through the rhythm and the sound of the words, something physically and conceptually of the rushed confusion of a battle charge, "line to line" (words that make explicit the congruence between the lines of soldiers and lines of Dobell's poem). The affective experience here comes remarkably not through the literal definitions of the words but through the impress of rhythm and sound on the reader of the poem. These are the "certain modes of verbal *motion*" that Dobell advocates in his 1857 lecture, "certain *rhythms* and measures [that] are metaphors of ideas and feelings" (55).

One need not call this great poetry to see the daring of its experimentation. Dobell's goal, essentially, is to capture in language the chaotic motions of the human mind and thus to transmit to his readers the actual, felt experience he describes. To do this, according to Dobell, requires getting beyond words to the inner ideas and feelings that words are meant to conjure.[13] "We are all irretrievably word-struck," he writes sometime around 1850 (Jolly, 1:161): "We are too apt to confound words with language. Are not visible images or the ideas of them the only language in the highest sense? Words are the outward noises by which we recall the inward shape. . . . [t]o reason by ideas, to compare ideas with ideas, to speak from the first-hand idea, to call up in the hearer a picture, not a sentence, should be our great aim" (Jolly, 1:155, 162). Dobell says much the same in his 1857 lecture: "Words rhythmically combined affect the feelings of the poetic hearer or utterer in the same way as the fact they represent: and thus by a reflex action the fact is reproduced in the imagination" (Dobell 1876, 36–37). This is the governing project of "An Evening Dream," in which rhythmic impulses ultimately supersede the poem's words. Dobell maximizes the rhythmic effects of the concluding battle charge, quoted above, by opening the poem with fairly regulated fourteener couplets:

> I'm leaning where you loved to lean in eventides of old,
> The sun has sunk an hour ago behind the treeless wold,
> In this old oriel that we loved how oft I sit forlorn,
> Gazing, gazing, up the vale of green and waving corn.
>
> (DPW, 1:315)

Dobell's image of physical "leaning" underscores the physiological press of rhythm, the measured lines that gradually break apart and become increasing irregular as the speaker's dream moves from "the treeless wold" to a scene of invasion by the Russian army. Indeed, the iambic regularity of Dobell's opening couplet almost immediately disintegrates into the steady run of trochees marking line four. It is precisely at the point of the invasion, a "flood that swelled from some embowelled mount of woe," that Dobell most clearly breaks from metrical regularity (and note again in "embowelled" the excremental trope, which Dobell consistently links to rhythmic spasm):

> Waveless, foamless, sure and slow,
> Silent o'er the vale below,
> Till nigher still and nigher comes the seeth [*sic*] of fields on fire,
> And the thrash of falling trees, and the steam of rivers dry,
> And before the burning flood the wild things of the wood
>   Skulk and scream, and fight, and fall, and flee, and fly.
>
> (DPW, 1:318)

The confusion climaxes in the British charge, the "to and fro storm . . . blown from line to line," during which the metrical structure modulates freely, in the style of an ode, to maximize the physiological impact of rhythmic play.

One might highlight the effect of Dobell's dissolution of rhythmic consistency by reading "An Evening Dream" alongside Tennyson's nearly contemporaneous "Charge of the Light Brigade" (first published 9 December 1854). Even Charles Kingsley, generally a great admirer of the Poet Laureate, suggests that "[t]he dactyl is surely too smooth and cheerful a foot to form the basis of such a lyric" (Kingsley 1855, 272). But perhaps what makes the poem appear disturbingly "smooth and cheerful" is not Tennyson's use of dactyls, but the unwavering consistency of the rhythm. More than most poets, Dobell understood the psychological and physiological effects of rhythmic inconsistency. In a letter of December 1855, Dobell states, "[A]nyone who would wholly understand any of my poetry . . . must read it with the mind of a musician. I don't mean that it is *musical*, in the common sense, but that it is written on the principles of music, *i.e.* as a series of combinations that shall produce certain *states* in the hearer, and not a succession of words which he is separately to 'intellectuate' by the dictionary" (Jolly, 1:447). Certainly, "An Evening Dream" makes the most of this "musical" understanding of poetry, a movement away from words ordered metrically and toward an enactment of rhythmic epistemology, or physiological states of embodied, rhythmic passion. Embodied rhythm need not necessarily be linked to irregularity—Tennyson's consistent trochees might just as well induce a bodily response—but for Dobell, irregularity works best, offering unself-conscious, passionate experience in place of intellectual reflection.

Many of Dobell's contemporaries shared the poet's interest in physiology and the unself-conscious work of rhythm on the human body. Herbert Spencer's 1857 essay "The Origin and Function of Music," for example, argues—like Dobell's lecture on poetry from the same year—that "there is a direct connection between feeling and motion" (Spencer, 213). This connection, Spencer claims, is both "innate" and inexplicable: "Why the actions excited by strong feeling should tend to become rhythmical, is not very obvious; but that they do so there are divers evidences" (220, 223). If unsure of why rhythm and feeling reflect one another, Spencer is quite clear on the implications of this connection. Along with tonal modulations of voice (the essay is primarily on the effects of music and not specifically poetry), rhythm enables other individuals "not only to *understand* the state of mind" that inspired a composition but also "to *partake* of that state" (235). Such participation, Spencer argues (echoing the eighteenth-century commonplace), is "the chief med[ium] of *sympathy*" (236), the glue to hold together an increasingly complex and atomized social structure.[14] Whereas Mary Robinson proposes that a "poetic picture" might inspire a reader's sympathetic response through a kind of imaginative identification (as discussed in chapter 1), Spencer and Dobell move beyond this simple work of the imagination; aided by a far more sophisticated understanding of human physiology (specifically, nerve transmission), the heirs to Robinson's poetic theory relocate the process of sympathy from the isolated, thinking brain to the body at large, thereby enabling a more profound—because all-encompassing—identification between the individual and the work of art. Romanticism's fantasy of a communal poetics thus reaches new heights by way of the mid-Victorian physiological sciences.

Spencer's essay helps to explain why his close friend George Henry Lewes found Alexander Smith so compelling as a poet: "[H]is eager senses," Lewes wrote in 1853, "have embraced the world." Lewes's only criticism for Smith is that he should "deepen and extend the nature of his passion, making it the flaming utterance of his *whole* being, sensuous, moral, and intellectual" (Lewes 1853, 524). Such a fully corporeal and, simultaneously, intellectual project relies on the spasmodic imbrication of body and mind, rhythm and thought. In his later writings on physiology, Lewes proposes that "all our knowledge *springs from*, and is *limited by*, Feeling" (Lewes 1877, 311). For Lewes, any comprehension of objective nature comes necessarily through the individual human body; "subjective" bodily passions lead to "objective" knowledge, and each individual's subjective experience of passionate sensation puts him in touch with, or at least opens the door to, objectivity. Lewes's work here shows debts to William Whewell and the empiricist philosophers discussed in chapter 2; in many ways, Lewes's theories of mind and body—and the Spasmodic poetics he celebrates—take Lockean empiricism to its logical extreme. Shaftesbury's complaint that Locke finds "neither right nor wrong, virtue nor vice" to be "any thing in themselves" bears much in common with the complaints echoed by the critics of spasmody (Shaftesbury, 346).[15] But according to Lewes, this necessarily subjective approach to objective knowledge is the *only* way the world may be apprehended. Lewes values Smith because in his view the poet's "embrace

. . . [of] the world" demonstrates the potential for both a universal, objective synthesis of subjective knowledge and feeling and, through such a synthesis, the reinvigoration of sympathetic human relations.[16]

George Eliot likewise had much to say about the consequences of feeling in poetic thought. Through her regular and anonymous contributions to the Belles Lettres section of the *Westminster Review*, Eliot was an active and little-acknowledged participant in the poetic debates emerging out of the Spasmodic controversy. Eliot by and large shared Lewes's ideal of knowledge springing from feeling; indeed, in an essay from January 1857, she criticizes the eighteenth-century poet Edward Young precisely for his "disruption of language from genuine thought and feeling" (Eliot 1857b, 27). Later in the same issue of the *Westminster*, Eliot praises Elizabeth Barrett Browning's *Aurora Leigh* for accomplishing what Young so miserably fails at, the perfect melding of "what we may call [her poem's] poetical *body*" with "genuine thought and feeling": in *Aurora Leigh*, "there is simply a full mind pouring itself out in song as its natural and easiest medium" (Eliot 1857a, 307). It should come as no surprise, given this praise for Barrett Browning, that Eliot could not help but be swayed in part by the work of the Spasmodic poets. She insists in a brief review of Dobell's *England in Time of War* that she is "not [an] enthusiastic admirer . . . either of Mr. Dobell or of the school of poetry to which he belongs," yet she admits her appreciation for his occasional "passage[s] of simple pathos, [and] exquisite rhythmic melody laden with fresh and felicitous thought" (Eliot 1856b, 567, 568).[17] Eliot here intuits (before Dobell had publicized his rhythmic theory) that rhythm and thought in the 1856 volume are to be understood as one and the same; it is Dobell's rhythm, she writes, that bears his thought.

What these essays all gesture at is how, within a particular school of thought, Dobell's views on poetry must be seen as entirely commonplace. Dobell's rhythmic epistemology springs not out of the poet's rabid imagination, sui generis, but from an important body of midcentury scientific and philosophical thought. In part, Dobell's Spasmodism seems dangerous to his critics precisely because it is not anomalous (the mutterings of a madman might more easily have been dismissed). Yet it was a movement in which Dobell himself lacked confidence. Dobell stresses that a poet can never know, really, the effect his rhythmic utterances will have on readers of his poem. He may only surmise, as Mill asserts in *System of Logic*, "how the great *majority* of the human race, or of some nation or class of persons, will think, feel, and act" (Mill, 8:847; emphasis mine). Insofar as poetry is a "carrying out and efflorescence of a human soul, according *to its own laws*" (Dobell 1876, 64), the poet can only hope that those personal laws will translate into universal ones. Thus, if poetic rhythms resemble the long and short impulses of Morse code, they form a language that only some will be able to read, and that perhaps many will misread and others entirely fail to read, as if readers of poetry were each to hold a unique codebook for the incoming patterns of stressed and unstressed syllables. The critics had a point when they grumbled over having "here to lean on a cadence,—there to lend accent to the rhyme." *Balder* repeatedly calls attention to moments when rhythm necessarily fails to communicate, most notably in what has become a signal moment of Spasmodic excess, Balder's thirteen repetitions of "ah!" (SDB, 250, xxxviii). These lines scan equally well as iambs or trochees, anapests alternating with pyrrhics or solid runs of spondees; any attempt at scansion necessarily resorts to guesswork, and this seems to be Dobell's point. Each reader will determine his or her own rhythmic pattern for the line, thereby rendering moot the possibility of its bearing a predetermined form of knowledge or feeling. At a certain point, then, the analogy between rhythm and the electric telegraph breaks down, as does the notion of interpersonal intimacy facilitated by poetic rhythm. Much as Dobell wants to align his rhythmic epistemology with the scientific work of Alexander Bain, Sir Charles Wheatstone, Ernst Chladni, and Felix Savart, the play of rhythm on individual human bodies remains in the end too variable for consistent objective analysis.

"Spasmodic," then, is a surprisingly appropriate term for Sydney Dobell's poetry. Insofar as Dobell's poetry resembles the "spasmodic contractions" that Darwin describes in animals suffering from "nervous excitement," readers of the poems are meant to react without conscious thought to the exciting effects of rhythm. The convulsive nature of rhythmic spasm is what gives poetry its communicative strength. Unself-conscious rhythm, like the reflex actions of Bain's physiological studies, communicates what Dobell called the living "flesh and blood" of the poet; when permitted, perhaps, Spasmodic rhythm transmits knowledge across time and space as a universal physiological experience. We turn now to the critical responses to Dobell's rhythmic poetics, and to the return to poetic formalism that accompanied the reaction against Spasmodic poetry.

RHYTHMIC DISCIPLINE

Particularly distressing to William Edmondstoune Aytoun, the most vocal critic writing against the Spasmodics, was that Spasmodic poetics was anything but an isolated phenomenon. This was made painfully clear to the Scottish critic by the publication of Tennyson's *Maud* (1855). In his *Blackwood's* review of the poem, Aytoun mournfully compares "the glorious rhythm of *Locksley Hall*" (1842) to the "hideous cacophony" of *Maud:* "The contrast between the breathings of an Æolian harp and the rasping of a blacksmith's file is scarcely more palpable" (Aytoun 1855, 312, 314, 315). Though the plots of "Locksley Hall" and *Maud* are famously alike, Aytoun admires the earlier poem and despises the latter almost entirely on the basis of rhythm. In *Maud*, the Poet Laureate seems to indulge in what Coventry Patmore was to call "the entire dissolution of metre displayed by some of the writers of our own century" (PE, 9).[18] According to Aytoun, who lectured on poetry throughout the mid-1850s at the University of Edinburgh, all such "Spasmodic writings" indicate not "health and strength," as good aesthetic works should, but are "on the contrary . . . symptomatic of disease" (n.d., MS. 4908, f. 161). The "state of anarchy and abject terror" that Aytoun claimed would come of pushing reform beyond the measures enacted in 1832 could arise with comparable ease through the promulgation of an aesthetic philosophy based on disorder (Aytoun 1852, 371). Hence, Aytoun's favored poetic form is the ballad, because, as he understands it, ballad poetry unites readers and listeners through a common culture and, in its highly regulated metrical forms, speaks to the "universal ear" (Aytoun 1867, 231). Spasmodic poetry, in contrast, encourages precisely those individual and introspective practices that, if spread too widely, and especially among the working classes and women, lead too easily down the path of cultural and political anarchy.[19] Like Carlyle, who worries about the "sharp, ran-tan" rhythmic beating of the French insurrectionists, Aytoun worries about the "impression of ill-regulated and spasmodic power" (n.d., MS. 4908, f. 146).

Indeed, Aytoun's literary criticism must be read in the context of mid-Victorian politics, especially the Chartist uprisings that lingered uneasily

in the public imagination in the 1850s. Aytoun had witnessed a riot dur-
ing the 1832 elections, and he recounts the experience in his 1861 quasi-
autobiographical novel *Norman Sinclair:* "[A] collection of ruffians . . .
roared, whistled, whooped, and yelled. . . . There were colliers from the
mines, carters from the villages, weavers from the streets, and cobblers from
their stalls, all in their working clothes, swarthy and begrimed, gesticulating
like madmen, wrestling for the foremost seats, and uttering diabolical howls
for no apparent reason except the exercise of their hideous voices" (1:140).
Within the novel—and Aytoun's life, it seems—this scene cements in place
the protagonist's conservative, Tory political views; the working classes,
uncontrollable "madmen," must be restrained and kept from positions of
authority. Whereas Carlyle would discuss, with apparent sympathy, the "'deep
dumb inarticulate want' of the English people" (Plotz, 137), Aytoun refuses
to commiserate with the working classes, and instead views their inarticu-
lateness as proof of their "diabolical" nature.

But Aytoun does offer an alternative vision of the working classes: for
example, in a ballad of 1844 that highlights the correlation between aes-
thetic and cultural order. Published originally in *Blackwood's,* "The Execu-
tion of Montrose" centers on James Graham, Earl of Montrose, as he passes
through a crowd of Scottish peasants—the "rabble"—on the way to his
execution. The year is 1650, and Montrose is to be hanged for, among other
things, having supported the royalist cause during the English Civil War
(the loyal Montrose is clearly a martyr for Aytoun). In the poem, the Whig
lords urge the peasants to jeer at Montrose as he passes, but the people
unexpectedly find themselves caught in a wave of genuine sympathy for the
doomed man:

> The rabble rout forbore to shout,
>   And each man held his breath,
> For well they knew the hero's soul
>   Was face to face with death.
> And then a mournful shudder
>   Through all the people crept,
> And some that came to scoff at him
>   Now turned aside and wept.
>
>   (Aytoun 1921, 19)

The Edinburgh crowd, Aytoun shows us, needs no complicated process of reflection to experience their sympathy for Montrose: "a mournful shudder" moves spontaneously "[t]hrough all the people." Such an electric-like transmission of feeling seems a physiological experience nearly indistinguishable from spasmodic rhythmic communication. But the distinction is nonetheless crucial. Whereas Dobell locates communication in rhythm itself (or, more distinctly, in rhythm as a vehicle for feeling), Aytoun concentrates on the pathos of a tableau: Montrose's resignation to death, and the crowd's sympathy. Aytoun's crowd arrives at its shared feeling because each individual understands the gravity of coming "face to face with death." As a universal sentiment, then, Aytoun's vision of emotional experience resists the chaotic, uncontrolled passions typical of many mid-Victorian crowd scenes. Social harmony develops from communal sympathy within the poem's formal order, as if the passions of the Scottish crowd might be contained within the ballad's textbook metrical structure. *Balder* and *Maud* feature individuals engaged in passionate (and, to Aytoun, dangerous) excesses, excesses that are mirrored in, and perhaps enabled by, their rhythmic indeterminacy.[20] Aytoun, in contrast, offers a tableau of tearful, communal sympathy as a noble and redeeming reflection of metrical stability.

Aytoun's literary reviews, published through the 1850s in *Blackwood's*, focus with utter distaste on irregular poetic rhythms, consistently linking rhythmic experience and political—specifically class—dynamics. For example, he attacks *Aurora Leigh* insofar as Elizabeth Barrett Browning "makes no distinction between her first and her third class passengers, but rattles them along at the same speed upon her rhythmical railway." Aytoun refers here to the various squalid subplots of Barrett Browning's poem—the kidnapping and rape of Marian Erle, for example—and he suggests that a better poet would not have "dignif[ied] ignoble thoughts or common sentiments" by composing them in verse (Aytoun 1857, 37). Not only does *Aurora Leigh* depict "ignoble thoughts" in verse, but also the meter seems not to cohere formally; Aytoun suggests as much by quoting a passage from the poem as though it were prose—that is, not demarcating Barrett Browning's line breaks (30). Is there really a difference, Aytoun implicitly asks, between *Aurora Leigh* and a prose narrative? Various subsequent critics have asked the same question, but the issue for Aytoun is always more than simply formal or aesthetic; Aytoun links what he perceives to be weak metrics with the violation of poetic decorum, all of which facilitates (through a figure such as Marian Erle) a politically suspect work of art. The first- and third-class passengers of *Aurora Leigh* thus find themselves equally vulnerable to the poet's formal carelessness.

Aytoun might have forgiven Barrett Browning some of her extravagances (she is "[e]ndowed with a powerful intellect," he notes [25]) had not *Aurora Leigh* followed on the heels of the Spasmodic controversy. Aytoun makes reference to the Spasmodics at the close of his *Aurora Leigh* review, unequivocally connecting Barrett Browning with poets such as Sydney Dobell and Alexander Smith: "[O]ur 'new poets,' as they love to style themselves . . . come upon their imaginary stage, tearing their hair, proclaiming their inward wretchedness, and spouting sorry metaphysics in still sorrier verse, for no imaginary reason whatever" (40). Note here the rhetorical parallel to Aytoun's description in *Norman Sinclair* of the 1832 riot, which featured workers "gesticulating like madmen . . . and uttering diabolical howls for no apparent reason." Both sketches concentrate on, first, a seeming lack of physiological control ("tearing their hair," "gesticulating like madmen"), followed by senseless vocal "spouting" and "howl[ing]." Both feature an inner emotional turmoil that struggles—and ultimately fails—to find coherent verbal expression. Aytoun tries to dismiss Spasmodic poetry as contemptible, a mere vehicle for "sorry metaphysics," but we can detect the more serious anxiety underlying his critique of spasmody through the rhetorical connection between the "new poets" of the 1850s and the working-class rioters of the 1830s. The Spasmodic poets, largely working class in origin, offer a challenge to mid-Victorian aesthetics that was interpreted, correctly, as a political challenge. Dobell's concentration on physiological experience, as well as the relative irrelevance of conscious thought in his poetic philosophy, intentionally opens poetry to a universal audience, a move with unmistakable class implications.[21] Barrett Browning did not share, and most likely was not even aware of, Dobell's specific views of rhythm, but her often casual approach to blank verse was enough to inspire Aytoun's reproach.

The mildly accusatory tone of Aytoun's *Aurora Leigh* review seems kind in light of the attacks the Scottish critic had launched against the Spasmodics a few years earlier. In May 1854, Aytoun published in *Blackwood's* a burlesque review of a nonexistent Spasmodic verse-drama, *Firmilian: A Tragedy*, meant to highlight the absurdities of Spasmodic poetry in general and *Balder* in particular. The review garnered so much attention, with some critics even taking it to be the review of a real poem, that Aytoun decided to write the (faux) poem itself, which he published as a separate volume in July under the pseudonym T. Percy Jones: *Firmilian; or, The Student of Badajoz, A Spasmodic Tragedy*.[22] In *Firmilian*, Aytoun illuminates through caricature what he sees to be the faults of Spasmodic poetry. Firmilian, a poet of Aytoun's creation, follows in Balder's footsteps, only to more drastic ends. Like Balder, Firmilian searches for a radical event that will make him feel passionately. Whereas Balder fixes on murdering his daughter, Firmilian decides to blow up a cathedral:

> 'Twas a grand spectacle! The solid earth
> Seemed from its quaking entrails to eruct
> The gathered lava of a thousand years,
> Like an imposthume bursting up from hell!
> In a red robe of flame, the riven towers,
> Pillars and altar, organ-loft and screen,
> With a singed swarm of mortals intermixed,
> Were whirled in anguish to the shuddering stars,
> And all creation trembled at the din.
>
> (Aytoun 1854b, 86)

Aytoun boasted enthusiastically of how in writing *Firmilian* he could "go slapdash, without thinking!" (Martin, 146). Yet even amidst the "grand spectacle" of the eructing cathedral, a parody of Balder's excremental poetics, Aytoun struggles against the draw of iambic pentameter; he is overcome, finally, in the closing line: "And all creation trembled at the din." Aytoun's point is clear enough. The "quaking entrails" of Firmilian's cathedral "eruct" like poetic form in the hands of Spasmodic poets. With "all creation trembl[ing]," the reader might reconsider the implications of irreverent formlessness. Aytoun concludes his drama with Firmilian fleeing from the memories of all those he has killed in his poetic endeavors, including four friends he poisoned and a rival poet whom he pushed from the top of St. Simeon Stylites' pillar. Worrying that he will be burned to death for his crimes, he insists—in an unmistakable gesture to Arnold—that he would rather "dare, / Like rash Empedocles, the Etna gulf, / Than writhe before the slaves of bigotry" (Aytoun 1854b, 147). Only a few pages later, the Spasmodic poet falls to his death in an abandoned quarry while a chorus of his victims dances nearby (153).

Aytoun's serious poetry—including two volumes of ballad poetry and an excruciatingly long dramatic monologue, *Bothwell* (1856)—complements the conservative thrust of *Firmilian*, though with far less ingenuity. In all of his poems, as we might expect, Aytoun offers insistent formal regularity as a model for cultural stability. When Bothwell, the imprisoned third husband of Mary, Queen of Scots, soliloquizes from his cell, Aytoun contains his speaker's passion within perfectly formed ballad stanzas. As the *Times* put it, Aytoun "has come forward to write a tale that shall be passionate, not spasmodic; and he has chosen to fetter himself by an adoption of the form [the dramatic monologue] which in the hands of the other poets leads directly to spasm" (27 December 1856, 4). Hence, Bothwell is imprisoned both literally, within a prison cell, and formally, within the poem's restraining ballad meter:

> O, that the madness, which at times
>   Comes surging through my brain,
> Would smite me deaf, and dumb, and blind,
>   No more to wake again—
> Would make me, what I am indeed,
>   A beast within a cage,
> Without the sense to feel my bonds,
>   Without the power to rage—
>
>   (Aytoun 1921, 136)

Even in near madness, Bothwell's speech flows out in perfect iambs. Bothwell's physical imprisonment "within a cage" mirrors exactly the regulation of his spasmodic individuality by the poem's constant ballad meter, meter too steady even for Aytoun's Victorian critics. "[Mr. Aytoun] has the poetic temperament," notes the *London Quarterly Review*, "but lacks the creative power of poetry. His genius is no living well, no bubbling and perpetual spring" (review of *Bothwell*, 206, 208). *Fraser's* is even more direct: "[Mr. Aytoun] has produced nothing of poetry, save metrical speech sometimes becoming musical" ("Aytoun's 'Bothwell,'" 357). The poem makes evident the distance between ordered meter—"metrical speech"—and the rhythmic, impassioned music central to Dobell's idea of poetry. Aytoun wants poetry to reflect a better world, but in *Bothwell*, which stretches to several thousand lines of verse, the lesson in national order seems overshadowed by one in monotony.

Aytoun was far from alone in his conservative response to spasmody. One example not regularly associated with the Spasmodics is Ruskin's essay "Of the Pathetic Fallacy," published in 1856, which engages notably with the rhetoric emerging out of the Spasmodic crisis. Reflecting the anxieties of the day, Ruskin's notion of the pathetic fallacy measures a poet's ability to write truthfully by regulating passion. Poets who engage in pathetic fallacy, defined by Ruskin as "falseness in all our impressions of external things," are "borne away, or over-clouded, or over-dazzled by emotion" (Ruskin, 5:205, 208). To avoid being "over-dazzled," poets must stand at a distance from passionate experience; "the high creative poet" must have "a great center of reflection and knowledge in which he stands serene, and watches the feeling, as it were, from afar off" (5:210). Ruskin echoes here the Wordsworthian ideal of powerful feeling recollected in tranquility, yet distinguishes himself from his Romantic predecessor in warning of the "diseased and false" "expressions and modes of thought" (5:210) that might result from unmediated powerful feeling (Wordsworth only suggests vaguely that "there is some danger that the excitement [induced by poetry] may be carried beyond its proper bounds" [459]). Ruskin summarizes his position: "A poet is great, first in proportion to the strength of his passion, and then, that strength being granted, in proportion to his government of it" (Ruskin, 5:215).

Tennyson, too, ultimately determined Spasmodism too excessive, though he originally found some of the Spasmodic productions compelling. According to biographer Charles Tennyson, Tennyson "spent a good part of the last months of [1846] in London, being much fêted and dined, and expressing great admiration for the now forgotten poem, Bailey's *Festus*, which he declared contained many grand things—grander than he himself had written" (C. Tennyson, 215). Philip James Bailey was among the first of the Spasmodic poets, and *Festus*—a long rewriting of the Faust legend—maintained a certain cult status through much of the nineteenth century.[23] Given Tennyson's ambivalent relation to Hallam's poetics of sensation (as discussed in chapter 2), one should not be surprised that Tennyson was both drawn to and anxious about the Spasmodic style; while admiring *Festus*, he also feared that the poem might make him "fall[ ] into extravagance" (quoted in Weinstein, 173). Tennyson owned a copy of *Balder*, inscribed to the Poet Laureate by the author, but the pages of the volume in Tennyson's library remain largely uncut; Tennyson appears to have read through scene 5 before deciding not to proceed. Alexander Smith's *Life-Drama*, in contrast, is fully cut, and Tennyson's light marginalia mark a handful of especially assonant passages, moments in the poem when Smith sounds most like Tennyson (Tennyson marks, for example, in scene 4, "The full-faced moon sits silver on the sea, / The eager waves lift up their gleaming heads, / Each shouldering for her smile").[24] Tennyson's enthusiasm for Smith and tacit dismissal of Dobell point to the by-now-familiar negotiation of poetic extremes that marked the laureate's career.

It was in *Maud* that Tennyson came closest to appropriating the Spasmodic style, and the poem clearly exhibits—and is indeed a thoroughgoing engagement with—the poet's lifelong anxious relation to extreme feeling.[25] Most critics were horrified by the poem's raving speaker, and they responded as though betrayed by the Poet Laureate. But *Maud* in fact only flirts with Spasmodism, and ultimately comes—à la *Balder*—to reject the Spasmodic style. In linking *Maud*'s irregularities to madness, Tennyson firmly rejects both Spasmodic physiological poetics and Hallam's sensational poetics. W. E. Aytoun was thus oddly right in suggesting that the poem's opening eight stanzas are "an ill-conceived . . . screed of bombast, set to a metre which has the string-halt" (Aytoun 1855, 315). String-halt, an affliction of a horse's hind legs that causes its muscles to contract spasmodically, appropriately diagnoses Tennyson's rhythm, which runs at an irregular, spasmodic canter ("The *red-ribbed led*ges *drip* with a *si*lent *hor*ror of *blood*" [ALT, 2:519, part 1, line 3]). How better to suggest both frenzied individuality and mental instability than with an unpredictable and jarring rhythmic tread? Tennyson explains in a letter that in composing *Maud* he "took a man constitutionally diseased and dipt him into the circumstances of the time and took him out on fire"; he describes the poem to Henry van Dyke as "the unfolding of a lonely, morbid soul, touched with inherited madness" and concludes, defensively, that "[t]he things which seem like faults belong not so much to the poem as to the character of the hero" (ALT, 2:517).

At least two of Tennyson's contemporaries, Charles Kingsley and Coventry Patmore, saw through to the poet's designs. Kingsley writes that "the purpose of the poem," which is to argue for "a fixed purpose . . . righteous duty, and hopeful toil and self-sacrifice" and against "self-will and selfishness," rightly balances *Maud* "against its defects" (Kingsley 1855, 271, 270). Patmore—whose connections to spasmody are examined in chapter 4—insists that "we may be sure" that the extreme thought and passion of the poem's speaker is meant to be "irony; and, that it should have been mistaken for anything more, is a remarkable illustration of the carelessness of modern habits of reading and thinking" (Patmore 1855, 509). In *Maud*, Spasmodism is an isolating madness through which the speaker must pass on his way toward sanity and companionship (as Dobell's Balder was meant to in the unwritten sequels to that poem). *Maud*, then, is both Tennyson's most significant excursion into physiological poetics and his most vehement rejection of those aesthetic principles.

Tennyson makes the connections among passionate introspection, physiological sympathy, and mental instability most explicit in the scene of the speaker's madness:

> Dead, long dead,
> Long dead!
> And my heart is a handful of dust,
> And the wheels go over my head,
> And my bones are shaken with pain,
> For into a shallow grave they are thrust,
> Only a yard beneath the street,
> And the hoofs of the horses beat, beat,
> The hoofs of the horses beat,
> Beat into my scalp and my brain,
> With never an end to the stream of passing feet,
> Driving, hurrying, marrying, burying,
> Clamour and rumble, and ringing and clatter
> $\qquad$ (ALT, 2:576–77, part 2, lines 239–51)

Here Tennyson connects the beating pulses of the horses' hoofs and the "stream of passing *feet*" to both madness and the physiological, rhythmic experience of poetry. The speaker's madness seems inseparable from the poem's rhythmic indeterminacy. As Kirstie Blair has argued, Tennyson draws attention to pulsing beats from the poem's beginning: "And my pulses closed their gates with a shock on my heart" (520, part 1, line 15).[26] As madness approaches, the images of beating multiply and take on increasingly sinister implications. At first, beating suggests a happy resonance between the speaker and the natural world–

> Beat, happy stars, timing with things below,
> Beat with my heart more blest than heart can tell[.]
>
> (557, part 1, lines 679–80)

> My heart would hear her and beat,
>   Were it ever so airy a tread,
> My heart would hear her and beat,
>   Had I lain for a century dead[.]
>
> (565, part 1, lines 918–21)

Beating after the speaker's duel and subsequent exile, however, becomes a frantic echo of Maud's "passionate cry":

> A cry for a brother's blood:
> It will ring in my heart and my ears, till I die, till I die.

> Is it gone? my pulses beat—
> What was it? a lying trick of the brain?
>
> (567, part 2, lines 34–37)

The mad scene follows shortly thereafter, by which point the "beat, beat" of horse hoofs press indelibly upon the speaker and exacerbate his psychological torment. Beating "feet" are impressed "into [his] scalp and [his] brain," a sinister literalization of Hallam's idea that poetry "places us at once in the position of feeling" (Hallam, 94). The speaker of *Maud* imagines himself buried by the overwhelming, horrifying rhythms of the surrounding world. He feels the physiological press of rhythmic feet on his body, and it drives him mad. His fate is that of the poet of sensation who has failed to distance himself appropriately from his own passionate lyricism.

Tennyson finally delineates the conflict of *Maud* as one between Spasmodic passion and scientific restraint, each an unwelcome extreme:

> The man of science himself is fonder of glory, and vain,
> An eye well-practised in nature, a spirit bounded and poor;
> The passionate heart of the poet is whirled into folly and vice.
> I would not marvel at either, but keep a temperate brain;
> For not to desire or admire, if a man could learn it, were more
> Than to walk all day like the sultan of old in a garden of spice.
> (ALT, 2:531, part 1, lines 138–43)

On the one hand, the man of science is "bounded and poor" for being too exact in his impressions of the world about him; the passionate poet, on the other hand, falls victim to "folly and vice." Tennyson's speaker, predictably enough, desires "a temperate brain," something between scientific restraint and poetic passion. But in comparing such a state to the perambulations of a sultan, *Maud* suggests the fantastic, near impossibility of this poetic balance—or at least how distant balanced poetry seems from Tennyson's native England.

Looking back to the 1850s from 1877, Edmund Gosse acknowledges the importance of Spasmodic verse to the development of mid-Victorian poetics, even if that importance manifests for Gosse as an example of how *not* to write poetry. To Gosse, poetry makes "immortal art out of transient feeling," and it does so by "chisel[ing] material beauty out of passing thoughts and emotions," an exercise of "conscious artifice" and "constructive power" (Gosse 1877, 53). The true poet, then, must "dismiss . . . purely spontaneous and untutored expression" such as that of the Spasmodics, who left behind "a baneful influence, a tradition of formlessness" (53, 54). By 1877, Gosse had come to believe that the Spasmodic tradition had passed, as poets such as William Morris and Dante Gabriel Rossetti reinvigorated formal structures, returning technical dexterity to the fore of poetic composition: "The actual movement of the time, then, appears certainly to be in the direction of increased variety of richness of rhyme, elasticity of verse, and *strength of form*. The invertebrate rhapsodies of Sydney Dobell, so amazing in their beauty of detail and total absence of style, are now impossible. We may lack his inspiration and his insight, but we understand far better than he the workmanship of the art of verse" (55; emphasis mine). However, the return to form that Gosse heralds carries with it unmistakable traces of Dobell's physiological aesthetics, the belief that rhythm and meter transmit universal knowledge and feeling with even more ease, in many cases, than words on a page. The following chapter shows how the "invertebrate" structures of spasmody—literally boneless, lacking in structure—find new poetic form in the stressed systems of Gerard Manley Hopkins and the isochronous intervals of Coventry Patmore's 1877 volume, *The Unknown Eros*. Chapter 5 continues this inquiry into the post-Spasmodic years with an examination of the poetry of Algernon Swinburne and Mathilde Blind. Their poetry, as with much of the poetry composed in the post-Spasmodic years, negotiates anxiously between Aytoun's style of formal regularity and what Mathilde Blind, following Dobell, considered the "primal and universal in the fate and feelings of man" (Blind 1874, 320). Sydney Dobell's "invertebrate rhapsodies" echo persistently and with surprising strength through the late Victorian period.

CHAPTER FOUR

Patmore, Hopkins, and the Uncertain Body of Victorian Poetry

[Y]ou ought, in my opinion, to say once clearly what English accent is[.]

—Gerard Manley Hopkins to Coventry Patmore (1883)

Time is thus the real basis of this metre, and
syllables are comparatively unimportant.

—T. S. Omond, *A Study of Metre* (1903)

THIS BOOK HAS SO FAR LOOKED AT THE DEVELOPMENT OF physiological poetics and its engagement with the electrical sciences, starting in the late eighteenth century with the movement toward thinking about the body as a place for poetic communication, and culminating with the Spasmodic poets of the 1850s and their hypotheses on a language of poetic rhythm. In the second half of chapter 3, we saw how one kind of conservative reaction against spasmody manifested as a return to strict poetic form—a conservative structure that, for W. E. Aytoun and others, was meant to mimic a conservative political and cultural ethos. Poetic theory in the latter half of the nineteenth century retreated from physiological poetics toward what some have called "The New Prosody," and it is to this new strand of poetic theory, along with the political and cultural implications inherent in its practice, that we now turn.[1]

Central to this New Prosody is the work of Coventry Patmore, whose theory of poetry both depends on and insistently departs from that of the Spasmodics. Like the Spasmodics, Patmore imagines how poetry might communicate in ways extraneous to the meaning of words on a page. As William Cadbury observed in 1966, Patmore "found it perfectly obvious, though his readers did not, that poetry is . . . still a predominantly nondiscursive form" (Cadbury, 238); poetry, that is, never functions simply as semantic presence. Unlike the Spasmodics, however, Patmore does not see the human body filling in the gaps left by language. Rather, Patmore looks to metrical form as a guide, experienced intuitively by the mind, to what would otherwise be an irrational and senseless mess of words and rhythmical impulses. Patmore thus shares with Dobell a belief in poetry's unconscious work, but he disagrees entirely with Dobell's understanding of physiological poetics. In so departing from the Spasmodic association of bodily impulse with poetic communication, Patmore stands for a generation of poets who made similar, and sometimes coordinated, retreats from Spasmodic rhythm to metrical structure. Electric poetics function for these writers as a foil, a style of composition to be avoided. This chapter will first examine Patmore's poetic theory and its aesthetic and cultural implications. It will then look to the work of Gerard Manley Hopkins as an effort to synthesize Spasmodic rhythm with the principles of the New Prosody.

BODILESS PATMORE

Rumor had it in 1844 that the volume of poetry just released by one "Coventry Patmore" was in fact the work of Alfred Tennyson, whose 1842 *Poems* had made a stir in the literary world (Champneys, 1:59). Patmore held Tennyson in high regard, and must have been pleased to be mistaken for him. The young poet, only twenty-one at the time of his first publication, had been raised in a literary household, and—though the 1844 volume was not a success—he committed himself to a life of letters, the most famous product of which was to be the epic and quintessentially "Victorian" *The Angel in the House* (1854–56). But Patmore was also a committed essayist and reviewer, and his writings on poetry, which span the 1840s to the 1890s, stand as an indispensable barometer of the Victorians' shifting literary tastes.

Like Aytoun, Patmore was a thorough critic of the Spasmodic poets. His 1856 *Edinburgh Review* essay on those he dismissively called the "New

Poets" attacks the "violence and incongruity" of Dobell, Smith, Bailey, and others, arguing that their poems offer an occasional "beautiful phrase" but that such exceptions are marred "by the context of tawdriness, bombast, and imbecility" (Patmore 1856, 340, 342). "Tawdriness" surely gestures to the various plot turns that Aytoun parodied in *Firmilian;* "bombast" points to both the Spasmodics' rhetorical style and their formal assertiveness; and "imbecility," to Patmore, is the inevitable result of combining tawdriness and bombast in a work of art. Patmore's poetry of this period, most of which comprises *The Angel in the House,* was meant explicitly to challenge the aesthetics of his contemporaries, and the Spasmodics in particular. Conservative in both its unerring iambic tetrameter and its morally austere narrative of courtship, Patmore's *Angel* is in many ways the antithesis to a poem such as *Balder.* According to Edmund Gosse, Patmore intended all along to rein in Spasmodic formlessness through his own example: "Patmore was often attacked by the critics [of *The Angel*] for using this humdrum, jigging measure, and he was once challenged to say why he had chosen it. He replied that he did so of set purpose, partly because at that particular time the Brownings and even Tennyson, with the Spasmodists in their wake, were diverging into the most quaint and extravagant forms, and he wished to call the public back to simplicity" (Gosse 1905, 58). Like Aytoun, Patmore believed in the power of poetry to "inflame and propagate" dangerous thoughts and feelings (Patmore 1856, 361). Metrical regularity was both a means of containing such inflammation and, more important, a way to regulate the intellectual and emotional disposition of the content.

Patmore's *Angel* thus makes much reference to rhythmic experience—rhythm is understood, at some level, to be a necessary feature of all life—but it urges readers toward restraint. The poem's heroine, Honoria, becomes a model for readers not only through her "feminine grace" (Bristow, 132), but also as a result of her rhythmic adherence to a larger, metrical pattern:

> She seem'd expressly sent below
>   To each our erring minds to see
> The rhythmic change of time's swift flow
>   As part of still eternity.
>
>   (PCP, 67)

Everyone feels the rhythmic sway of daily events, Patmore suggests here, but through Honoria, we see the larger metrical totality, the consistent whole through which rhythmic variations become not violent disruptions but mere quivers in the larger eternal fabric of time.[2] Patmore elaborates on this view of rhythm and meter in his 1857 *Essay on English Metrical Law*, a direct response to the Spasmodic controversy that was perhaps the most important Victorian study of prosody.

Patmore's *Essay* has received some belated attention in recent years, as scholars of the Victorian period have returned to thinking about poetic form.[3] What critics thus far have overlooked, however, is how Patmore's work responds to and engages with his Spasmodic peers. Seen from the distance of our current moment, Patmore's *Essay* reads as a fairly dry, if studious and important, attempt to make sense of English meters. Seen within the context of the Spasmodic controversy and the physiological sciences to which Spasmodics such as Dobell were responding, the *Essay* comes to life as a crucial aesthetic and politically relevant document. Patmore's primary goal in the *Essay* is to understand how the Classical approach to prosody, whereby meter is determined by duration (by the actual time required to speak or to sing patterns of words), might be reconciled with English prosody, which tends to focus on patterns of stressed and unstressed syllables. As Derek Attridge has shown, British prosodists had long made gestures to such quantitative poetics, dating back to George Gascoigne's 1575 *Certayne Notes of Instruction* and William Webbe's 1586 *Discourse of English Poetrie* (Attridge 1982, 18).[4] A. A. Markley has suggested that Tennyson, too, played with meters that would "approximate for the English reader the experience of reading Greek and Latin poetry" (Markley, 60). Patmore's argument, essentially, is that the best poets never truly left behind the Classical model, and that most English poetry is organized on a principle—unconscious though it may be—of "isochronous" intervals: intervals equal in time, having a consistent duration. Within this understanding of poetry, one focuses primarily on the time it takes to read the poetic line, rather than on the number of syllables in a foot or the placement of stressed syllables. Patmore draws from musical theory to explain that his notion of meter "takes the isochronous *bar* for the metrical integer, and uses the same kind of liberty as is claimed by the musical composer, in filling up that space" (PE, 33). Chopin, for example, writes as many notes as he wishes within any one measure of a waltz;

what matters is that the notes should last the length of the measure's three beats, no more and no less. So, too, should poets take liberty with syllables, making sure only that each line lasts for as long as the meter—understood as a temporal structure—dictates.

Among other things, what isochronous intervals provide is a decorporealized system for understanding poetry. In Patmore's theory, meter is a structure for intellectually intuited duration, rather than for physiologically experienced pulses. This is what leads Dennis Taylor, in a recent book on Hardy and Victorian prosody, to locate Patmore as central to what, in Taylor's opinion, was the Victorians' signal prosodic accomplishment: "an understanding of the abstract nature of metrical form and the dialectic way in which it interplayed with the spoken language" (Taylor, 5). In other words, Patmore sees meter as functioning primarily in one's own head, a pattern that each individual keeps going—consciously or not—like an internal metronome. The key passage in the *Essay* reads thus: "I think it demonstrable that, for the most part, [meter] *has no material and external existence at all*, but has its place in the mind, which craves measure in everything, and, wherever the idea of measure is uncontradicted, delights in marking it with an imaginary 'beat'" (PE, 15). What does not receive attention in Taylor's argument is the reactionary nature of Patmore's metrical abstraction, along with the anxiety behind Patmore's italicized insistence on meter's immateriality. Were it not for the Spasmodics' celebration of the "physical principles of sound," as Dobell put it in his 1857 lecture (Dobell 1876, 24), Patmore would not have struggled so persistently to diminish the importance of poetry's corporeality. We can know this, in part, because both *The Angel in the House* and the *Essay on English Metrical Law* offer views of poetry and poetic form seemingly at odds with work that Patmore composed both before the Spasmodic crisis and in the decades following its dissolution. Patmore's work in the 1850s, that is, strikes the reader of the full corpus of his writings as incongruous, and this is so not only for the social conservatism of the work, but also for its utter disdain for rhythm.[5] Like *The Angel*, which privileges metrical structure over rhythmic experience, Patmore's *Essay* locates the true experience of poetry in meter and relegates to the sidelines "the corporeal element," rhythmic sensation: "Art, indeed, must have a body as well as a soul; and the higher and purer the spiritual, the more powerful and unmistakable should be the corporeal element;—in other words, the more vigorous and various the life, the more stringent and elaborate must be the law by obedience to which life expresses itself" (PE, 7). The rhythmic experience of the poem, then, must be secondary to the "spiritual" or intellectual metrical concept, the "law" that structures "life." Patmore continues by noting that meter "ought not only to exist as the becoming garment of poetic passion, but, furthermore, it should continually make its existence recognized. . . . The language should always seem to *feel*, though not to *suffer from* the bonds of verse"; rhythm must be subject to the lawful restraints of meter (8).

One does not have to look far in Patmore's 1844 volume, *Poems*, to see a different approach to poetic experience. Patmore came to regret this early publication, referring to the poems as "trash" and "rubbish" (Champneys, 1:57), a position no doubt encouraged by a colorful *Blackwood's* review that brandished words such as "simpering," "impotence," and "sickly"; "Mr. Coventry Patmore's volume," the essay concludes, "has reached the ultimate *terminus* of poetical degradation" (Ferrier, 333, 334, 342). But Patmore also abandoned his first efforts for his own aesthetic reasons. The poems are both rhythmically coarse and metrically tedious; E. Bulwer Lytton suggested that Patmore had not "attended sufficiently to variety and sustained music in rhythm" (quoted in Champneys, 1:56). The result is structural monotony— the same droning patterns over and over again—crossed with rhythmic irregularity, which makes many of the lines hard, if not impossible, to scan (the unerring rhythms of *The Angel*, in contrast, fall entirely in line with its meter). In addition to these formal concerns, the 1844 *Poems* spotlights a language of sensation that Patmore in the 1850s came to find repugnant. John Maynard has shown the extent to which Patmore "obliterated" his early poetic self: "Poem after poem of the 1844 volume is thrown out, rewritten, or torn in pieces for later volumes" (Maynard 1993, 165). I would point out that this process of expurgation and revision takes place along a timeline running parallel to the rise and fall of the Spasmodic poets. "Lilian," a poem from 1844, allows us to see more clearly the young Patmore's poetic sensibility, and to understand more distinctly how and why Patmore abandoned this approach and arrived at the remarkable poetic formulations of the 1857 *Essay*.

In the words of the unflattering *Blackwood's* review, "Lilian" might at first be viewed as a poem "designed to illustrate the bad effects produced on the female mind by the reading of French novels" (Ferrier, 336). In the poem, Percy, a friend of the narrator's, watches in horror as his beloved Lilian falls for Winton, a handsome man recently returned from France who puts aside "healthy study" in favor of novels, "French chiefly," that make "his blood . . . boil and gush" (Patmore 1844, 64). Lilian's blood boils as well, as a result of both the fiery Winton and his sensational books, and she ultimately leaves Percy behind. What "Lilian" seems most concerned in asking, finally, is whether poetry too—or even most especially—inspires in readers the kind of spark that sets Lilian aflame. As Maynard suggests, "Lilian" argues that writing itself might be seen as "the source of sexual problematics" (Maynard 1993, 169). Within a decade of Patmore's first volume, the Spasmodic poets would popularize (and politicize) the view that poetry moves its readers through the bodily experience of sensation, and through rhythm in particular. If physiological poetics in "Lilian" might be read as an unfortunate moral conundrum, Patmore came ultimately to see such interplay of poetic form and bodily sensation as both politically and aesthetically irresponsible.

We can observe both anxiety and inspiration in the bodies of "Lilian," from silences that are "read" (Patmore 1844, 51) to "thoughts unworded" that the speaker discerns in Lilian's expression:

> On her face, then and forever, thoughts unworded used to live;
> So that when she whisper'd to me, "Better joy earth cannot give"—
> Her lips, though shut, continued, "But earth's joy is fugitive."
>
> (60)

A kind of silent speaking, Lilian's body language depends on the speaker's interpretation, and perhaps stems entirely from the speaker's imagination. Patmore's rhythm here also seems up for interpretation, failing to maintain a coherent pattern. Breaking from the poem's standard iambic rhythms, these three lines seem a jumble of substitutions, many of which could be read in a variety of ways. Are we meant to feel "On her face" as an anapest or as part of a larger trochaic pattern (*On* her *face*, then *and* for*e*ver)? Either choice has awkward consequences: the former leads one to stumble over "then" (stressed or unstressed?), whereas the latter seems to put undue emphasis on "and." Consistent trochees also break too dramatically from the rest of the poem's iambs. When Patmore revised "Lilian" for publication as "The Yew-Berry" in his 1853 volume *Tamerton Church Tower*, he acknowledged the stanza's troubling indeterminacy by editing out some of the stumbling blocks (other awkward rhythms in the poem were also smoothed over):

> On her face, when she was speaking, thoughts unworded used to live;
> So that when she whisper'd to me, 'Better joy Earth cannot give,'
> Her following silence added, 'But Earth's joy is fugitive.'
>   (PCP, 3)

An anapestic "On her face" now leads comfortably into an iambic line, and this rhythmic pattern (an anapest followed by six iambs) repeats itself in the second line; as in the original, the mostly iambic third line scans perfectly well.

The point here is not simply that Patmore's ear for rhythm developed over time, though this is certainly true. In "The Yew-Berry," Patmore is also in far more control of his poem's meaning; in clarifying the poem's rhythmic movements, he lessens the authority—or the whim—of his reader and instead guides interpretation. Paralleling this on a thematic level, "The Yew-Berry" excises most of the French-novel plot, which in "Lilian" worked to demonstrate the significance of readerly interpretation; the earlier poem's moral instructs us to distance ourselves from fictional romance, lest we fall victim to passion. The narrator of "Lilian" wonders whether degenerate novels really can change a person who otherwise would have led an ethical life. The young Lilian, the narrator suggests, must have been passionate to begin with, and it took only some encouragement for those desires to surface: "are souls worth saving / Which are lost with so much ease!" (Patmore 1844, 54). *Blackwood's* echoes this point in a critique of Patmore's ambivalence: "[I]t evidently did not require the application of such a spark as the seducer Winton . . . to set her tinder in a blaze—any other small contingency would have answered equally well" (Ferrier, 336). By 1853, however, Patmore has lost any indifference he might once have felt with respect to individuals falling (or not) according to their own dispositions. The poems of *Tamerton Church Tower* are a step toward the didacticism of *The Angel in the House;* the poems impress on their readers clear moral and aesthetic structures. Patmore knew back in 1844 the dangers inherent in reading: "We are all fools of language," the narrator of "Lilian" intones (Patmore 1844, 88). By the early 1850s, he had learned that metrical structure, and rhythmic adherence to that structure, can offset some of those dangers. Along with W. E. Aytoun, Patmore came to see metrical clarity as a guide for the wayward reader toward ethical and moral virtue.

This evolution in Patmore's thinking is more explicit in three reviews he wrote of Tennyson's poetry, from 1848 to 1855. Each review represents a step toward the theory of isochronous intervals that Patmore would elaborate in his 1857 *Essay*. In his 1848 review of *The Princess* and the fourth edition of Tennyson's *Poems*, Patmore has yet to embrace the formal conservatism that the Spasmodics would soon inspire. With language that might surprise those who know only Patmore's later works, the essay criticizes the older poet's lack of spontaneity, the "constant predominance of thought over feeling . . . manifest throughout" Tennyson's earliest poems (Patmore 1848, 24). The solution to uninspired poetry is not, Patmore stresses, the abandonment of thought, but the subjection of "external law"—that is, aesthetic laws that "exist in the mind of the poet in expressed forms and full consciousness"—to the active will of the poet (28). The poet should write as he sees fit, not according to established poetic practice. This does not mean that the poet should write without deep thought and self-consciousness; Patmore notes that a "true poet" will be occupied for "half an hour with [the] analysis" of a "single line, which you imagine he had struck off, as it were, at a blow" (28). The issue here concerns the nature of the poet's thoughts as he rigorously forms this single line. Does he worry over the predominant aesthetic designs of his day, or reach deep inside to determine how best to express his thoughts and feelings? Great works of art inspire by engaging the mind, "by inducing the mind actively to take upon itself, for the time at least, a new and excellent shape, namely, that of the artist's work, as the only clue to the comprehension of it" (27). A new thought requires a new poetic form; the poet leaves an impression on his reader because he has literally changed the way his reader thinks. For Patmore, Tennyson's early poetry falls short of genius because it does not require the reader to make such a change: "[A] certain defect of spontaneousness . . . tends to limit the force of the impression to the time during which it is being made" (24). Tennyson's early poetry fails to stick with us, because it adheres to familiar patterns of thought.

But Tennyson ultimately overcomes these problems, according to Patmore's 1850 review of *In Memoriam*. By 1850, Patmore has clearly started thinking more seriously about meter. Whereas in the 1848 review, Patmore writes only of "law" in a vague sense ("laws exist, as living and actuating ideas, in the mind of the poet" [28]), in 1850 Patmore defines poetic law as largely metrical in nature: "All beauty, from the highest to the lowest . . . is *life expressed in law.* . . . By the superinduction of metre, language is lifted out of the sphere of prose expression altogether, and a free poetical diction becomes not only allowable, but necessary, in order to balance and relieve the artificial law" (Patmore 1850, 288). Note here how with "superinduction" Patmore borrows electric terminology to describe the effects of meter on language. *Superinduction* had long been a term for describing the adoption of a characteristic or possession "in addition to one already existing"—for example, the taking on of a second wife "within the lifetime of the first (or, by extension, shortly after her death)" (*OED*, "superinduce"). *Induction* as a scientific term was used from the end of the eighteenth century to describe how an electric or magnetic object will "bring about" a similar electric or magnetic state in neighboring objects, simply "by . . . proximity (without actual contact)" (*OED*, "induction"). Patmore thereby sees meter as electrical insofar as it "superinduc[es]" a new kind of life and beauty onto language; it makes language resonate. In his 1848 essay, quoted above, Patmore suggests that artists—in a general sense—use their work to "induc[e] the mind[s]" of others; by 1850, this process of induction has become specifically metrical in nature. With *In Memoriam*, Patmore claims, Tennyson has found a metrical structure, a formal law, that allows his emotion and intellect free play; the meter "lift[s]" the language rather than containing it: "Few poets have equaled the author of 'In Memoriam,' in the complete conquest and subdual of metre and language to the service of thought and feeling" (Patmore 1850, 296). Spontaneity seems no longer an issue because Tennyson's iambic tetrameter quatrains, electrical in their influence on the poem as a whole, offer both lawful form and subjective flexibility.

Patmore's 1855 review of *Maud* advances these ideas and arrives, finally, at a theory of isochronous intervals. The essay again praises *In Memoriam* for its "metrical discipline" (Patmore 1855, 505), and it suggests, predictably, that "the qualities we appreciate most highly in [*In Memoriam*]"—that is, its metrical grace—"are precisely those which are most wanting in [*Maud*]"

(506). But Patmore notes the obvious distinctions between *In Memoriam* and *Maud* not to disparage the latter poem, but to elaborate his developing theory of isochrony. Patmore makes reference to this theory in his 1850 review, suggesting that in Wordsworth's "Intimations" ode, as in most irregular odes, "each line, however many syllables it may contain, ought to occupy the same time in reading, according to the analogy of bars of music" (Patmore 1850, 292). In 1855, with the same idea clearly in mind, he calls passages from *Maud* "music without notes":

> This kind of poetry which is almost a modern invention, and of which Mr. Tennyson is probably the greatest master, asks to be read as it was written, in a mood in which reflection voluntarily abandons for a time its mental leadership; and thought follows instead of guiding, the current of emotion. A vague spiritual voluptuousness takes the place of distinct conceptions; and we should as soon think of judging such verses by the ordinary laws of language as of determining the merit of a drama by the melodies of an opera. A sustained passage of this sort is perhaps one of the rarest if not the highest triumphs of poetry, "that sweeter and weaker sex of truth." It is only after a very complete mastery has been obtained in the lower excellences of his art, that the poet can trust himself thus completely to the direction of his feelings and his instinct of rhythm. (Patmore 1855, 512)

Patmore's overall project through the 1850s is to abstract poetry from bodily experience, but this passage borders on an endorsement of what I have been calling physiological poetics. Patmore has to work overtime to assert the "spiritual" nature of *Maud*'s "current of emotion." Tennyson's "instinct of rhythm," Patmore wants us to believe, sidesteps physiological voluptuousness because the poet has so "complete[ly] master[ed] . . . the lower excellences of his art," the various formal components that structure the poem. Three pages later, Patmore identifies Tennyson's technique as a "complete return to the Anglo-Saxon principle of isochronous bars, of which the filling up is left to the will of the poet" (515). The Poet Laureate, once captive to external laws of form and possessing an unfortunate lack of spontaneity (according to Patmore's 1848 review), has risen to the height of poetic composition first by attending to the law of meter, which permits freedom of expression within a strictly governed form (Patmore's 1850 review of *In Memoriam*), and finally by transitioning from a metrical system based on stress to a metrical system determined by duration and in which rhythm achieves nearly free play (the 1855 review of *Maud*).

When we return from Patmore's views of Tennyson to the critic's own poetry, a significant incongruity emerges between Patmore's theory and practice. To begin, it should be apparent how vastly Patmore's poetic theory differs from the standard conservative responses to spasmody—for example, the principles of metrical regularity that Aytoun encouraged in *Blackwood's* and in poems such as *Bothwell*. If we were to read only Patmore's *Angel*, we could rightfully group the poet with Aytoun's insistent regularity, and his dogged alignment of metrical structure with moral rectitude. We have seen, too, how Patmore's move from "Lilian" in 1844 to "The Yew-Berry" in 1853 privileges metrical regularity and the didactic/moral role of the poet. But at the same time that Patmore's own poetry was moving toward the regulation and restraining of rhythm, his poetic theory was creating a space for something altogether different: rhythm entirely liberated from the traditional stressed systems of English meter. It would be difficult to imagine Aytoun countenancing isochrony as a guiding principle for poetic meter; the structure leaves too much to the reader's imagination. Patmore notes that the isochronous system requires "the filling up" of rhythmic impulses to be subject "to the will of the poet," but it also puts a great deal of trust in the reader, who must intuit (physically? intellectually?) the poem's metrical structure. Reviews of *Maud* (as discussed in chapter 3) demonstrate that most readers of the 1850s, even those trained in the poetic arts, could not fathom the poem's metrical principles. To put it bluntly, if the point of meter is to subdue and to regulate, then isochrony must largely fail the test: what sort of regulation might come from a poem that most readers cannot scan? Patmore's drive toward the order of *The Angel in the House* thus finds itself at odds with the formal insights of his critical work.

Were it not for the popularity of the Spasmodic poets, Patmore might not have been compelled toward such contradiction. Faced with the profound physicality of Spasmodic poetics, Patmore turned to a Hegelian notion of poetry as the "most spiritual mode of representation" (Hegel, 95). Patmore notes that Hegel, "whose chapters on music and metre contain by far the most satisfactory piece of writing I know of on the subject, admirably observes, that versification affords a necessary counterpoise to the great spiritualization of language in poetry" (PE, 7). Patmore's isochronous system follows Hegel in understanding meter as "abstract" (to borrow Dennis Taylor's term) and in shifting poetic experience from the physical body to the thinking mind. "Poetry," writes Hegel, "is the universal art of the mind which has become free in its own nature, and which is not tied to find its realization in external sensuous matter, but expatiates exclusively in the inner space and inner time of the ideas and feelings" (Hegel, 96). Patmore, of course, understands the necessary place of the body in poetic experience and interpretation—"Art, indeed, must have a body as well as a soul" (PE, 7)—but the body in Patmore's scheme must remain under the influence of a forceful metrical (that is, abstract) law. Thus, "the 'body' of language," as Yopie Prins notes, "materialize[s]" for Patmore only "through the marking of meter," through the strict regulatory control that meter asserts (Prins 1999, 150). Such control develops as a result of both Patmore's personal aesthetic sense and his deep concerns for the time in which he lived: "this very dangerous and critical period" (Gosse 1905, 44). Richard Garnett, who worked with Patmore at the British Library through the 1850s, later recalled "conversations" with Patmore "in which [Garnett] learned lessons invaluable for prose as well as verse. . . . The subordination of parts to the whole, the necessity of every part of a composition being in keeping with all the others, the equal importance of form with matter, absolute truth to nature, sobriety in simile and metaphor, the wisdom of maintaining a reserve of power—these and kindred maxims were enforced with an emphasis most salutary to a young hearer just beginning to write in the heyday of the 'spasmodic school'" (Champneys, 1:108). Patmore agonized over the role that poetic theory and practice had to play within the cultural and political dynamics of his day. If *The Angel in the House* is paradigmatic of mid-Victorian sensibilities, it is also a retreat from the Spasmodic experiments that both challenged those sensibilities and suggested new directions for prosody and poetic experience.

But Patmore was clearly frustrated by the divide in his work between theory and practice, and in the post-Spasmodic years he set about attempting to reconcile the two. By the mid-1860s, poets such as Dobell and Smith had fallen from public favor, and Patmore found the liberty to write the sort of poetry he had long hypothesized. The poems that would eventually make up Patmore's volume of 1877, *The Unknown Eros,* were thus long in the making and the result of great thought and labor. They bear little resemblance to Patmore's earlier works, and they have been largely ignored by scholars of the period.[6] The poems are astonishingly challenging both thematically and formally, and they ought to be better known. That said, my interest here is not to exhume the whole of this very difficult and multivalent work, but to showcase the final stage of Patmore's formal evolution; I thus focus on just one example from the forty-two odes. Maynard identifies this poem, "The Day after To-Morrow," as "almost certainly the most expressive and sensual love poem Patmore ever wrote" (Maynard 1993, 215). It is essentially a lyrical expression of desire for an absent lover, and a forecast of the pleasure the two will have when united. I quote at length here as the speaker apostrophizes the wind and the sea. The shocking formal departure from Patmore's *Angel* will be immediately apparent:

> Tell her I come,
> And let her heart be still'd.
> One day's controlled hope, and then one more,
> And on the third our lives shall be fulfill'd!
> Yet all has been before:
> Palm placed in palm, twin smiles, and words astray.
> What other should we say?
> But shall I not, with ne'er a sign, perceive,
> Whilst her sweet hands I hold,
> The myriad threads and meshes manifold
> Which Love shall round her weave:
> The pulse in that vein making alien pause
> And varying beats from this;
> Down each long finger felt, a differing strand
> Of silvery welcome bland;
> And in her breezy palm
> And silken wrist,
> Beneath the touch of my like numerous bliss
> Complexly kiss'd,
> A diverse and distinguishable calm?
> What should we say!

(PCP, 357)

Making sense of the content here is not difficult, but understanding the meter—and how each line's rhythm makes sense within that meter—is an altogether different proposition. Patmore's early biographer Basil Champneys writes with some exasperation that "[t]he new metrical system seems to be founded on no theoretic principle, nor can it be explained by analysis" (Champneys, 1:243). Only recently have critics returned to Patmore's *Essay* for guidance as to how the odes should be read, looking especially to Patmore's understanding of metrical pauses, or catalexes. Patmore again uses the analogy of music to describe the work of catalexis, whereby "a good reader . . . by instinct" will feel a pause within a poetic line (PE, 23). A helpful example, and one that T. S. Omond uses in his 1903 study of prosody, is Tennyson's "Break, Break, Break," which features a strong terminal catalexis in most of its lines: "Break, break, break, [pause] / On thy cold gray stones, O Sea! [pause]." Patmore seems to have found catalexis appealing because, like music, it depends more on temporal experience than rhythmic impulse; we feel the pause not as the absence of a stress, but as a space of time that allows the line to finish its natural duration. Omond follows in Patmore's footsteps in writing that time "is thus the real basis of this metre, and syllables are comparatively unimportant"; "the poet . . . use[s] his words as indices of time" (Omond, 6, 17). Catalexis plays a central role in isochrony by encouraging readers to rely on temporal, and not stressed, experience; catalexis thus facilitates Patmore's turn from rhythm toward an "abstract" understanding of metrical experience.

Even with an understanding of catalexis, however, Patmore's odes remain difficult to read formally. Robert M. Pierson notes that "we may infer that Patmore wanted us to feel [catalexis] in his own poetry," but it is "doubtful" that such pauses might "always . . . be observed in accordance with Patmore's theory" (Pierson, 507). Attridge points to yet another problem in the quantitative approach: "Any account of metre based on the assumption that . . . objective reality [in determining a syllable's duration] exists is without foundation; verse rhythm is not created by time-sequences measurable in centiseconds" (Attridge 1982, 26). At the line-level, too, problems arise at nearly every step. In the lines quoted above, for example, it seems unlikely that a reader might pause long enough after "Tell her I come" to make the line last for as long as "One day's controlled hope, and then one more." Then again, perhaps we are meant to read the first two lines together, such that "Tell her I come, / And let her heart be still'd" lasts for a time equal to "One day's controlled hope, and then one more." Several lines in "The Day after To-Morrow" can be juggled in this way to make the time lapses work, leaving only occasional examples of truly drawn-out catalexes (such as that following "Yet all has been before," which to my ear then requires the equivalent of two full pauses). Patmore was clear that "the great point" of the odes is "the form," and he writes excitedly that this form "flashed upon" him, as a sudden inspiration (Champneys, 1:253). The content of the lines also regularly points to the formal elements, as in the references in the passage above to a "pulse in that vein making alien pause / And varying beats." Patmore's odes are largely iambic, but they are far from consistent, offering "varying beats" alongside the catalectic pauses that for many readers must seem "alien." Patmore praised *Maud* for its "vague spiritual voluptuousness [that] takes the place of distinct conceptions," but one wonders whether "The Day after To-Morrow" abandons the spiritual in favor of the purely voluptuous, tugging and pulling rhythmically in the style of Dobell's poems on the Crimean War. Indeed, in reading *The Unknown Eros*, one begins to question the degree to which Patmore's later works, and therefore his thoughts on isochrony and catalexis, are indebted to the Spasmodics and their highly subjective, physiological approach to poetic experience. Patmore wants the meter of his poems to be understood temporally (time intuited mentally), but the "varying beats" of the odes enable—necessitate, even—rhythmic experiences that are compellingly physiological. Most important, the poet of such odes cannot claim to be in control of his reader's experiences.

What the odes of *The Unknown Eros* make perfectly clear is the extent to which Patmore's *Essay* overstates the case for metrical immateriality. Yes, meter is abstract insofar as it takes place not on the page but within the individual who experiences the poem. But that experience, as the Spasmodics well knew, is never entirely "in the mind" but finds its place in the body as well, in the muscles that tap or sway to the beat, or—more profoundly—in the brain's formulation of the idea of meter (the brain, as discussed in chapter 3, having recently been determined to function as a physiological organ, not a spiritual or abstract receptacle). Patmore acknowledges this in "The Day after To-Morrow" with a language of physiological sensation, consistent through the poem, and a structural elasticity that encourages us to feel—to experience bodily—that physicality. Coventry Patmore was not a Spasmodic poet, but his prosodic theory depends far more than he ever would admit on the physiological mode that the Spasmodics celebrated. Toward the end of his life, Patmore more openly acknowledged the balancing between intellect and body, and between meter and rhythm, often framing the tension in gendered terms. In an essay from 1891, for example, he writes that "[m]asculine law is always, however obscurely, the theme of the true poet; the feeling, with the correspondent rhythm, is its feminine inflection, without which the law has no sensitive or poetic life" (Patmore 1898, 20); in another piece from the same year, he suggests that poetry "is the mind of *man*, the rational soul, using the female or sensitive soul, as its accidental or complementary means of expression" (Patmore 1898, 24). This is precisely the kind of balancing that served as an ideal for poets in the post-Spasmodic years, a necessary meeting of isochrony and spasmody, mind and body, "spiritual" and physiological. Patmore even attempted, just prior to his death, to recuperate some of Sydney Dobell's work, "to aid in securing, if possible, a place in future anthologies" for his poems. Patmore notes—in a passage that at first shocks, accurate as it is—that "Dobell wrote some passages which, had they been found in Wordsworth or any other of our great poets of humanity, would have been famous." Dobell's verses still "annoy[] and pain[]" Patmore with their "pretentious strain and unconscious failure," but the poet of *The Angel in the House* has clearly experienced a sea change in his approach to physiological poetics (Patmore 1921, 116–18). It was through *The Unknown Eros* that Patmore most nearly sympathized with the Spasmodic style, even though isochrony was in large part an effort to move English poetics away from the Spasmodics.

HOPKINS'S ELECTRIC HORROR

Hopkins's system of "sprung rhythm" bears important structural similarities to Patmore's isochronous intervals, even if at first it seems exactly the opposite in practice. Simply put, sprung rhythm focuses on accent only and disregards quantity: "Its principle," writes Hopkins to his friend Richard Watson Dixon in 1880, "is that all rhythm and all verse consists of feet and each foot must contain one stress or verse-accent." Additionally, and most important, "the stress alone is essential to a foot and . . . therefore even one stressed syllable may make a foot and consequently two or more stresses may come running" (Hopkins 1955a, 39). Like Coleridge's "Christabel" meter, in which readers are meant to count the accents (four to a line) and not the syllables, Hopkins's sprung rhythm rejects syllable-counting in favor of a singular, governing accent for each foot. The result is that a metrical foot might just as easily consist of one stressed syllable or a combination of three unstressed and one stressed syllables: the time it takes to read a foot is inconsequential, as everything focuses on the accent. For obvious reasons, then, Patmore found Hopkins's poetry distasteful: "I do not think," Patmore writes to Hopkins in 1884, "that I could ever become sufficiently accustomed to your favourite Poem, 'The Wreck of the Deutschland' to reconcile me to its strangeness" (Hopkins 1956, 352). For his part, Hopkins found much to dispute in Patmore's 1857 *Essay* (I quote at length from a letter of 1883 to show Hopkins's persistence at confronting the issue):

> The treatment of English spoken accent here is unsatisfactory: you nowhere say what it is. Now if, as you say, the learned are pretty well agreed what the old Greek accent was, which no living ear ever heard, we must surely be able to know and say with certainty what the English is, which we cannot even dispute about without exhibiting as fast as we open our mouths. If some books say it is long quantity, that is so grossly stupid as to need no refutation. . . . It is plain and, so far as I know, it is commonly agreed that it [English accent] is stress. The Greek accent was a *tonic accent*, was tone, pitch of note: it may have included a stress, but essentially it was pitch. In like manner the English accent is *emphatic accent*, is stress. . . . Stress appears so elementary an idea as does not need and scarcely allows of definition; still this may be said of it, that it is the making of a thing more, or making it markedly, what it already is; it is the bringing out its nature. Accordingly stress on a syllable (which is English accent proper) is the making much of that syllable, more than of others; stress on a word or sentence (which is emphasis) is the making much of that word or sentence, more than of others. I have written a great deal on this head, but all comes to this, that you ought in my opinion, to say once clearly what English accent is and not, after quoting different views, leave the truth unexpressed as if there could be or in fact were any doubt about the matter. (Hopkins 1956, 326–28)

Hopkins gets immediately to the heart of the problem with Patmore's metrics. Like it or not, English meter relies on stress; accent is central to English metrical practice. Hopkins's irritation with Patmore's coy avoidance of the issue burns through his letter, indicating that this was a matter of no small concern for the younger poet.

Yet the long correspondence between Patmore and Hopkins—their elaborate exchange runs from 1883 to Hopkins's death in 1889—suggests that the two were not entirely, or not simply, at odds with one another in thinking about meter. The parallels between the two systems emerge in their structure, not their practice. Both isochrony and sprung rhythm open English meter to a wider range of possibilities while still insisting on what Patmore called the "law" of verse. Whereas the poet using isochrony writes as many syllables as fit within a given time frame, the poet using sprung rhythm focuses only on stress, and thereby understands slack syllables in a way similar to that of the poet using isochrony: as a kind of "filling up" of space. Both isochrony and sprung rhythm, then, offer a kind of freedom (the liberty to interpolate unstressed syllables almost at will) while holding firmly to an overarching metrical structure (a temporal structure for Patmore, a strong-stress structure for Hopkins). The two systems also show clear debts to the physiological poetics of the midcentury: Patmore's isochrony in its absolute rejection of the Spasmodic enterprise, Hopkins's sprung rhythm in its innovative turning of Dobell's principles to different— that is, more spiritual and less purely physiological—ends. If Patmore represents the opposite of Spasmodic corporeality, Hopkins works to locate a middle ground, a space from which to appreciate both the necessary connections between rhythm and the human body *and* the possibility within poetry for some form of transcendence.

Hopkins regularly turned to electricity when attempting to locate this middle ground. Electricity becomes a figure in Hopkins' poetry for the work that he imagines poetic form—and stress in particular—to accomplish. Recent critics have pointed to Hopkins's thoroughgoing interest in the sciences, including his study of John Tyndall's work on sound and midcentury developments in electromagnetism.[7] Jude V. Nixon has argued for the importance of energy in Hopkins's poetry: "heat, fire, and light" (Nixon, 131). Daniel Brown has suggested that Hopkins found inspiration in electromagnetic field theory, a subject I address more thoroughly in chapter 5 (Brown 1997,

238–41). Building on this work, I wish to suggest that electricity was an especially helpful figure for Hopkins in negotiating what he saw to be an uneasy relationship between the material and the spiritual worlds. In a series of notes taken in 1868, for example, he writes of words expressing mental ideas by means of a "physical" and "refined energy accenting the nerves" (Hopkins 1959, 125). Words in Hopkins's view are physical things, and they effect change by "accenting the nerves" with their "energy." Rhythm facilitates this connection, with the "accenting" of stress ideally embodying the nature of the word's referent (M. Campbell, 191); Hopkins's terms *inscape* and *instress*, among others, work in different ways to describe this phenomenon. That said, Hopkins remained wary of a simple one-to-one or deterministic relationship between a word and its physiological experience. As he writes in an undergraduate essay, "The Probable Future of Metaphysics" (1867), "it is all to no purpose to show an organ for each faculty and a nerve vibrating for each idea, because this only shows in the last detail what broadly no one doubted, to wit that the activities of the spirit are conveyed in those of the body" (Hopkins 1959, 118). Electricity appeals to Hopkins insofar as he views it as both concrete physical communication—words "accenting the nerves"—and as a sign of "the spirit" as it moves through the body. The challenge as Hopkins sees it is to develop a poetics that reflects this double nature, avoiding a deterministic model for an individual's encounter with language and instead opening poetry to experiences both earthly and transcendent. As Armstrong puts it, a poem for Hopkins "must fuse thinking and feeling or, if possible, thought and sensation in an irreducibly concrete configuration of particulars seized as epiphany and oneness" (Armstrong 1982, 15). Electricity is Hopkins's figurative vehicle for this fusion, the work of poetic embodiment.

Let us then consider the opening stanza of Hopkins's "Wreck of the Deutschland" (1875–76), the poet's first full-out experiment with sprung rhythm:

> Thou mastering me
> God! giver of breath and bread;
> Wórld's stránd, swáy of the séa;
> Lord of living and dead;
> Thou hast bóund bónes and véins in me, fástened me flésh,

And áfter it álmost únmade, what with dréad,
Thy doing: and dost thou touch me afresh?
Óver agáin I féel thy fínger and fínd thée.
(GMH, 119, lines 1–8)[8]

In terms of its substance, the passage depicts the speaker's questioning en-
gagement with the Christian deity. Ostensibly an elegy on the death of
five nuns aboard a foundered ship, Hopkins's poem is more significantly an
inquiry into the pain of existence on the one hand and the sensuousness of
bodily life on the other. The poem "seeks to clarify," as Julia Saville puts it,
"in terms of a long-standing Catholic hermeneutic tradition, the meaning of
intense suffering" (Saville, 63), while at the same time acknowledging what
Norman White calls the "sensuous pleasure about martyrdom" (White,
252).[9] That it is also an explicit challenge to Victorian prosody almost goes
without saying. Consider first the distance between Hopkins's depiction of
touch and the hesitant, largely figurative touching of Felicia Hemans's
poetry. As discussed in chapter 1, Hemans imagines a kind of physiological
touching in "The Lyre's Lament"—and many other poems—but the lyric
ultimately fails to make that touch a literal act. Elizabeth Barrett Browning
makes a similar gesture toward physicality in *Aurora Leigh* when she cele-
brates poetry's "divine first finger-touch" (EBB, 4, book 1, line 851), but this
too remains almost exclusively a figurative endeavor.[10] Aurora experiences
feeling and transmits that feeling to her readers; she "touches" us emotion-
ally. Her poetry, though identified as Spasmodic by Aytoun (Aytoun 1857,
40), avoids the sheer physicality that would allow readers literally to feel her
touch. Hopkins gives us no choice: "I féel thy fínger and fínd thée" instructs
us precisely how to feel, both through its alliteration and the accompanying
stress marks. If the speaker is touched "afresh," so too is the reader of the
stanza; Hopkins's intent is to bring together these different modes of touch-
ing (rhythmic, physiological, spiritual), such that the speaker's experience of
touch becomes the reader's experience of the poem.[11]

"The Wreck of the Deutschland" ultimately proposes two kinds of
poetic touching—one destructive, the other healing—and it imagines elec-
tricity as a figure for each. The more violent form of electricity emerges in
the second stanza, when the "fire of stress" (GMH, 119, line 16) comes to
the speaker through "líghtning and láshed ród":

electricity," Isobel Armstrong notes, stress for Hopkins "brings together and fuses the material and the non-material, spirit and sense, form and matter" (Armstrong 1993, 422). In this, Hopkins sympathizes more with Sydney Dobell than with Patmore. There are important connections, for example, between Hopkins's notion of instress and Dobell's suggestion that poetry "is actually in tune with our material flesh and blood," that it embodies "certain modes of verbal *motion* . . . certain *rhythms* and measures [that] are metaphors of ideas and feelings" (Dobell 1876, 22, 25). Hopkins also follows Dobell in believing poetry and religious affect to be similar in nature. As Emma Mason has shown, Dobell finds poetry to be "religious" because "it reconciles the 'spirit' with 'Matter,' securing our physical reality in a world we only come to know through the immaterial feelings that give rise to language"; rhythm thereby acts as a "numinous" force of communication between the earthly and the spiritual (Mason 2004b, 544, 546). Patmore's insistence on metrical immateriality, his celebration of duration over stress (both, as I have argued, a response against Dobell), places him at odds with Hopkins's model of electric poetics, the "fire of stress" that for Hopkins epitomizes what poetry does best.

Only through the lens of culture might one make sense of Hopkins's attention to Patmore and the New Prosody, with which he disagreed so forcefully, and his concurrent avoidance of the Spasmodics (specifically, Dobell's theory of rhythm). Hopkins's implicit rejection of Dobell's poetics might best be understood alongside his outright dismissal of Whitman, another poet with whom Hopkins shares obvious formal sympathies. In 1881 Hopkins writes, famously, "I always knew in my heart Walt Whitman's mind to be more like my own than any other man's living. As he is a very great scoundrel this is not a pleasant confession. And this also makes me the more desirous to read him and the more determined that I will not" (Hopkins 1955b, 155). Hopkins acknowledges the similarities between his style and Whitman's but insists on important distinctions as well. As Saville has noted, Whitman is Hopkins's "repudiated double," in terms of both style and sexual expression (Saville, 173). Hopkins continues, "Of course I saw that there was to the eye something in my long lines like his, that the one would remind people of the other. And both are in irregular rhythms. There the likeness ends. The pieces of his I read were mostly in an irregular rhythmic prose: that is what they are thought to be meant for and what they seemed to me to be. . . . [I]n short what he means to write—and writes—is rhythmic prose and that only" (Hopkins 1955b, 155–56). Aside from calling him a "great scoundrel," then, Hopkins resists engaging with the content of Whitman's poetry, concentrating instead on formal concerns. In his criticism of Swinburne, too, Hopkins glances over the subject matter to dwell at length on issues of style: the poems show "passion but not feeling" and "genius without truth"; Swinburne "has no real understanding of rhythm" (Hopkins 1955b, 79, 303). In all these examples, poetic form stands in as illustrative of poetic content. Swinburne is one of the "plagues of mankind" (Hopkins 1955b, 39), but judging from Hopkins's letters this is so because of his poetic style, not his penchant for writing about necrophilia, for example, or sadomasochism. Hopkins thus formulates his distance from Whitman and Swinburne in terms of style and form, not character and cultural values.

In the end, Hopkins sympathizes most with those who urge a retreat from physiological poetics, including Edmund Gosse's 1877 call (discussed briefly in chapter 3) to "dismiss the purely spontaneous and untutored expression" of poetry (Gosse 1877, 53).[14] Gosse closes his essay with a rhetorical flourish, hoping that he "may be dead before the English poets take Walt Whitman for their model in style" (71). Hopkins hews to the conservative line because he cannot stomach identifying with those who, like Whitman and Swinburne, use poetic innovation to challenge contemporary culture in addition to aesthetic taste. In this way, Patmore's attention to meter offers an antidote to the physiological poetics to which Hopkins was by nature drawn. Hopkins insists on the metrical regularity of "The Wreck of the Deutschland"; even "the long, e.g. seven-syllables, feet of the *Deutschland*," he writes to Bridges, "are strictly metrical" (Hopkins 1855b, 45). Following the rule of sprung rhythm, Hopkins determines regularity by the number of stresses in each line, not the number of syllables.[15] As I have been suggesting, it is in this way that Hopkins's sprung rhythm sympathizes with Patmore's isochronous method, another metrical system that disregards almost entirely syllable-counting. Sprung rhythm and isochrony open poetic form to a kind of limited freedom, resisting the complete liberty of spasmody or Whitmanian "rhythmic prose" while also avoiding the strict meters advocated by Gosse and other post-Spasmodic critics. There was much in Patmore that Hopkins found distasteful or simply in bad aesthetic taste (the feeling was entirely mutual), but the two were more alike than different in their attempts to locate a poetic middle ground.

In 1932, F. R. Leavis claimed that the "Wreck" shows clearly "that Hopkins has no relation to . . . any nineteenth-century poet." For Leavis this is a compliment, writing as he does at a time that largely anathematized the Victorians, and he justifies the point by noting Hopkins's "association of inner, spiritual, emotional stress with physical reverberations, nervous and muscular tensions" (Leavis, 26). However, it is exactly because of this association of the "inner, spiritual, emotion" with the "physical" and physiological that Hopkins emerges as a representative poet of his day. Hopkins's developments in physiological poetics take place within a literary culture struggling to reconcile a range of new scientific data—on the human body, on the physical sciences—with shifting aesthetic values and tastes. Chapter 5 continues this discussion with a reading of two post-Spasmodic poets—Algernon Swinburne and Mathilde Blind—who were more willing than Patmore or Hopkins to consider the benefits of Dobell's style. Swinburne and Blind also write in a post-Darwinian era, wherein form comes to be seen within an evolutionary model, a structure in which form enables development and thus takes on even more cultural weight.

Rapture and the Flesh, Swinburne to Blind

> We on the earth's surface live night and day in the midst of ethereal
> commotion. The medium is never still. . . . The sources of this
> vibration are the ponderable masses of the universe.
>
> —John Tyndall, "The Constitution of Nature" (1865)

N THE 1820s, SCIENTISTS BEGAN TO SPECULATE ON THE existence of electromagnetic fields: lines of force traversing all of physical space, interacting with everything in their path. Just as iron filings fall into wavelike patterns when placed around magnets, any late-Victorian amateur scientist might have told you, we all encounter—and perhaps respond to—electromagnetic forces, whether we are conscious of them or not. Tyndall's idea that we are all, every day, "in the midst of ethereal commotion" (Tyndall 1905, 12) has its origins in the work of Michael Faraday and James Clerk Maxwell, the two British scientists most responsible for innovations in electric field theory (in the 1830s and '40s, Faraday determined the relationship between electricity and magnetism; in the 1850s and '60s, Maxwell devised mathematical equations to describe that interaction).[1]

As Bruce J. Hunt has argued, Faraday's experiments had the result of making space seem "not . . . empty and inert but . . . the locus of power and activity" (Hunt, 313), a place where bodies bump up against and interact with unseen forces.[2] In addition, a growing consensus within the Victorian scientific community suggested that electricity, magnetism, light, and heat were interconnected—were all, in fact, different manifestations of a more general property that might be called "energy." Faraday thus announced during an 1845 address to the Royal Institution that he had established, "for the first time, a true, direct relation and dependence between light and the magnetic and electric forces"; his experiments, he went on to argue, "tend to prove that all natural forces are tied together, and have one common origin" (Faraday 1965, 19, 20).[3] Human beings occupy this highly interactive space; we are constantly bumping up against light, heat, electricity, or magnetism, and even participating in the transfer of energy—the conversion, for example, of electricity or light into heat. "This," writes Tyndall, "is the rhythmic play of Nature as regards her forces. . . . Thus beats the heart of the universe, but without increase or diminution of its total stock of force" (Tyndall 1905, 25–26).

One finds this language of rhythm, beating, and resonance not only in Victorian studies of the physical world but in the work of biologists as well, and that of Charles Darwin in particular: rhythm plays a crucial role in the development of species. Whereas Alexander Bain (as discussed in chapter 3) highlighted the role of telegraph-like electric charges in the human nervous system, Darwin emphasizes the importance of rhythm in the process of sexual selection, and thus the evolutionary process as a whole. The reader of *The Descent of Man* (1871), for example, will learn of the "vibratory movement" of peacocks and birds of paradise that in the process of mating "rattle their quills together," and of the male North American grouse, who "drums rapidly" with his wings against either tree stumps or his own body so as to lure female grouses from hiding (Darwin, 2:61–62). To the extent that these animals rely on rhythmic patterning as part of their mating rituals, vibratory experiences enable their continued development as species. This is true, Darwin suggests, for humans as well: "[T]he suspicion does not appear improbable that the progenitors of man, either the males or females, or both sexes, before they had acquired the power of expressing their mutual love in articulate language, endeavoured to charm each other with musical notes and rhythm" (337). Darwin consistently identifies rhythmic utterances as important substitutes for "articulate language," as when he quotes from an eighteenth-century scholar to describe the patterning of a hen's clucking: "[W]hen she has laid an egg, [she] 'repeats the same note very often, and concludes with the sixth above, which she holds for a longer time'; and thus she expresses her joy" (51). Rhythm, then, is a kind of language, one more universally accessible than written or spoken words because it is felt physiologically rather than processed intellectually. Darwin recognizes the evolutionary importance of such physiologically experienced rhythm inasmuch as rhythm facilitates the communication required among animals for procreation.

Darwin also gestures in these descriptions toward his belief in a necessary truth to rhythmic form. We see this readily, for example, in his casual attribution of joy to the rhythmically clucking hen. Why must the cluck necessarily indicate joy and not, say, relief, or any number of other possible emotions? Darwin assumes that every hen expresses the very same emotion by way of her patterned clucking; there is a truth, according to this way of thinking, in rhythmic patterning such that a hen's clucking *will* mean the very same thing no matter which particular hen lays the egg. A similar style of thinking, variously expressed, can be seen in the poetics of Patmore and Hopkins (as discussed in chapter 4), both of whom believe that rhythm—in either "isochronous" or "sprung" form—communicates specific feeling from one individual to another. From this perspective, the song of a sparrow will, on average, articulate a comparable message to any other sparrow, and perhaps even to other animals. According to Darwin and his Victorian contemporaries, in other words, particular patterns of stressed and unstressed—or long and short—beats translate necessarily into particular thoughts, ideas, and feelings. The clucking of a hen will indicate the very same joy from one hen to another, a concordance of experience made possible by all hens' comparable physiological structures.

In what follows, I propose a model for late-Victorian formal poetics that looks equally to Darwinian ideas of evolution and to the electric field theories of midcentury. On the surface, these two intellectual developments have little to do with one another. However, they share a belief in the connectedness of things, a confidence that we are not isolated in the universe, but attached through a variety of webs and networks both to one another and to the larger physical world of things.[4] The rhythms of Darwin's mating rituals pulse within a universe resonant with Faraday's electromagnetic fields; these phenomena connect living things physically, through the bodily experience of space, and they inspire psychical and emotional connections as well. I call this idea of connectedness "rapture," and I argue that poetic rapture—a moment of physiological, emotional, and intellectual union imagined by way of poetic form and content—was an ideal shared by many poets in the closing decades of the nineteenth century. Romanticism had fantasized a similarly universal experience of the world, what the young Tennyson in "Armageddon" (circa 1824) called "the deep heart of every living thing." But the late-Victorian poet of rapture neither reflects the world (like a mirror) nor casts illuminating light on the world around him (like a lamp), but instead jumps headlong into a world of chaotic flux, a space of colliding energies and rhythmic forces.[5] If seemingly riotous and unpredictable, both the physics of energy and Darwinian evolution nevertheless suggest an ordered, logical network undergirding the universe of things. Mathilde Blind calls access to this network "the rapture of communion"; to reach such sympathy with the order of things is Algernon Swinburne's primary goal in many of his greatest works (BCB, 36). As a universal and universalizing phenomenon in an increasingly secular world, rapture for Swinburne and Blind comes to stand as a substitute for religious belief. I will show why this ideal should be understood specifically as a poetic practice, and how this practice brings to a close the work of Victorian physiological poetics so far examined in this book.

SWINBURNE IN THE FLESH

Like Hopkins's sprung rhythm, though in importantly distinct ways, Swinburne's idea of poetry relies on its kinship with the human body. He reports in an 1866 preface to an edition of Byron that "[a]cross the stanzas of 'Don Juan' we swim forward as over 'the broad backs of the sea'" (ACS, 15:123), much as he celebrates "the peculiar passion" of Elizabeth Barrett Browning's poetry, "the rush and glow and ardour of aspiring and palpitating life" (ACS, 16:4). The best poetry, for Swinburne, offers readers a physical experience, a journey into the palpitating life of *Aurora Leigh*, or over Swinburne's own living sea in "The Triumph of Time" (1866), "Where faint sounds falter and wan beams wade, / Break, and are broken, and shed into showers" (ACS, 1:171). The intense beauty of these lines comes in no small part from

and post-Christian framework.[10] When Wordsworth in the Intimations Ode looks at the "immortal sea" from which he believes all human "Souls" to have come, he positions himself at a distance:

> Though inland far we be,
>   Our Souls have sight of that immortal sea
>   Which brought us hither[.]
>
> (Wordsworth, 190)

Swinburne, in contrast, takes a more active role, leaping with rabid energy into the chaotic flux of life, the present moment. Wordsworth's visual metaphor, the "sight" he imagines from afar, becomes in Swinburne's lines an energetic, interactive experience.

The central part of the poem thus presents the "rapturous plunge" of the speaker into the titular Lake of Gaube. Through bodily submersion, a kind of pagan baptism, Swinburne confronts both mortality and the insignificance of individual existence within the larger framework of the universe. Deep beneath the cold water, the body enjoys the overwhelming experience of sensation without sight:

> Death-dark and delicious as death in the dream of a lover and
>   dreamer may be,
> It clasps and encompasses body and soul with delight to be living
>   and free:
> Free utterly now, though the freedom endure but the space of a
>   perilous breath,
> And living, though girdled about with the darkness and coldness
>   and strangeness of death:
> Each limb and each pulse of the body rejoicing, each nerve of the
>   spirit at rest,
> All sense of the soul's life rapture, a passionate peace in its
>   blindness blest.
>
> (ACS, 6:201)

As in "A Nympholept" (1891), a poem often read as a complement to "The Lake of Gaube," Swinburne's language here captures a synesthetic joining of thought and sensation that plays out syntactically as a confusion between active and passive engagement (McGann 1972, 188). The "It" of the second line, for example, refers to the water of the lake, which "clasps and encompasses body and soul." What, though, possesses the subsequent "delight to be living and free": the speaker's body, or the clasping, encompassing lake, or both? "It clasps and encompasses body and soul with delight to be living and free": Swinburne intentionally conflates the speaker's experience with that of the lake, such that the syntax emphasizes the poem's argument for synthesis, what Catherine Maxwell calls Swinburne's "symbiosis between the individual and the natural world" (Maxwell 2006, 121). It matters not whether the lake or the speaker delights to be living, because both speaker and lake exist as part of the same universe of sensation. Such oneness Swinburne emphasizes as well through his near-manic use of alliteration, the percussive *d*, *p*, and *b* sounds that create for the reader a sonic web of experience.

The profound physicality of "The Lake of Gaube" echoes those poems from Swinburne's first volumes—the *Poems and Ballads* of 1866 and *Songs before Sunrise* of 1871—that were famously derided as "fleshly" by the Scottish critic Robert Buchanan. Though Dante Gabriel Rossetti was the primary object of Buchanan's attack, Swinburne—"a little mad boy letting off squibs" (Buchanan, 338)—received his fair share of attention. As Gowan Dawson has shown, Buchanan's attack on Rossetti and his cohorts resonated within Victorian culture because it made explicit the connections between "fleshly" poetry and scientific materialism, the belief—advocated by scientists such as Thomas Henry Huxley and John Tyndall—that "nothing exists independently of matter, with even human consciousness being at some level a correlate of the mechanical activities of the nervous system" (Dawson 2003, 114). Such materialist claims for the truth of bodily experience stretch back, in various forms, to the associationist and empiricist philosophers of the eighteenth and early nineteenth centuries. Materialist anxiety rests at the heart of the trouble with Dr. Jeffray's experiments on the executed criminal, which threaten the idea of what constitutes human emotion. These concerns play out in the field of poetic theory, as Mill and Hallam used the language of sensation to link bodily and poetic experience. Tennyson's tentative steps toward enacting these materialist theories climaxed in the Spasmodics' enthusiastic embrace of physiological poetics, which inspired the conservative backlash against the Spasmodics; Patmore's isochronous intervals then attempted to return poetics to a more intellectually governed and thereby "bodiless"—which is to say, immaterial—structure.

Buchanan's attack on the "fleshly" poets participates in this narrative, bringing to a new height the sort of anxiety anent the privileging of bodily experience that had inspired John Wilson's condemnation of Tennyson, Aytoun's devastating parody of Dobell, and Patmore's 1857 *Essay on English Metrical Law*. Within this context, Buchanan's language and mocking tone sound entirely familiar: "[T]he fleshly gentlemen have bound themselves by solemn league and covenant to extol fleshliness as the distinct and supreme end of poetic and pictorial art; to aver that poetic expression is greater than poetic thought, and by inference that the body is greater than the soul, and sound superior to sense" (Buchanan, 335). Whether or not this is an accurate description of Swinburne's or Rossetti's poetry, the framework within which the critic writes is perfectly clear, from Wilson's 1832 claim that "every thing is poetry which is not mere sensation" (J. Wilson, 721) to Darwin's suggestion that "the progenitors of man" used "musical notes and rhythm" as part of their mating rituals "before they had acquired the power of expressing their mutual love in articulate language." At stake is not only the nature of poetry and poetic communication, but also human nature and the place of humankind within the natural—and, for some, the supernatural—world. From the perspective of those hostile to materialism, "fleshly" poetics rest uncomfortably alongside Darwinian evolution and electrodynamic physics as threats to transcendent views of human existence.

Buchanan was in fact correct to link Swinburne to materialist thought. Swinburne expressed enthusiasm for Tyndall's infamous 1874 Belfast address to the British Association for the Advancement of Science: "My mind is very full just now of Tyndall's magnificent address which I have read with great care and greater admiration" (SL, 2:334). Tyndall's speech was best known at the time for challenging the value of religion and endorsing in its place what the *Edinburgh Review* called the "nihilism of the latest school of German materialists" (quoted in Dawson 2003, 114). Among the more remarkable features of Tyndall's speech is his elision between "[t]he theory of the origin of species" and "the doctrine of the Conservation of Energy." Nineteenth-century science is marked by these "great generalizations," Tyndall asserts, and the "ultimate philosophical issues" arising from these ideas "are as yet but dimly seen . . . bringing vital as well as physical phenomena under the dominion of that law of causal connection which, as far as the human understanding has yet pierced, asserts itself everywhere in nature" (Tyndall 1874, 65). Evolution and electromagnetic theory, that is, are but pieces of a larger framework—the greater laws of nature—that scientists have yet to understand. Swinburne finds inspiration in this suggestion that the universe might be held together by a "law of causal connection." He suggests to his friend Theodore Watts that "[s]cience" as presented by Tyndall gives him "a sense as much of rest as of light." Furthermore, he sees religion rather than science as that which most inspires "doubt, discord and disorder": "Even my technical ignorance does not impair, I think, my power to see accurately and seize firmly the first thread of the great clue, because my habit of mind is not (I hope) unscientific, though my work lies in the field of art instead of science, and when seen and seized even that first perception gives me an indescribable sense as of music and repose. It is Theism which to me seems to introduce an element—happily a factitious element—of doubt, discord and disorder" (SL, 2:335).[11] Swinburne clearly does not shy from what others decried as "materialism" or "fleshliness"; in both his life and his poetry, the poet celebrates the present, physical reality in which he finds himself.[12]

To negotiate the unease that many of his contemporaries located in "fleshliness," Swinburne turns in part to aesthetic structure, and specifically to meter. George Saintsbury writes in 1895 of "the astonishing revelation of the metrical powers of English" that one experiences while reading Swinburne (Saintsbury, 76). Swinburne's metrical versatility says as much about the poet's aesthetic sense as it does about the larger philosophical questions governing his compositions. Poetic form becomes throughout Swinburne's work a reasoned space from which to confront the exigencies of a brutal and unpredictable natural world. Swinburne's poetics show sympathy with Grant Allen's 1877 *Physiological Aesthetics*, which locates the modern individual as standing, "as he never stood before, face to face with the naked realities of nature. Solitary in a boundless universe, alone on a little isthmus of historic time between the vast sea of vague geological aeons and the unknown future of cosmic cycles, he finds himself awe-struck and ignorant, ready to fall prostrate before the terrible forces of nature, which work out unswerved their fatal will in apparent disregard of his happiness or misery, of his prayers or imprecations" (Allen, 277). In response to this uncomfortable new awareness of "the naked realities of nature," Allen directs his readers to works of aesthetic wholeness: poems in which the author "has gathered together, as in a treasure-house, all that is glorious and beautiful, without and within, in the boundless universe or in the soul of man." Allen emphasizes the importance of "the spontaneous choice of a metre that harmonises with [the poet's] theme," even as he discourages poetry offering only "a rambling, disconnected stream of 'spasmodic' images" (281, 283). Swinburne himself suggests a keen awareness of this gap between metrical harmony and spasmodic detachment. Edmund Gosse writes of how, as a college student in the 1850s, Swinburne had been "violently attracted and then repelled by Sydney Dobell's *Balder*" (Gosse 1927, 73).[13] One suspects that the attraction originated in Dobell's physiological poetics, which in some ways Swinburne mimics, and that the subsequent repulsion developed after Swinburne recognized Dobell's lack of aesthetic structure. In an 1857 letter to John Nichol, Swinburne describes the "exquisite passages" of Dobell's *England in Time of War* that, though "as musical and gorgeous in *words* as . . . ever," still have the effect of doing Dobell an "immense injustice" (SL, 1:10).

Swinburne's 1880 poem "By the North Sea" brings together the different strands of argument elaborated above: philosophical and cultural concerns about materiality; aesthetic form; and the relationship between the individual and the natural world. The poem is an especially clear example of Swinburne's thoughts because it leaves aside the narrative elements that—in poems such as "Laus Veneris," "Anactoria," and "The Leper," to name just a few—distract from the poet's larger philosophical and aesthetic concerns. Written after Swinburne had taken up residence with Theodore Watts at The Pines, which gave the poet breathing space from the tumult of London (Rooksby, 234–39), "By the North Sea" is a meditation on the place and value of human life in a seemingly indifferent natural world. The poem is set on the English coast near Dunwich, a great port city in the early Middle Ages that had long since eroded into the sea, as described in James Bird's 1828 *Dunwich: A Tale of the Splendid City:*

Where the lone cliff uprears its rugged head,
Where frowns the ruin o'er the silent dead,
Where sweeps the billow on the lonely shore,

Where once the mighty lived, but live no more,
Where proudly frowned the convent's massy wall,
Where rose the gothic tower, the stately hall,
Where bards proclaimed, and warriors shared the feast,
Where ruled the baron, and where knelt the priest,
There stood the City in its pride—'tis gone—
Mocked at by crumbling pile, and mouldering stone,
And shapeless masses, which the reckless power
Of time hath hurled from ruined arch and tower!
O'er the lone spot, where shrines and pillared halls
Once gorgeous shone, the clammy lizard crawls;
O'er the lone spot where yawned the guarded fosse,
Creeps the wild bramble, and the spreading moss:
Oh! time hath bowed that lordly City's brow
In which the mighty dwelt—where dwell they now!

                                        (Bird, 1–2)

Bird's sense of loss for a city destroyed and absorbed by the power of the sea is very much at the heart of Swinburne's poem as well. More than Bird, however, Swinburne uses the Dunwich tableau as a backdrop for more profound metaphysical considerations.

    Among the most gruesome focal points of "By the North Sea" is Swinburne's attention in the poem's sixth section to dead bodies buried in a church graveyard that has gradually eroded into the sea. "The whole picture is from life," wrote Swinburne to Richard Monckton Milnes, "salt marshes, ruins, and bones protruding seawards through the soil of the crumbling sandbanks" (SL, 4:179). As the earth slips into the devouring waters, the bones of the dead break free from their tombs, "cast out" from their resting places into the violent sea:

Now displaced, devoured and desecrated,
    Now by Time's hands darkly disinterred,
These poor dead that sleeping here awaited
    Long the archangel's re-creating word,
Closed about with roofs and walls high-gated
    Till the blast of judgment should be heard,

Naked, shamed, cast out of consecration,
   Corpse and coffin, yea the very graves,
Scoffed at, scattered, shaken from their station,
   Spurned and scourged of wind and sea like slaves,
Desolate beyond man's desolation,
   Shrink and sink into the waste of waves.

Tombs, with bare white piteous bones protruded,
   Shroudless, down the loose collapsing banks,
Crumble, from their constant place detruded,
   That the sea devours and gives not thanks.
Where hope and prayer and sorrow brooded
   Gape and slide and perish, ranks on ranks.

                        (ACS, 4:343–44)

Unlike "The Lake of Gaube," in which submersion in water allows for the ex-
perience of greater life, or "The Triumph of Time," in which the speaker
imagines his body embraced ecstatically by the living seas, the sea here brings
primarily violence and destruction. The horror of the scene might best be
captured by the twofold meaning of *consecration* in the second stanza: "cast out
of consecration." Taken in its religious sense, the line means literally that the
body has been removed from the church ground, the consecrated land (land
"set apart . . . as sacred to the Deity" [*OED*, "consecrate"]). But "to consecrate"
can also mean to "devote or dedicate to some purpose," not strictly religious
in nature, as in "His whole life was consecrated to letters" (*OED*, "conse-
crate"). In this sense, the bodies of Swinburne's poem have been "cast out of
consecration" insofar as their displacement raises a more fundamental ques-
tion of their purpose, the point of their having been alive and buried at all.
Shrinking and sinking "into the *waste* of waves," one confronts the apparent
purposelessness of human life, the great indifference of anything spiritual—or
natural, for that matter—to the goings-on of human beings. In this reading,
the dead bodies serve as a microcosm for the city of Dunwich as a whole: gen-
erations of human labor eroded into the sea, now nearly indiscernible to
human eyes. What, Swinburne's poem asks implicitly, is the point of it all?
   The dead bodies of section six point readers back to the third part of "By
the North Sea," when Swinburne references Ulysses' encounter in Hades

with his dead mother. Unlike the very material presence of rotting bones in section six, Ulysses' experience with Anticleia, his mother, is famously immaterial; though he tries to embrace his mother's spirit, he cannot touch her body:

> Parted, though by narrowest of divisions,
>   Clasp he might not, only might implore,
> Sundered yet by bitterest of derisions,
>   Son, and mother from the son she bore—
> Here? But all dispeopled here of visions
> Lies, forlorn of shadows even, the shore.
>
> All too sweet such men's Hellenic speech is,
>   All too fain they lived of light to see,
> Once to see the darkness of these beaches,
>   Once to sing this Hades found of me
> Ghostless, all its gulfs and creeks and reaches,
>   Sky, and shore, and cloud, and waste, and sea.

(ACS, 4:334)

As Kerry McSweeney has suggested, Swinburne's speaker offers the image of Ulysses and Anticleia in part as a contrast to his own experience of the Dunwich coast. Ulysses may mourn his inability to embrace his mother, but he at least enjoys an exchange of sorts with the ghosts of the dead. Dunwich, by comparison, "holds no message" for Swinburne's speaker "and no sign of any transcendent reality capable of transforming the poverty and oppressiveness of the purely naturalistic world of the shore" (McSweeney, 226). But in truth the speaker finds recompense neither in the immateriality of Ulysses' encounter (the scene as Swinburne presents it is unmistakably tragic) nor in the stark physicality of the disinterred bones; something more is needed, a compromise to fill the loss central to each scene.

Swinburne locates the answer to this dilemma in the brutal, highly physical give and take of the natural landscape as it is mediated by the form of the poem. Through rhythm, rhyme, assonance, alliteration, and other sonic effects, Swinburne believes poetry engages with nature at its most profound and inspiring, what he calls "the higher things of nature" (ACS, 15:128). Of

Swinburne's contemporaries, "Victor Hugo alone" had the gift of composing poetry in this "loftiest form"; Shelley and Byron only came close, with work that "recall[s] or suggest[s] the wide and high things of nature; the large likeness of the elements; the immeasurable liberty and the stormy strength of waters and winds" (ACS, 15:128, 125).[14] These are the qualities Swinburne aims to capture in his own poetry, and "By the North Sea," according to a letter he wrote to Edmund Gosse, best exemplifies this "metrical and antiphonal effect" (SL, 2:158). The poem is a masterpiece of echoing sounds and rhythms, both within and among stanzas. "By the North Sea" assaults its readers sonically, from its unforgiving alliterations—"displaced, devoured and desecrated . . . by Time's hands darkly disinterred"—to rhymes that emphasize the bleakness of the scene: "cast out of consecration," for example, becomes "scattered, shaken from their station," and then, finally, "[d]esolate beyond man's desolation." Most famously, at the poem's exact midpoint, Swinburne transforms the opening desolation of "A land that is lonelier than ruin, / A sea that is stranger than death," into a landscape with the desire, perhaps, for redemption: "A land that is thirstier than ruin, / A sea that is hungrier than death" (ACS, 4:325, 336). David Riede notes that "By the North Sea" thus "*becomes*" through its formal maneuvering "its very subject" (Riede, 181); by the end of the poem, the speaker has achieved not merely a psychic sense of peace with the world as he knows it, but an aesthetic form of resonance and sympathy. Swinburne thereby bestows transcendent value on what at first seem only material forms and sounds; the press and release of language suggests for the poet a sympathetic place for humankind in the natural world, much as Faraday and Maxwell determined a kind of order behind the apparent flux of electricity, magnetism, light, and heat. In "By the North Sea," words not only "yearn after an unreachable and unknown beyond which transcends their limits," as Isobel Armstrong suggests of Swinburne's poetry in general (Armstrong 1993, 405), but also point to the only sort of transcendence Swinburne believes possible: the recognition of humankind's material, fleshly position within the universe.

In the final, redemptive section of the poem, Swinburne turns his focus to Apollo, the sun god, also the god of poetry and the natural world. This pagan deity—"our father," Swinburne provocatively calls him—offers a path toward human transcendence:

Our father is lord of the day.
Our father and lord that we follow,
  For deathless and ageless is he;
And his robe is the whole sky's hollow,
    His sandal the sea.

                                        (ACS, 4:345)

Apollo is all at once "father and saviour and spirit" (ACS, 4:346) because he
links together the physical world, the aesthetic sense, and the eternity of time
(the days pass by his rising and setting). The sun "[m]akes music of earth,"
and for this Swinburne's speaker "rejoices" in song:

I, last least voice of her voices,
  Give thanks that were mute in me long
To the soul in my soul that rejoices
For the song that is over my song.

                                        (ACS, 4:347)

The resonances of this passage—all the echoing *l* and *s* sounds, the repeti-
tion of "voice," "soul," and "song"—enact the greater resonance that
Swinburne attributes to the natural world. Though this world may crush
bones with brutal strength, the speaker recognizes an overarching unity,
and a synthetic force of nature, that contains that violence and, by nature
of its omnipresence, makes sense of it. The fall of Dunwich fits at last
within a greater pattern of give and take, stress and release, that Swinburne
imagines as a kind of music: a rhythmic and sonic pattern into which he
gladly plunges.

     For Hopkins, rhythmic experience is a strategy for achieving a sort of
intimacy with the divine, whereas Swinburne's physiological poetics aim to
accomplish a nearly opposite form of transcendence, that of intimacy with
the living, breathing universe of things: "All death and all life, and all reigns
and all ruins" ("Hertha"; ACS, 2:142). Shelley was in part responsible for
Swinburne's fantasy of universal intimacy (Beach, 464), but the path from
Shelley to Swinburne passes through several decades of physiological science.
Shelley writes in *Prometheus Unbound* of "[l]anguage" creating "harmony"
out of "thoughts and forms, which else senseless and shapeless were" (Shel-

ley, 2:256, IV, lines 415–17). Swinburne builds his harmony less on language and the ideas inherent in words than on the scaffolding of poetic form and the physiological experience of rhythm and sound. For Swinburne, it is primarily through the feeling body (rhythm and sound), not the thinking mind (words and meaning), that the individual engages with the universe. In this way, Swinburne attempts to universalize physiological poetics. Buchanan suggests that this "fleshly feeling" (Buchanan, 339), taken to an extreme, results in "an abnormally intense concern with the sensuous world" and "a depraved celebration of the earthly pleasures of the physical form" (Dawson 2003, 116). The depravity here comes not simply from the connections between fleshliness and sexuality (Buchanan was famously affronted by Rossetti's depiction of "the most secret mysteries of sexual connection" in the sonnet "Nuptial Sleep" [Buchanan, 338]) but, more important, from the infusing of a "fleshly" aesthetic into poetic production, such that the poet's overriding concern is for the intensity of his own feelings. "Whether [Rossetti] is writing of the holy Damozel, or of the Virgin herself, or of Lilith, or Helen, or of Dante, or of Jenny the street-walker," wails Buchanan, "he is fleshly all over, from the roots of his hair to the tip of his toes; never a true lover merging his identity into that of the beloved one; never spiritual, never tender; always self-conscious and æsthetic" (343). The "true lover" in Buchanan's view must abandon both his ego and his physical desires, to enable a more "spiritual" union with his beloved. Oddly enough, Swinburne shares Buchanan's concerns, though he chooses different means by which to address them. Like Buchanan, Swinburne carries with him the burden of a culture desperate to make sense of human existence in light of an ascendant "materialist" scientific establishment. Unlike Buchanan, though, who retreats from the corporeal to an idealized "spiritual" realm, Swinburne attempts to make the best of the bodily world in which he finds himself—by situating bodies, his own and others, within the context of a vaster universe of feeling.

Swinburne is a "fleshly" poet, then, only in a way quite distinct from the category Buchanan describes. Though he admired elements of Spasmodic poetry, he also rejected the excesses of Dobell's style for being too self-absorbed, too blind to the larger universe of things. The same values that inspired this rejection ultimately led Swinburne to imagine, and to attempt in his writings, a different sort of poetic transcendence. Swinburne's passionate endorsement of Republican politics, recently the subject of much excellent scholarship, helps explain the poet's desire to negotiate a new style of connection between the individual and the community.[15] Poetic rapture as Swinburne practiced it is a mode of physiological and aesthetic experience through which the interdependency between all living things and the forces of the universe might be both realized and elevated, held up as an ideal model for individuals in a post-Spasmodic, post-Darwinian world. The fusion of the individual with the poem simulates, and thereby facilitates, the fusion of the individual with the surrounding world: fleshly, yes, but equally transcendent, and perhaps all that anyone has left in a universe otherwise unconcerned with the goings-on of human beings.

LYRIC SPASMS: MATHILDE BLIND

The poet and literary critic Mathilde Blind was among Swinburne's friends and intellectual correspondents. Until recently overlooked by scholars, Blind was part of a social and artistic network that included the Rossetti and Hunt families. Along with poets such as Alice Meynell, Amy Levy, and Graham R. Tomson, she attended meetings of the Literary Ladies, a group formed in 1889 "to support women's participation in the profession as equals and to give women writers some of the advantages enjoyed by men at their clubs" (Hughes 2005, 88). Blind and Swinburne exchanged letters and volumes of poetry. Blind reviewed Swinburne's *Songs before Sunrise* in 1871, clearly inspired by Swinburne's mix of passionate lyricism and republican politics. "They were fellow republicans, atheists, and aesthetes," writes James Diedrick, "and for a short period in the 1870s, it seemed to some of their friends that they should be lovers" (Diedrick 2002, 365).[16] Like Swinburne, Blind struggles to imagine a form of poetry that might capture the resonances between human individuals and the natural world. "The poet only truly lives," she writes in 1893, "when he feels the rapture of communion; when his soul mirrored in a sister soul is doubled like the moon glassed in the Lake of Nemi" (BCB, 36). Blind here alludes to the belief that from the shores of Lake Nemi, located just southeast of Rome, one might witness a perfect reflection of the moon upon the lake's still waters. Like the moon that casts its light down on the lake, the ideal poet radiates outward toward her readers, experiencing with them "the rapture of communion," a flash of sympathetic confederacy. Blind regularly singles out moments of passionate communication, such as lines of D. G. Rossetti that set one's "nerve[s] tingling" (MS. 61928; letter to Richard Garnett, 10 October 1881), and Shelley's poetry, which she deems like an "electric telegraph of thought flashing its fiery spark through the dull dense world of sense" (Blind 1870, 97). Like Swinburne, Blind believed that the best poetry fuses an "intensity of feeling, [a] depth of thought, music, and form" (MS. 61927; letter to Richard Garnett, 27 January 1870) so as to resonate most effectively with what Tennyson called "the deep heart of every living thing."[17]

But Blind is not always confident in the likelihood for communion in the modern world. Earlier in 1893, Blind had mourned "the present state of disorganization" apparent in an increasingly secularized and atomized culture. She suggests that "one may be chilled to the Soul by . . . complete isolation from the pulse of a collective life. Nay, the Soul may gradually perish for want of appropriate nourishment" (BCB, 24). Having been raised in a household of frustrated revolutionaries—Blind was the stepdaughter of Karl Blind, a political exile from Germany involved in the failed republican insurrections of 1848; Marx, Garibaldi, and Mazzini were all frequent visitors to the Blinds' London home—Blind's poetry reflects on and participates in her lifelong desire to strengthen sympathetic relations among individuals, even as it acknowledges the difficulty, and near impossibility, of achieving such a goal.[18] Blind wonders whether human culture might remove individuals from the natural, sympathetic networks described by Maxwell and Tyndall, for the "pulse of a collective life" seems increasingly difficult to access in a world of violence and indifference. What follows examines Blind's complex ideal of rapturous communion from the perspective of Darwinian thought and electrodynamic theory, focusing in particular on the poet's nuanced juxtaposing of poetic form with evolutionary theories of development.

Blind has rarely been acknowledged as an important voice in Victorian arguments concerning evolution and poetics, yet one would be hard pressed to find a poet more preoccupied, both formally and thematically, by late-nineteenth-century evolutionary theory.[19] Blind's 1889 *The Ascent of Man* achieved a degree of popularity, if not notoriety, through its use of varied metrical structures, driving rhythmic impulses, and vivid imagery to portray the drama of human evolution. Blind "hurries her reader along, breathless and perspiring perhaps, but never anxious to stop," writes a critic for the *Athenaeum*. "We have known her book to be read in the Underground

Railway, and the reader to be so absorbed in its contents as to be carried un-
awares several stations past his destination" (review of *The Ascent of Man*,
87). Rhythm and meter are important not only for the poem's ability to ab-
sorb its readers, even to the point of distraction, but also, and more signifi-
cantly, as part of Blind's understanding of evolution. More than most
poems, *The Ascent of Man* upholds Alice Meynell's claim that "[i]f life is not
always poetical, it is at least metrical" (Meynell, 1). In the poem, life on
earth progresses ineluctably toward something like metrical form, from "[a]
pulse stirred in the plastic slime" to "[h]armonies of confluent sound" that
"[l]ift you at one rhythmic bound / From the thraldom of the ground" (BPW,
159, 188). In Blind's evolutionary model, humankind achieves "a flaming
world embrace" by accessing the metrical uniformity of a "universal heart,"
a rhythmic beating with which every human being might sympathize (189).

   Much as Darwin points to an essential truth of rhythmic experience—
recall the rhythmically clucking hen—Blind believes wholeheartedly in the
truth of poetic form. Not merely a facile analogy, the organizing, structur-
ing efforts of poetry stand in Blind's view as crucial work in the evolution of
the human race. At the very opening of *The Ascent of Man*, Blind envisions

> a rhythmical chain
> Reaching from chaos and welter of struggle and pain
> Far into vistas empyreal
>
>   (157)

—an image of steady advancement through poetic rhythm that remains an
ideal both in the poem and in Blind's work more generally considered.[20]
Though a religious skeptic, Blind had great faith in what she calls, in her
commonplace book, "the righteousness of the Cosmic Order" (BCB, 36).[21]
In so taking the world's "chaos and welter" and rendering it a structured
"rhythmical chain," poetry participates in a world-making process, enabling
the human individual to access something of "the Cosmic Order." The
"ascent of man," as Blind insistently calls it, is a movement toward form
facilitated by poetic structure and made possible by the universality of rhyth-
mic experience.

   Appropriately enough, then, the first section of Blind's *Ascent* narrates
the earth's chaotic, early formation by means of strictly governed dactylic

hexameter lines. Blind the poet exerts her structuring power over nature's pulsating overflow:

> Struck out of dim fluctuant forces and shock of electrical vapour,
> Repelled and attracted the atoms flashed mingling in union
>   primeval
> And over the face of the waters far heaving in limitless twilight
> Auroral pulsations thrilled faintly, and, striking the blank heaving
>   surface,
> The measureless speed of their motion now leaped into light on
>   the waters.
>   (BPW, 158)

Blind's primeval atoms of "measureless speed" fall into highly measured and exacting metrical patterns. "Auroral pulsations" of unpredictable rhythmic impulses fit within the stanza's strict metrical form; when they "strik[e] the blank heaving surface" of the hexameter line, they emerge through Blind's mediation in neatly ordered dactyls. Blind's meter echoes the Greek hexameter line as Homer practiced it (generally five dactyls followed by a spondee), thereby emphasizing the epic nature of the evolutionary scene: "*struck* out of *dim* fluctuant *for*ces and *shock* of e*lec*trical *vapour*." In depicting these various forces, electrical and otherwise, that combine to form the world as we know it, Blind references the field-theory hypotheses of scientists such as Faraday and Maxwell even as she emphasizes the formal, ordered (metrical) nature of those ideas. The narrative continues:

> And lo, from the womb of the waters, upheaved in volcanic
>   convulsion,
> Ribbed and ravaged and rent there rose bald peaks and the rocky
> Heights of confederate mountains compelling the fugitive vapours
> To take a form as they passed them and float as clouds through
>   the azure[.]
>   (158)

Blind has much to say about such convulsive, ravaging phenomena, what she calls in an essay on Darwin and Shelley "the irresponsible forces of Nature"

(Blind 1886, 19). The work of evolution, she argues, involves subjecting un-
ruly instinct, or natural disorder, to disciplined control: "[T]urning these
elemental forces, that filled [humankind's] progenitors with fear and terror,
into the nimblest of servants" and ultimately allowing for "higher stages of
moral and mental development" (Blind 1886, 19). One sees the possibility
for such work in the "fugitive vapours," from the lines quoted above, that by
chance "take a form." So too, through a combination of happenstance and
conscious labor, Blind imagines the human species evolving toward ever
higher levels of moral and intellectual sophistication through the imposi-
tion of or accession to formal structure.

In Blind's *Ascent*, the first human enters the scene notably devoid of
metrical regularity:

> And lo, 'mid reeking swarms of earth
> Grim struggling in the primal wood,
> A new strange creature hath its birth:
> Wild—stammering—nameless—shameless—nude;
> Spurred on by want, held in by fear,
> He hides his head in caverns drear.
>
> (BPW, 163)

Uncoincidentally, the wild and stammering rhythms of Blind's fourth line
interrupt an otherwise consistent iambic tetrameter stanza, with graphic
dashes highlighting the rhythmic breaks; this "new strange creature" has yet
to learn its position within a metrically ordered universe. Only after consid-
erable development—after learning how to manipulate fire and grow crops,
for example—does the human race begin to discern structure behind the
apparent chaos of nature:

> For Man, from want and pressing hunger freed,
> Begins to feel another kind of need,
> And in his *shaping* brain and through his eyes
> Nature, awakening, sees her blue-arched skies;
> The Sun, his life-beggetter, isled in space;
> The Moon, the Measure of his span of days;
> The immemorial stars who pierce his night

With inklings of things vast and infinite.
All shows of heaven and earth that move and pass
Take form within his brain as in a glass.
The tidal thunder of the sea now roars
And breaks symphonious on a hundred shores;
The fitful flutings of the vagrant breeze
Strike gusts of sound from virgin forest trees;
White leaping waters of wild cataracts fall
From crag and jag in lapses musical,
And streams meandering amid daisied leas
Throb with the pulses of tumultuous seas.

(169; emphasis mine)

From the sun and the moon, humans learn to determine periodicity, through which metrical oscillations the natural world begins to make formal sense. The breaking of the sea on the shore, for example, now seems a rhythmic movement within a grander metrical scheme. The throbbing stream echoes the pulsing rhythms of the "tumultuous seas," and an ordered metrical structure governs what at first appeared to be fitful rhythmic motions. "Periodicity," writes Alice Meynell in a nearly contemporaneous essay, "rules over the mental experience of man" (Meynell, 1).[22] So too for Blind, human life is necessarily a metrical experience.

In Blind's *Ascent*, however, this necessary periodicity does little to save humankind from a history of passion and violence, and the poem proceeds for several hundred lines recounting, among other brutal historical episodes, the fall of Rome and the Reign of Terror. Even with a "shaping brain" and an understanding of natural order, "the spasm of life" still wrests control from the human species (BPW, 182). That is, uncontrolled rhythmic impulses reign supreme, even in the face of persistent resistance from art. Poets in particular (perhaps inevitably, given Blind's metrical predisposition) represent the highest stage of development away from unruly spasm, and it is through their verses that the latent order of the universe ultimately comes into greatest focus:

But see, he comes, Lord of life's changeful shows,
    To whom the ways of Nature are laid bare,

Howls of babes, the drunken father's damning,
Counter-cursing of the shrill-tongued wife.

(BPW, 209)

Slamming doors, crying children, and verbal abuse, conjured in part by
the stanza's cutting alliterations, all help cast a skeptical eye on the place
of rhythmic communication—Darwin's "articulate language"—in modern
human civilization. What once appeared as patterns of sympathetic rhyth-
mic beating now manifest as violent interactions, miserable cries, and ag-
gressive shouting. Blind's 1891 collection of dramatic monologues, *Dramas
in Miniature*, details such savage discord in the lives of destitute women:
mothers separated from dying children, girls forced by economic necessity
into lives of prostitution, women gone insane and forcibly removed from
those they love. The tragedy of these women's lives comes less from their
capitulation to rhythmic individualism, though this is important, than from
defective social structures, the failure of human communities to provide a
sympathetic "world embrace" within "universal law" like that fantasized in
the more optimistic moments of *The Ascent*. Whereas Blind's evolutionary
narrative found metrical order for the "dim fluctuant forces and shock of
electrical vapour" that comprised the earth's earliest moments, the poet
seems at a loss to accommodate in regulated meter the spasmodic fluctua-
tions of women in the modern world.

Blind brings into focus the modern deficiency of sympathetic embrace
in the first poem of *Dramas in Miniature*. "The Russian Student's Tale," a
dramatic monologue spoken by the eponymous Russian student, narrates
the young man's seduction and betrayal of an impoverished woman. When
the woman admits to having turned to prostitution to avoid starvation, the
student is distraught and sympathetic: "A sob rose to my throat as dry / As
ashes" (226–27). Yet the student abandons the woman, refusing to take on
the social stigma tied to fallen women. Predictable as it is in terms of Victo-
rian social conventions, Blind's tale distinguishes itself through the song of
a nightingale the student overhears at intervals throughout his narrative.
The nightingale emerges as a figure—as constructed by the student—for
the abandoned young woman:

And through the splendour of the white
Electrically glowing night,

Wind-wafted from some perfumed dell,
Tumultuously there loudly rose
Above the Neva's surge and swell,
With amorous ecstasies and throes,
And lyric spasms of wildest wail,
The love-song of a nightingale.

(225)

These lines, the poem's spasmodic refrain, expand or contract rhythmically depending on the number of syllables one accords to words such as *electrically* and *tumultuously*. "The Russian Student's Tale" culminates with a variation of the refrain that marks the death of the lovelorn nightingale:

With lyric spasms, as from a throat
Which dying breathes a faltering note,
There faded o'er the silent vale
The last sob of a nightingale.

(229)

The woman thus dies, or at least she dies metaphorically, from having been abandoned by her lover, the result of both the conditions of working-class urban existence and Victorian ideals of feminine propriety.

But let us consider in more detail the student's vision of the singing nightingale. The night glows "[e]lectrically," and the river, the Neva, "surge[s]" and "swell[s]"; the physical world seems alive with pulsing, rhythmic energy, and from these pulsing patterns the nightingale's spasmodic lyric song emerges. If anything, the nightingale's spasms seem at one with the surrounding, pulsating world. The wind carries the song, the "ecstasies and throes" of which parallel and even sympathize with the "surge and swell" of the river. Hence the nightingale, and the abandoned woman whom the nightingale represents, embodies a kind of ideal of sympathetic vibration, as though it were connected through "universal law" to the world around it. Such a vision accords with Darwin's view of rhythmic communication, as well as with ideals of rhythm articulated by physiological theorists from Alexander Bain to Grant Allen, in which rhythm is universally understood. Blind's connection of universal rhythm to electricity affirms more than a century's worth of thinking about the omnipresence of electric charge and its affiliation with poetic experience. But the outcome of Blind's poem demonstrates the ultimate failure of this fantasy. The poor woman is abandoned, after all, not only by the Russian student but also by a culture and social structure with little room for the truly impoverished, especially those who through desperation turn to prostitution. Within this structure, the young woman dies and the nightingale's passionate song "fade[s] o'er the silent vale," unheard by any who truly would sympathize, let alone help. The evening's electric glow, no doubt the "white nights" of summer in St. Petersburg, does not embrace the fallen woman but instead offers light by which to witness her looming decline. What in Swinburne's poetry may have facilitated the lyric's rhythmic transmission—its connection, say, to the natural world's "surge and swell"— now disables its ability to communicate among human individuals. The nightingale's spasms fail to resonate with "universal law" insofar as it applies to the human community at large, and the lyrical bird dies.

Hard-hearted social values again come head to head with genuine feeling in "A Mother's Dream," a poem from the *Dramas* narrated by a woman who leaves her daughter, who was born out of wedlock, at a nunnery so she will not suffer from the "stain" of illegitimacy (259). Too late, the mother repents her decision and attempts to recover the little girl from the nunnery, believing that her daughter is "calling [out to her] without words, / Touching her nature's deepest chords" (260). The woman reaches the convent only to learn that her daughter has died and had indeed been calling for her mother as she lay on her deathbed (264). In responding to "nature's deepest chords," the narrator accedes to what Blind calls "universal law," turning belatedly from the artificial social structures that had separated her from her daughter. Like "The Russian Student's Tale," "A Mother's Dream" calls attention to and mourns the disjunction between social forms and genuine feeling. Whereas Blind wrote passionately of Shelley's ability to translate "the hidden laws of nature" into art and to communicate "thoughts [that] throb audibly through their solemn rhythms" (Blind 1870, 97), *Dramas in Miniature* forcefully shows how the modern world distorts Shelley's pulsing, rhythmic "throb[s]" into destructive, spasmodic jerkings. More often than not, it seems, rhythmic pulses go awry, and women especially suffer the consequences of such failure.

Blind, however, appears reluctant to forsake entirely the experience of rhythmic spasm. Undoubtedly, she wants structured patterning that communicates clearly, much as the "vibratory movement[s]" of male peacocks form part of an elaborate mating ritual clearly intelligible to their female counterparts. But at the same time, Blind demands lyric spontaneity that will, like Shelley's poetry, "penetrate . . . into the fiery depths of human passion" (Blind 1870, 90). Such balanced poetry Blind finds in the works of both Elizabeth Barrett Browning, who offers "a distinctively womanly strain of emotion in the throbbing tides of her high-wrought melodious song" (Blind 1904, 7), and Arthur O'Shaughnessy, of whose volume *Music and Moonlight* (1874) Blind writes glowingly.[23] In the works of both poets, formal structure governs the excesses of lyric spontaneity; Barrett Browning's song is "high-wrought," or finely structured, and the work of O'Shaughnessy, "a master of the formal art of poetry," is marked by "grace of diction, and an aërial delicacy of rhythm" (Blind 1874, 320). Blind turns critical when writing of poets who have mastered only one of the requisite components, either form or spontaneity. With respect to Frances Kemble, for example, Blind values the poet's "rare emotional force" and "irresistible . . . directness of utterance," but she notes disapprovingly that Kemble does not "carefully and assiduously cultivate . . . [her feelings] by the labour requisite to produce every highest product of art." Kemble does not contain her passion within finely structured meters; she overflows, like the spasmodic nightingale, onto the page with a force that is both "irresistible" and troubling (Blind 1884, 50–51). Blind cannot fully endorse Kemble's poetry, even as she cannot approve of those poets who lose all sense of spontaneity by adhering too stringently to metrical structure, as is the case in Blind's view of George Eliot's epic poem *The Spanish Gypsy* (1868); Eliot's "thoughts," writes Blind, "instead of being naturally winged with melody, seem mechanically welded into song" (Blind 1904, 223).

Any number of Victorian poets might have identified with Blind's astringent aesthetic logic, her ideal of balance between form and expression, objective sense and subjective sensibility, meter and rhythm. Few poets, however, elaborated so compelling a view of poetry as ineluctably intertwined with cultural values—in particular, the shifting cultural landscape of the post-Darwinian fin de siècle. In "The Russian Student's Tale," for example, the lyric spasms of Blind's nightingale suggest powerfully the post-Darwinian human condition, the state of being, in the words of Grant Allen, "[s]olitary in a boundless universe" and "cry[ing] like infants for the light" (Allen, 277). At the same time, the poem's formal structure, and especially the balladlike tetrameter couplets into which the lyric spasms fit, gestures to a cultural structure that fails to redress the pain of the nightingale's suffering. Many of the poems in *Dramas in Miniature* appear as modified ballads, part of a late-Victorian ballad revival driven especially by women poets, and Blind uses the form to critique British culture at the fin de siècle; more than any other poetic form, the ballad seemed to nineteenth-century readers an embodiment, or more likely a fantasy, of a unified British culture.[24] The problem with such unity, of course, rests with the ballad's inability to accommodate individual spasm, the "fiery depths of human passion" that Blind so valued in Shelley and that cannot be restricted to form, whether that form be poetic, cultural, or otherwise. The cultural structure implicit in the ballad's metrical form dooms Blind's young prostitute, even as her "lyric spasms of wildest wail" resonate thoroughly and unambiguously with the pulsing rhythms of the natural world. "This poor lost child," mourns the Russian student, "we all—yes, all— / Had helped to hurry to her fall" (BPW, 228). Thus results the poet's near-impossible negotiation between nature and culture, spasm and restraint, rhythm and meter: "[I]n the present state of disorganization," writes Blind in her moving judgment of modern life, "one may be chilled to the Soul by . . . complete isolation from the pulse of a collective life" (BCB, 24). Rhythmic pulses seem not to cohere into reasoned metrical structures, and those structures that do exist seem not to account for individual rhythmic pulses.

Blind's poetic ideal thus appears always beyond reach, except perhaps *as* an ideal to which she turns throughout her literary career. In her essay on Shelley, Blind uses the Pygmalion myth to describe the perfect melding of form and passion, the ideal that Shelley and few others come close to achieving:

> As it is fabled that Pygmalion was consumed by so potent a passion for the marble image that, clasping it, he mastered the cold repose of the stone itself, and won a response from its locked lips, even thus every true poet stands in his relation to Nature, and besieges her with prayers, tears, and entreaties, weary watches, and devouring aspirations, *till he feels at last the throb in the stony veins,* hears the murmur of the muffled voice, till, from the sun and the sea, the trees and beasts, yea, the very stones, there burst awful manifestations,

opening glimpses, strange and sudden, into the vast dumb mystery.
(Blind 1870, 92; emphasis mine)

In passionately embracing solid form, the poet accesses the "vast dumb mystery" of nature, through which he converts dead matter into a living, breathing being. The idea is not to abandon form—cultural form, metrical form, the "Cosmic Order"—but to "w[i]n a response from its locked lips," to bring life to form's "cold repose."

Such yearning for vital structure is very much the crux of Blind's speculation, quoted above, that "[t]he poet only truly lives when he feels the rapture of communion; when his soul [is] mirrored in a sister soul" like the moon's reflection on the lake (BCB, 36). The rapture that Blind values so highly comes by apprehending the wholeness of the moon's form, a phenomenon Blind explores more fully in a poem entitled "The Mirror of Diana" (it is from where the temple of Diana once stood on Lake Nemi's shore that one may best witness the fully doubled image of the moon on the lake's surface):

> She floats into the quiet skies
>   Where, in the circle of the hills,
>   Her immemorial mirror fills
> With light, as of a virgin's eyes
> When, love a-tremble in their blue,
> They glow twin violets dipped in dew.
>
>   (BPW, 367)

As the moon glides into place above the lake, forming its mirror-perfect image,

> In many a burst of sweet delight
> The love throb of the nightingale
> Swells through lush flowering woods and fills
> The circle of the listening hills.
>
>   (BPW, 367)

Not only the nightingale but all of nature—glowworms, fireflies, and "all the wild wind instruments / Of pine and ilex"—seems enthralled, captivated by the moon's perfect image:

O Beauty, far and far above
  The night moth and the nightingale!
  Far, far above life's narrow pale,
O Unattainable! O Love!
Even as the nightingale we cry
For some Ideal, set on high.

Haunting the deep reflective mind,
   You may surprise its perfect Sphere
   Glassed like the Moon within her mere,
Who at a puff of alien wind
Melts in innumerable rings,
Elusive in the flux of things.

(BPW, 368)

Like the sun that in Swinburne's "Lake of Gaube" shines down on "earth and air" as they "[l]ie prone in passion, blind with bliss," Blind's moon radiates over the natural world. The moon's rapturous form evaporates into "the flux of things," but not before inspiring an ideal vision of perfect beauty through perfect form. Yet the question remains for Blind—and, one suspects, for Swinburne as well—whether any poet in the modern world might translate such passionate experience into a poetic form, might bring, as Blind writes of Shelley, "the hidden laws of nature" into art and communicate to others with "thoughts [that] throb audibly through their solemn rhythms" (Blind 1870, 97).

The ideal of rapturous form, what Blind calls "the rapture of communion," fuses emotional affect with structural poetics. In so doing, it attempts to access a physiological experience that is both individual and communal. If such an ideal remains for the most part unattainable in the modern world, much like the lovelorn nightingale's impossible infatuation with the moon, it abides nonetheless as perhaps the only conceivable reconciliation between individual spasm and universal, formal structure. In forms of rapture, we may discern tangible shapes among the "dim fluctuant forces" mediating our modern lives. If "fleshly," such poetry nonetheless avoids the egoism Buchanan sees as predominant in the works of Rossetti and Swinburne. Instead, for Swinburne and Blind, their guiding philosophy is as Henry

Maudsley writes in his 1870 *Body and Mind:* "No, science has not destroyed poetry, nor expelled the Divine from nature, but has furnished the materials, and given the presages, of a higher poetry and a mightier philosophy than the world has yet seen" (Maudsley, 111). Blind makes little pretense to having achieved this "higher poetry," but her works look forward in anticipation of it. Swinburne perhaps imagines his innovative language and form to approach a rapturous ideal, a compromise between material structure and transcendent value. In the work of both poets, rapture persists as paradigmatic of what poetry has to offer a post-Darwinian, post-Maxwellian world: the passionate synthesis of individual and community, spasm and structure, that both Swinburne and Blind undoubtedly believe may yet be achieved.

Spiritual and Material Poetics

DOTEN, BARRETT BROWNING, AND BEYOND

I saw the spirit-sky—I felt the flood
  Of music lift me to that region clear
Of endless morning. . . .
. . . .
                  The very air
Thrilled me with ecstasy, for Love Divine
Flowed in it.

          —Thomas Lake Harris, *An Epic of the Starry Heaven* (1854)

IT WAS ONLY NATURAL FOR THE SPIRITUALIST POET THOMAS Lake Harris to set one of the scenes for his *Epic of the Starry Heaven* in the "Electrical Ocean of the Solar System between Earth and Mars" (Harris, 23). From the very beginnings of spiritualism, the mid-Victorian craze for communicating with the dead, the so-called spiritual telegraph was a popular figure in both America and England. L. Alph Cahagnet's *Celestial Telegraph* (1851) and the *Spiritual Telegraph*, a journal published in the United States from 1852 through 1857 and in Britain from 1855 through 1859, relied on electricity (specifically, the electric telegraph) as a model for ghostly communications. The "limitless possibilities of flowing electrical information," as Jeffrey Sconce puts it, "placed the technology at the center of intense social conjecture" (Sconce, 25); if electricity might be harnessed to send messages instantaneously across vast spaces, so the logic went, why not imagine extending its reach to the ultimate limit, the world beyond? The generation that came of age in the 1830s, according to Alison Winter, "set few limits on the powers that might be revealed in electricity, light, magnetism, and gases" (Winter, 35).[1] One must imagine oneself in such an enthused state of mind when reading the introduction to Harris's *Epic of the Starry Heaven*, wherein Harris's friend and fellow spiritualist S. B. Brittan explains the process by which Harris received, through spiritual inspiration, the whole of his poem: "[*Starry Heaven*] was spoken by THOMAS L. HARRIS in the course of fourteen consecutive days, the speaker being in a *trance state* during its delivery. . . . The general appearance and manner of the *improvisatore* while subject to the influence of Spirits, was much like that of a person in an ordinary magnetic sleep. . . . [Harris] remarked, during the progress of the work, that the invisible powers seemed to be singing it within him, and that all his nerves vibrated to the music" (Harris, vii). According to the story, Brittan wrote out the four thousand lines of the poem as Harris spoke them. Much of the poem reiterates Brittan's narrative, pointing repeatedly to the process by which Harris received his inspiration:

> The origin of Beauty, Love, and Truth—
> Of light, life, motion, and immortal youth—
> Of form, of music, sweetness, and delight,
> Flashes from God's own Image on my sight.
> I feel the pulses of the Eternal Soul
> In all my veins.
>
> (Harris, 28–29)

Most striking about Harris's lines, and spiritualist poetry in general, is their reliance on the language of physiology, even as their subject ostensibly celebrates the opposite of such materiality. *An Epic of the Starry Heaven* may concern itself primarily with "the Eternal Soul," but it approaches such immaterial subject matter by way of the physical body: pulses and nerves. Harris's poem was first published in early 1854, just months after Dobell's *Balder*, and his method of poetic expression resonates entirely with the physiological style of his Spasmodic contemporaries.

Not surprisingly, spiritualists were fond of attacking materialist culture, what Frederic Myers dismissed as "the mechanical theory of the Universe." As a poet, a founder of the British Society for Psychical Research, and in

1882 coiner of the term *telepathy*, Myers disdained "the reduction of all spiritual facts to physiological phenomena" (Myers 1904, 33).[2] But Myers also relied on physiology to report on psychic phenomena:

> It is reported that a spirit's encounter with another spirit higher than itself generates inevitably that feeling which on earth we know when the shock of some pure passion has whelmed all sense of the body in one selfless and pervading love. Strangely akin to this, moreover (as Plato knew), is the soul's shock and sense of consummation when even on earth she receives within her some majestic and vivifying truth. . . . The rapture of knowledge must heighten as the Cosmos opens more profoundly on our view; the oneness of spirits must be ever more interpenetrating as those spirits bring to the marriage a more eager and incontaminate fire. (44)

The paradox at the center of Myers's description captures perfectly what John Durham Peters has identified as "the heartland of the problem of communication: contact between people via an invisible or elusive material linkage" (Peters, 103). Both "material" and "invisible or elusive," this paradox was ultimately exploited by Victorian spiritualists, who convinced the public both that the spiritualist experience was more familiar than might be expected—Myers points to "that feeling which . . . we know"—and that there was something more to be had for those who opened themselves to its wonders: "rapture of knowledge," "a more eager and incontaminate fire." Myers speaks with equal assurance of physiological experience (the "shock" that "has whelmed all sense of the body") and of philosophical idealism ("as Plato knew"). The connection between spiritualist poetry and physiological poetics is thus not nearly as tenuous as the term *spiritualism*—calling to mind a necessary immateriality—at first suggests. Eliza Richards has rightly noted that the "centrality" of poetry to spiritualism "has rarely been noted or interpreted" (Richards, 118). Equally true is that spirit poems have rarely been acknowledged as having a role to play within the broader context of Victorian poetry and poetic theory. Spiritualist poetry in fact offers a forceful and paradoxical limit case for poetic materiality as it manifested across the nineteenth century, from Romantic sensibility to Tennyson's engagement with sensation through the Spasmodic experiments of the 1850s and on to Hopkins's sprung rhythm and Swinburne's rapturous lyricism.

Most compelling among Victorian spirit poets was the American Lizzie Doten, infamous for communicating poetry from dead writers such as Shakespeare and Poe. Born in 1829, Doten came to be known as an "inspirational speaker" and "an improviser of poetry, which she produce[d] with little or no intellectual effort, claiming that it [was] dictated to her by spirits" (Wilson and Fiske, 2:209). The preface to her *Poems from the Inner Life* (first published in 1863) describes how she came into contact with dead poets by way of her keen sensibility:

> My brain was fashioned, and my nervous system finely strung, so that I should inevitably catch the thrill of the innumerable voices resounding through the universe, and translate their messages into human language, as coherently and clearly as my imperfections would allow. . . . I was, for the time being, like a harp in the hands of superior powers, and just in proportion as my entire nature was attuned to thrill responsive to their touch, did I give voice and expression to their unwritten music. (Doten, viii, xii)

Much like Felicia Hemans's lyre awaiting "the touch to give [it] life," Doten imagines herself in the role of passive vehicle; her body makes tangible the ethereal, "disembodied intelligences" of the spirit world. Doten often made public displays of her "spiritual telepathy," performing for audiences her communication with the dead. The poem "Resurrexi," for example, was given "impromptu" and under the influence of Edgar Allan Poe, after reading a lecture in Boston. The dead Poe here speaks through Doten:

> Now I come more meekly human,
> And the weak lips of a woman
> Touch with fire from off the altar, not with burnings as of yore;
> But in holy love descending,
> With her chastened being blending,
> I would fill your souls with music from the bright celestial shore.
> (Doten, 105)

The poem thematizes the act of its own transmission, such that what we get has little to do with "The Raven," the poem it so laboriously wants to echo (other stanzas celebrate the "burning inspiration" that "in a fiery flood [will] pour," and Poe's spirit "leap[ing] from out its prison door" [105, 107]). "Poe" instead elaborates on the nature of spiritualist poetics, the means by which a voice might traverse the metaphysical space between life and afterlife. This "telegraphic" process of communication, as Richards suggests, "derive[s] largely from [the poem's] metrical and figurative aspects" (Richards, 119); rhythm and sonic echoing permit the harplike Doten to receive "Resurrexi" as a physiological impression—she "thrill[s] responsive to [Poe's] touch."

Spiritualist communication thereby repeats with only a slight difference the physiological poetics of the Victorian period. The poetic experiences of Harris and Doten suggest a convergence of Tennyson's "indefinable pulsa-tion / Inaudible to outward sense, but felt / Through the deep heart of every living thing" with Dobell's notion of poetry as "the word of Man made flesh and dwelling amongst us."[3] Each imagines a form of poetic transcendence that might resonate universally among all living beings, and for each there is also a clear spiritual component to universal transcendence (Tennyson's moment arrives at the time of judgment as it is described in the Bible; Do-bell paraphrases from the Bible to explain his ideal of poetic composition).[4] The paradoxes in Tennyson and Dobell—pulses that are indefinable yet recognized by all, language taking on physiological qualities—are at one with the paradoxes of spiritualism. According to Doten, spiritualist poetry can be fully understood only if one allows one's "soul . . . [to] be transported to that sphere of spiritual *perceptions*, where there is no *audible* 'speech nor language,' and where the 'voice is not *heard*'" (Doten, xxiv; Doten quotes here from her own poem, "The Farewell to Earth"). Such melding of self and world, physical and metaphysical, characterizes as well Hopkins's notion of instress, and—from a secular perspective—Swinburne's ideal of poetic rapture. A fantasy of synthesis and union among words, ideas, and physical bodies links these writers within a distinct school of poetic practice.

Victorian poetry is thus more engaged with spiritualism than is gener-ally acknowledged. Many Victorians turned for spiritualist inspiration to the theories of Emanuel Swedenborg (1688–1772), whose influential texts recount the Swedish scientist's purported conversations with angels. Swe-denborg's work was published in England in the 1840s, and his ideas have

clear ties to the emergence of spiritualism at the end of the decade (Gold-
farb and Goldfarb, 29). As Leigh Eric Schmidt argues, however, whereas
the eighteenth-century Swedenborg emphasized the "opening up of the
interior senses" as a way of communicating with supernatural entities, the
new Victorian spiritualist practices featured "voices from the spirit-land
that . . . were increasingly materialized and incarnated" (Schmidt, 201).
Tennyson heavily annotated his copy of Swedenborg's *On the Intercourse of
the Soul and the Body* (1844), underlining passages that blur the line between
body and spirit: for example, "the spiritual world flows into the natural world,
and actuates it in all its parts" and "[f]or the *rational sight* of man, which is
the *understanding*, without forms organized for the reception of *spiritual
light*, would be an abstract nothing" (Swedenborg, 8, 19).[5] On the verso of
Swedenborg's final page, Tennyson responds by asking, "What is the nature
of the 'substantial body' . . . in which the soul is clothed after death?" Fred-
eric Myers echoes these musings with interesting effect in "To Tennyson,"
a poem composed shortly after the Poet Laureate's 1892 death. Myers
imagines Tennyson exerting a kind of lyrical influence over the heavens:

> Once more he rises; lulled and still,
>   Hushed to his tune the tideways roll;
> These waveless heights of evening thrill
>   With voyage of the summoned Soul.
>
>   (Myers 1904, 117)

Rolling and thrilling to Tennyson's progress, the lines borrow thematically
from both "The Passing of Arthur" and "Crossing the Bar," poems in which
Tennyson figures death as movement across water. Tennyson thus may not
have fully believed in Swedenborg's theories or in spiritualism more broadly
conceived, but his work leaves open the possibility for spiritualist readings;
at the very least, the Poet Laureate endorses the spiritualist belief in cosmic
resonance and appears to Myers sympathetic to the spiritualist cause.[6]

The ranks of nineteenth-century poets similarly absorbed into spiritual-
ism, whether they meant to be or not, are long and noteworthy. They in-
clude Wordsworth—who according to Myers demonstrated the ability to
"renew for a while [a] sense of vision and nearness to the spiritual world"
(Myers 1902, 134)—and Emily Brontë, whose contributions to the 1846

Poems by Currer, Ellis, and Acton Bell gesture regularly to an otherworldly presence:

> So stood I, in Heaven's glorious sun,
>   And in the glare of Hell;
> My spirit drank a mingled tone,
> Of seraph's song, and demon's moan;
> What my soul bore, my soul alone
>   Within itself may tell!
>
>   ("My Comforter"; E. Brontë, 30)

Even the profoundly secular Mathilde Blind makes frequent reference to a sort of communication that might be understood as spiritualist in nature. As we saw in chapter 5, the plot of "A Mother's Dream" depends on the call of a dying girl to her mother, which is miraculously heard across the English Channel. Blind presents the call as a sign of nature's universal resonance, but her Victorian readers more likely would have understood it within the context of spiritualism, which was still much in vogue at the end of the century.[7]

Chief among the respected Victorian poets who also dabbled in the world of spiritualism is Elizabeth Barrett Browning, whose connection of poetry to the otherworldly stretches back to her early childhood: "My Muse come forth and touch the Heavenly lyre / Breathe the wild accent of celestial fire" (Barrett Browning 1984, 1:29). Composed in 1816 at the age of ten, this poem introduces the trope of the "[h]eavenly lyre," which was to remain among Barrett Browning's favorites as a child.[8] Barrett Browning presents the lyre, the quintessential figure for poetry, existing in a nearly supernatural state of incorporeal being, simultaneously physical and immaterial. We will look briefly now at how this paradoxical notion of touching a material yet spiritual poetic instrument informs Barrett Browning's later writings and helps to situate her work within both spiritualist and electric poetics.

TOUCHING BARRETT BROWNING

According to Barrett Browning, Swedenborg was "a man of genius": "[H]is scheme of the natural and spiritual worlds and natures appears to me, in an internal light of its own, divine and true" (quoted in McAleer, 596).[9] Barrett Browning's interest in spiritualism has been much noted, including her 1855 visit to Daniel Dunglas Home, the most renowned medium of the day (Robert Browning's abhorrence of all things spiritualist has also been much discussed, largely by way of his 1864 parody of Home, "Mr Sludge, 'The Medium'").[10] Having taken an interest in mesmerism in the early 1840s (Winter, 235–45), Barrett Browning welcomed spiritualism, in Dorothy Mermin's words, "as the inauguration of a new antimaterialist age" that would have the effect of erasing "barriers of nation, class, sect, and gender," as well as "the greatest barriers of all: between life and death, the human and the divine" (Mermin, 179).[11] More than this, spiritualism for Barrett Browning confirmed her ideal of poetry as bridging the material and the immaterial worlds, and as such it provided for Barrett Browning a model for her role as a poet. Tricia Lootens has suggested that the reclusive Barrett Browning was viewed by midcentury critics as lacking a "corporeal presence"; Lootens quotes from an 1853 review by the American George Stillman Hillard, who writes that he "[has] never seen a human frame which seemed so nearly a transparent veil for a celestial and immortal spirit. She is a soul of fire enclosed in a shell of pearl" (Lootens 1996, 126). Barrett Browning becomes, in this description, something of a medium herself, bearing through her fragile physical body—her "shell of pearl"—poetry that emanates from the "celestial and immortal" sphere.[12]

Within this context, Barrett Browning's "A Vision of Poets" (1844) reads unmistakably as an early manifestation of spiritualist poetics. The poem offers an extended narrative of connection between a poet and the spirit world. In brief, an insomniac poet goes walking in a nearby forest and arrives, after a series of turns, in a "great church" wherein reside, among various angels, spirits of the greatest poets in the western tradition: Homer, Sappho, Sophocles, Dante, Shakespeare, Milton, Goethe, Shelley, Keats, and many more (EBB, 2:318–26, lines 220–426). Most critics addressing the poem focus on the suffering visible in each poet's spirit—"where the heart of each should beat, / There seemed a wound instead of it, / From whence the blood dropped to their feet" (326, lines 427–29)—and on the poem's analogy between poetic suffering and the biblical martyrdom of Christ.[13] Barrett Browning's preface to her 1844 *Poems* states that she "endeavoured" in the poem "to indicate the necessary relations of genius to suffering and self-sacrifice" (EBB, 2:147). The poets in Barrett Browning's "Vision of Poets" are all "[c]ontent" to suffer in order that "harmony" might be brought to the world (331, lines 559, 555). Poets function for Barrett Browning as a unifying force, forging communities out of individuals and joining together elements of the universe that would otherwise be experienced as distinct. The preface to her 1826 *Essay on Mind*, for example, describes "one who could try the golden links of that chain which hangs from Heaven to earth, and shew that it . . . is placed there to join, in mysterious union, the natural and the spiritual, the mortal and the eternal, the creature and the Creator" (EBB, 1:59). This, in short, is the ultimate vision of the 1844 "Vision of Poets": that such union might come of poetic suffering.

Within the poem, Barrett Browning suggests the power of this unifying vision by way of organ music, which an angel plays for those assembled in the church. Notice in the following passage how the poem blurs distinctions between physical and spiritual, and between inner experience and aesthetic manifestation:

> the poet gazed
> Upon the angel glorious-faced
> Whose hand, majestically raised,
>
> Floated across the organ-keys,
> Like a pale moon o'er murmuring seas,
> With no touch but with influences:
>
> Then rose and fell (with swell and swound
> Of shapeless noises wandering round
> A concord which at last they found)
>
> Those mystic keys: the tones were mixed,
> Dim, faint, and thrilled and throbbed betwixt
> The incomplete and the unfixed:
>
> And therein mighty minds were heard
> In mighty musings, inly stirred,
> And struggling outward for a word:
> . . . .

> . . . The music was
> Of divine stature; strong to pass:
>
> And those who heard it understood
> Something of life in spirit and blood,
> Something of nature's fair and good.
> (EBB, 2:328–29; lines 466–80, 497–501)

Barrett Browning's early wish to "touch the Heavenly lyre" and "Breathe the wild accent of celestial fire" develops here as a paradoxical melding of earthly and otherworldly. The angel's music emanates as "shapeless noises" that nevertheless affect the poet physiologically: his body "thrilled and throbbed." The organ is not touched, but the keys respond to "influences." The "minds" of others are "heard," but their "musings" do not take the form of language: they "struggl[e] outward for a word." Swinburne and Blind would later identify such experiences, translated into a secular frame, as "rapturous": the melding of feeling and form, body and mind. But for Barrett Browning, this ideal poetic experience cannot be imagined outside the spiritual context, as she views the very object of poetry to be the enrichment of the mundane by way of the divine.

This ideal of union informs Barrett Browning's poetry from her earliest juvenilia to *Aurora Leigh*, which George Eliot rightly praised for joining "melody, fancy, and imagination—what we may call its poetical *body*" with an idea of "[a] *soul*, namely . . . genuine thought and feeling" (G. Eliot 1857a, 307). One suspects that Barrett Browning would have reversed Eliot's classification, identifying the poetical "body" as "genuine thought and feeling" and the poetic "soul" as the "melody, fancy, and imagination," linked necessarily to some sense of divinity: the spiritual. Through this taxonomy, Barrett Browning presents one of the key moments of *Aurora Leigh*, the young Aurora's first "touch" of poetic inspiration:

> As the earth
> Plunges in fury, when the internal fires
> Have reached and pricked her heart, and, throwing flat
> The marts and temples, the triumphal gates
> And towers of observation, clears herself
> To elemental freedom—thus, my soul,

> At poetry's divine first finger-touch,
> Let go conventions and sprang up surprised,
> Convicted of the great eternities
> Before two worlds.
>
> (EBB 4:28, book 1, lines 845–54)

Aurora imagines herself touched by a "divine" force, here via the nearly cataclysmic power of verse, in a tableau that recalls Michelangelo's famous finger-touch in the Sistine Chapel. The passage, however, is not strictly spiritual. Aurora's language allows for a more physical form of touching that parallels the spiritual, a touch to Aurora's "poetical *body*," as Eliot might have put it. Nearly masturbatory in its suggestion—the soul "sprang up surprised" at being touched so by poetry's finger—the image insists on a spiritual dynamic but relies for its power on the physiological, much as spiritualist poets such as Doten and Harris centered their otherworldly experiences in the trembling and pulsing of their own bodies. Poetry accesses "the divine," but it does so through the human, by touching the "internal fires" of our most intimate parts. A similar fusion of spiritual and sensual occurs toward the end of "A Vision of Poets," when the angel's organ song, "[l]ike measured thunders . . . fused together sense and mind" and, ultimately, "[s]oared . . . as a soul / Is raised by a thought" (EBB, 2:338–39, lines 742–44, 763–65).

Toward the end of *Aurora Leigh*, Barrett Browning endows her poet with the ability to communicate more directly, because more physically, with a divine force. Stopping one evening in an Italian church, Aurora yearns for a more immediate mode of exchange, wishing

> That He would stop His ears to what I said,
> And only listen to the run and beat
> Of this poor, passionate, helpless blood—
> And then
> I lay, and spoke not: but He heard in heaven.
> (EBB 5:124, book 7, lines 1269–72)

As Beverly Taylor argues, "Aurora now represents the poet-woman's utterance as the body that speaks to God, through its throbbing pulse inscribing woman's experience" (Taylor 1992, 24). Borrowing from the language of spiritualism, Barrett Browning imagines Aurora's blood to be a celestial telegraph, pulsing a message more accurate, and more effectively heard, than any written or spoken language.[14]

Barrett Browning is therefore more an enthusiast of poetry's materiality than her investment in spiritualism and otherworldliness at first suggests. Herbert Tucker rightly points to the "embodied intuition" of *Aurora Leigh*, much as Matthew Campbell suggests that "Aurora authenticates her utterances through a sounding of the rhythms of her own body" (Tucker 2004, 444; Campbell, 43).[15] Richard Hengist Horne's 1844 *New Spirit of the Age*, which Barrett Browning effectively coauthored, concludes with the speech of a "rough beard[ed]" working man who champions just the sort of aesthetic materiality consistent throughout Barrett Browning's works. "A modeller and a mason," he in "one hand . . . holds a chisel, in the other a lump of clay" (Horne, 2:306), and he voices a theory of art entirely of a piece with "A Vision of Poets," which was published in the same year:

> Nothing [says the working man] will now be received which has not some distinct principle, a clear design, a shapely structure. Characters, passions, thought, action and event, must all be within a circle and citadel of their own, bounded by no hard line of horizon, and opening large portals on all sides to the influences and sympathies of the outer world. The only artist-work that does good in its day, or that reaches posterity, is the work of a Soul that gives Form. But without the impassioned life of that soul, the best-reasoned form and structure are but cold vanities, which leave man's unstirred nature just where they found it, and therefore are of no service on earth. (309–10)

The ideal of Horne and Barrett's working man, aesthetic form embodying "the impassioned life of [the] soul," is very much the ideal of Victorian poetics as I have charted it through this book. Barrett Browning's poetic model resonates with the physiological poetics of the Spasmodics, poets whom she by and large supported.[16] Her ideas appear as well in the works of Swinburne and Hopkins, poets who discovered new ways for literary form to be both physical and malleable: rhythm shaping itself around or being shaped by the contours of human action and feeling, as well as—for Hopkins—a transcendent, spiritual intuition.

Barrett Browning also reflects her age in understanding the political significance of this new, physiological poetic mode; not for nothing is the artist of the *New Spirit of the Age* a burly working man. In the first part of *Casa Guidi Windows* (1851; composed 1847), among the most explicitly political of her poems, Barrett Browning uses the context of the Italian *risorgimento*—and, not incidentally, the figure of electricity—to draw together ideas about physiological poetics, spiritualism, and political idealism. The passage that follows, as Matthew Reynolds has argued of the poem as a whole, offers a "prophecy" for the future; Barrett Browning "has assumed the prophet's task: to identify and to hymn an Ideal" (Reynolds, 91):

> Drums and battle-cries
>   Go out in music of the morning star—
> And soon we shall have thinkers in the place
>   Of fighters, each found able as a man
> To strike electric influence through a race,
>   Unstayed by city-wall and barbican.
> The poet shall look grander in the face
>   Than even of old (when he of Greece began
> To sing "that Achillean wrath which slew
>   So many heroes")—seeing he shall treat
> The deeds of souls heroic toward the true,
>   The oracles of life, previsions sweet
> And awful like divine swans gliding through
>   White arms of Ledas, which will leave the heat
> Of their escaping godship to endue
>   The human medium with a heavenly flush.
>
>   (EBB, 3:272–73, lines 725–40)

The poet in Barrett Browning's vision is thus a "human medium" who allows herself, Leda-like, to be penetrated by the divine spirit; poetry from this view is necessarily both material and spiritual in nature. Having acquired the "heavenly flush" of "godship," the poet then broadcasts her newfound "heat" to the world at large, "strik[ing] electric influence through a race." Shockingly sexual, the passage makes explicit the poetic conflation of sensuous body with divine spirit, employing the spiritual telegraph as the figurative vehicle for this communication. Zeus literally penetrates the unsuspecting Leda; Barrett Browning does not shy from suggesting that poetic inspiration follows from a kind of physical violation. One suffers, bodily, to acquire the "heavenly flush" and thereby to become a poet who might move the masses. To cultivate political strength, the poet must channel her vision through her own flesh. Barrett Browning's contemporaries thus might have thought her to lack a "corporeal presence," as Lootens suggests, but her poetry is as much physiological as it is "spiritual." Like the later spiritualist poets who relied on the physical body as a locus for experiencing the otherworldly, Barrett Browning telegraphs a spiritual ideal through the palpitating, eroticized flesh of the poet's physical body: a fully realized and corporeal electric poetess.

ELECTRIC POETICS AND BEYOND

By 1870, spiritualist poetry had made enough of an impression in Victorian Britain to warrant a full chapter in Alfred Austin's study, *The Poetry of the Period*. Austin, who would later become Britain's poet laureate, plays coyly with his readers as to how seriously he thinks we should take these spirit poets. Whether or not the poems are the product of communication with the dead, however, their "literary merits," he argues, "are obvious." Moreover, they are "worthy of the age which is [their] real parent, if scarcely of that invisible land to which [they] ascribe[] [their] birth" (Austin, 257–58). Indeed, nineteenth-century spirit poetry marks a logical, if extreme, end to the poetic theories governing the day, from those of Arthur Hallam and John Stuart Mill up through the Spasmodic manifestos that hit the Victorian poetic scene at precisely the same moment the spiritual fad reached its first climax, the early 1850s. The movement of a poem from the world beyond into the living world, whatever we might make of it today, resonated entirely with aesthetic theories that invested in poetry a nearly fantastical degree of interpersonal communicability. Poetry in the Victorian era was meant to overcome boundaries, to move through space, to penetrate individuals' minds, much as the spirit of Edgar Allan Poe was said to have entered the entranced mind of Lizzie Doten.

These views are still at play in Rudyard Kipling's 1902 short story "Wireless," which features a young chemist who inadvertently channels, apparently under the influence of electrical waves, Keats's poem "The Eve of St. Agnes." Kipling's chemist, Mr. Shaynor, does not mean to channel Keats, but is struck into a trancelike state, wherein—much like Doten and Harris before him—he delivers the poetic lines:

> His lips moved without cessation. I stepped nearer to listen. "And threw—and threw—and threw," he repeated, his face all sharp with some inexplicable agony.
>   I moved forward astonished. But it was then he found words—delivered roundly and clearly. These:
>   And threw warm gules on Madeleine's young breast.
>   (Kipling, 565)

As Pamela Thurschwell has suggested, Kipling's story puts early wireless radio technology (an experiment with a wireless telegraph takes place while Shaynor delivers Keats's lines) in dialogue with spiritualism "and pictures both as untrustworthy methods of information transmission" (Thurschwell, 30). Mr. Cashell, Kipling's wireless operator, notes that his receiver picks up "odds and ends of messages coming out of nowhere—a word here and there—no good at all," which makes the new technology much like "a spiritualistic séance" (Kipling, 573). Most remarkable about Kipling's story for the purposes of this conclusion is how explicitly it connects electric technologies and spiritualism to poetry. Shaynor's iambic stuttering—"And threw—and threw—and threw"—resembles the sounds of the "Morse instrument" that through much of the story "was ticking furiously" (572). Even into the early twentieth century, then, electricity—what Kipling's narrator calls the "Hertzian wave" (567)—is imagined as a vehicle for poetry, much as the human body remains a medium for both electric and poetic transmission. The particular means by which these phenomena interact with one another had yet to be understood completely in Kipling's day (arguments about the effects of electromagnetic radiation remain a favorite subject of local television news programs and tabloid magazines). But Kipling's connection of electromagnetism and spiritualism to poetry reflects a distinctly Victorian investment in electric poetics, and a period-specific ambivalence regarding the materiality of poetic production.

This anxiety about poetic materiality echoes into the twentieth century, though the Modernists and their successors framed the matter somewhat differently. Shaynor's sensibility to poetic impulses may well be read in the context of T. S. Eliot's 1921 essay, "The Metaphysical Poets," which famously but erroneously accuses nineteenth-century poets of suffering from "a dissociation of sensibility" (T. S. Eliot, 247). Tennyson and Robert Browning come under especial attack in this essay as poets who "think" but "do not feel their thought as immediately as the odor of a rose" (247). As Carol Christ has argued, Eliot here performs an act of misreading that says more about his anxieties than about Victorian poetry and poetic theory (Christ, 149). Worried that the precision and intellect of his own verses might get in the way of a unified sensibility, Eliot accuses his predecessors of not having achieved "a direct sensuous apprehension of thought, or a recreation of thought into feeling" (T. S. Eliot, 246). But Eliot's desire for a unified sensibility might have been lifted directly from Arthur Hallam's 1831 review of Tennyson and his call for a poetry of "sensation" and not "reflection" (Christ, 147). The moderns preferred to imagine their distance from the Victorians—we thus find Virginia Woolf "mus[ing] with kindly condescension over" *Aurora Leigh*, considering it a "token of bygone fashion" (Woolf, 203)—even as they remained true to an ideal of poetry much like Swinburne's and Blind's "rapture": a union of the bodily with the intellectual and spiritual. Charles Olsen's mid-twentieth-century efforts to imagine what he called "Projective Verse," discussed briefly in the introduction to this book, constitute yet another locus for this conversation. "[I]t is from the union of the mind and the ear that the syllable is born," writes Olsen, arguing that breath, speech, and voice must remain central to our understanding of a poem: "A poem is energy transferred from where the poet got it . . . by way of the poem itself to, all the way over to, the reader" (Olsen, 242, 240). Equally a poetics of sensation and a sensibility eminently *not* dissociated, Olsen's poetic theory demonstrates the staying power of Victorian physiological poetics, as well as the continued imbrication of physiological poetics with the language of electric charge.

It has been the project of this book to suggest how and why this confluence of ideas—poetry, electricity, and physiological experience—shaped the development of British poetry and poetics through the nineteenth century. To indicate one last time the cultural weight of what I have been calling electrical poetics, I offer an image (figure 6.1) from the *Illustrated London News* of 1846. As is well known, the first electric telegraph systems were marketed to railroad companies as tools for communicating information

pertaining to rail travel: for example, the delay of a train, or a broken track'
in need of repair. In this image, we can glean something of how the Victori-
ans conceived of the railroad and the telegraph as part of one vast network
reaching boldly across the British nation. The accompanying text reads "novel
use of the electric telegraph," and the cartoon was part of an essay by one
Albert Smith, who imagines musical notes "fastened" to telegraph wires,
such that passengers on board the trains passing by might "play [the notes]
as they travel": "The andante movements will be placed close to the sta-
tions, where progress is slow; and the tunes will be so arranged as to finish
at all the stoppages. . . . [G]aloppes will be chosen for the Express Trains;
sets of quadrilles for the stopping ones; and marches, or dirges, for the
luggage-class" (Smith, 200). Though facetious, this "novel use of the elec-
tric telegraph" is but one of innumerable Victorian fantasies of intimate
community seemingly enabled by telegraphic—and, more generally, elec-
tric—communication. There is something wonderful in the image of a train
full of passengers staring out their windows and playing or singing along to
musical notes as they pass by. Looking out on a pastoral setting, physically
propelled across the landscape as a single unit, the passengers on Smith's
train might discover a new sort of fellowship—perhaps a tonic to anxieties

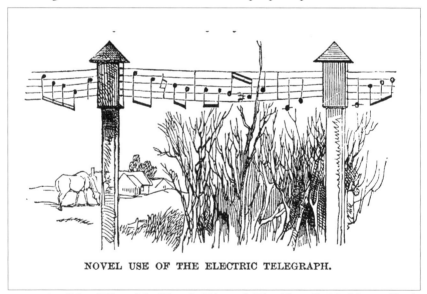

NOVEL USE OF THE ELECTRIC TELEGRAPH.

FIGURE 6.1. "Novel Use of the Electric Telegraph," by Albert Smith. Notes affixed
to telegraph lines, to be read by passengers on trains passing by. (*Illustrated London
News*, 21 March 1846, 200.)

about industrialization and fractured social cohesion. Henry Frith was thus to suggest in his 1888 *Marvels of Electricity and Magnetism* that the electric telegraph was "beginning to make the human race one vast family, throbbing with one heart, feeling an interest in one another never before possible" (Frith, v–vi); "The World in an electric Union blest," wrote Martin Tupper in an 1860 poem on the telegraph (Tupper, 168).

Victorian poets share this burden of cultural and political pressure and work toward similar ends: to bring together in new and compelling forms the vast multiplicity of a complex age. Mary Robinson, at the end of the eighteenth century, urged an isolated monk to rejoin the community of mankind, to heed the "electric spark" that might inspire a sense of collective sympathy. Poets across the nineteenth century followed her lead, discovering in the new electrical and physiological sciences figures through which such communities might be imagined. Tennyson's electrified girls, Dobell's spasmodic musings, Barrett Browning's material spiritualism (equally a spiritual materialism), Hopkins's flaming divine charge, the raptures of Swinburne and Blind, and Kipling's wireless resonances: these are the electric meters of Victorian physiological poetics. If idealized and—like the *Illustrated London News* cartoon—often a bit absurd, their fantasies reflect the desires of the age: the longing for connection and community at a time of profound technological, scientific, and cultural change.

NOTES

All quotations are cited parenthetically by author and page number, with the year of publication added to distinguish multiple works from one author. Longer poems include line references and, when appropriate, section divisions.

INTRODUCTION: PHYSIOLOGICAL POETICS

1. My thanks to Gerard Passannante for directing me to Poliziano's work. In Plato's *Ion*, Socrates explains the work of poetic experience—"an inspiration . . . divinity moving you"—to be "like . . . a magnet"; just as a magnetic force can pull through a chain of iron rings, so too the strength of "the Muse" works through the poet, by way of the poem, to the reader (Plato, 1:107).

2. On the politics of Victorian poetry, the most important recent studies include Armstrong 1993; Kuduk Weiner 2005; and Reynolds 2001. On the physiology of Victorian poetry, see Blair 2006b; M. Campbell 1999; and Prins 2000.

3. Basil Mahon describes the significance of Maxwell's equations: "The theory predicted that every time a magnet jiggled, or an electric current changed, a wave of energy would spread out into space like a ripple on a pond. Maxwell calculated the speed of the waves and it turned out to be the very speed at which light had been measured. At a stroke, he had united electricity, magnetism and light" (Mahon, 1–2). I am indebted to Michelle Boswell for introducing me to Maxwell's poetry.

4. James Munro's 1891 *Heroes of the Telegraph* describes the mirror galvanometer: "[It] consists of a very long fine coil of silk-covered copper wire, and in the heart of the coil, within a little air-chamber, a small round mirror, having four tiny magnets cemented to its back, is hung, by a single fibre of floss silk no thicker than a spider's line. The mirror is of film glass silvered, the magnets of hair-spring, and both together sometimes weigh only one-tenth of a grain. A beam of light is thrown from a lamp upon the mirror, and reflected by it upon a white screen or scale a few feet distant, where it forms a bright spot of light. When there is no current on the instrument, the spot of light remains stationary at the zero position on the screen; but the instant a current traverses the long wire of the coil, the suspended magnets twist themselves horizontally out of their former position, the mirror is of course inclined with them, and the beam of light is deflected along the screen to one side or the other, according to the nature of the current. If a *positive* electric current . . . gives a deflection to the *right* of zero, a *negative* current . . . will give a deflection to the left of zero, and *vice versa*" (Munro, 99–100).

5. Tennyson's version of the line—"O love, they die in yon rich sky"—highlights by contrast Maxwell's playfulness.

6. Tom Standage reviews Nollet's experiment and its aftermath in *The Victorian Internet* (1–2). On Nollet's relation to eighteenth-century science, especially his rivalry with Franklin, see Riskin 2002, 69–103; and Delbourgo 2006, 39–40.

7. Chapter 2 examines Mill in detail, with especial attention to the empiricist/associationist debate within his poetic theory. For more on Coleridge's ambivalent relation to materialism, associationist philosophy, and the sciences, see A. Richardson 2001, 39–65; and Roe 2001.

8. See Gilmore 2002a, 2002b, 2004; Menke 2005 and 2008; Otis 2001; and Stubbs 2003. Gilmore's thoughts on the connections between aesthetics and electricity have been especially helpful to my thinking.

9. Menke's *Telegraphic Realism*, for example, argues that "new media and information systems offered inspiration for reimagining how the world might register *in prose*" (Menke 2008, 7; emphasis mine); those studies that bring poetry into the conversation, such as Menke's "Media in America" and Gilmore's "Telegraph in Black and White," discuss the thematic appearance of electric technologies in nineteenth-century poetry but not their formal implications.

10. Kittler elaborates his views on nineteenth-century technologies of communication in *Gramophone, Film, Typewriter* and *Discourse Networks*. Clayton roundly critiques Kittler's dismissive account of the telegraph (2003, 65–70).

11. See also Prins's reading of Swinburne's use of rhythm and meter (Prins 1999, 121–56) and Alice Meynell's late-Victorian experiments with a "poetics of pauses" (Prins 2005, 264). Other important recent work on Victorian rhythm includes Catherine Maxwell's work on Swinburne (2003 and 2006) and Catherine Robson's reading of Felicia Hemans's "Casabianca" (2005).

12. Alexander Bain's *English Composition and Rhetoric* (1866) includes a lengthy chapter on poetry (257–94); I discuss George Henry Lewes's important review of Alexander Smith's *A Life-Drama* (1853) in chapter 3; and E. S. Dallas authored one of the key midcentury studies of poetry and poetic form, *Poetics* (1852).

13. Tsur 1998; Elfenbein 2006. See also Attridge 1982 and Stewart 2002. Elfenbein's essay embraces both novel theory and poetics.

14. As I discuss in chapter 4, F. R. Leavis claimed (erroneously) that "Hopkins has no relation to . . . any nineteenth-century poet" (Leavis, 26).

15. There are, of course, exceptions. Recent work on the Spasmodic poets has done much to overturn the longstanding prejudices against them (see LaPorte and Rudy 2004). Romantic women poets have benefited from some recent and long-overdue critical attention (see especially Armstrong 1993; Leighton 1992; Lootens 1996; Mason 2006; Ross 1989; and Wolfson 2006).

16. See Prins 2000 for an overview of the period's experimentation.

17. On the physiology of sensibility, see especially Barker-Benfield 1992.

CHAPTER 1: THE ELECTRIC POETESS

1. On the eighteenth-century "ideal of metaphysical harmony" inspired by electricity, see Ritterbush 1964, 6.

2. On the emergence and characterization of sensibility, see also Abrams 1953; Barker-Benfield 1992; Ellison 1999; Frye 1986; McGann 1996; and Todd 1986.

3. For more on Galvani, Volta, and the distinctions between their work, see Heilbron 1979, 491–94; Pancaldi 2003, 178–210; Para 1992; and Spillane 1981, 111–63.

4. Abernethy writes in 1817 that "a subtile substance of a quickly and powerfully mobile nature, seems to pervade every thing, and appears to be the life of the world, and . . . therefore it is probable a similar substance pervades organized bodies, and is the life of these bodies" (Abernethy, 26). Ruston's chapter on the "vitality debate" helpfully narrates the details of the controversy (Ruston 2005, 24–73). Alan Richardson's analysis of what he calls "Neural Romanticism" is also important (Richardson 2001, 1–38).

5. Quotations from *The British Album* are cited by page number and original publication date.

6. Jacqueline Labbe concludes that Della Cruscan love has thereby "been relocated to the Mind, which has been redesignated the receptor of sensation" (Labbe, 56). On the Della Cruscan poets, see also Pascoe 1997, 68–94; and McGann 1996, 74–93. W. N. Hargreaves-Mawdsley's quirky *The English Della Cruscans and Their Time* is occasionally helpful.

7. Jerome McGann notes that Della Cruscan verse is "self-consciously theatrical and spectacular" (McGann 1996, 78).

8. Herbert Tucker writes of the "adhesive correspondences" between "Mariana's phenomenal world . . . and Tennyson's 'phonemenal' one" (Tucker 1988, 73).

9. The poems are only notionally ekphrastic—that is, not modeled on actual works of art. On ekphrasis at the turn of the nineteenth century, see especially Scott 1994.

10. For Tennyson, see chapter 2; for Hopkins, see chapter 4.

11. Compare Rudy 2006.

12. I use the Tractarian term *reserve* intentionally; Hemans was influenced by the centrality of this concept to the poetry of contemporaries such as John Keble. On the doctrine of reserve and women's poetics, see Mason 2004a; Gray 2006; and Scheinberg 2002.

13. Compare John Stuart Mill, "Thoughts on Poetry and Its Varieties" (1981, 1:343–65), originally published in the *Monthly Repository*, January and October 1833, as "What Is Poetry?" and "The Two Kinds of Poetry."

14. On Hoffmann's aesthetics, see Bonds 2006: "Hoffmann declared instrumental music to be the highest of all art forms, for it opened up to listeners the realm of the infinite. . . . Precisely *because* of its independence from words, music could express that which lay beyond the grasp of conventional language" (8).

15. Adela Pinch, for example, writes that "[i]f sentimental verse was inevitably a woman's genre in the late eighteenth century, it was so only by making the feelings expressed *not* her own" (Pinch, 8; emphasis mine). Following in this line of thought, Yopie Prins suggests that "there is no 'I' to speak of" in nineteenth-century women's poetry; in "the abyss of female authorship . . . the Poetess proves to be the personification of an empty figure" (Prins 1999, 184). See also Jackson and Prins 1999.

16. Marlon Ross writes of Hemans's "heightened consciousness" that manifests in her poems as both "the capacity to know one's own heart" and "to know how it is linked to others' feelings"; Ross also identifies Hemans's "goal [as being] the feminization of culture at large. Bringing her readers to tears is not simply a way of sensitizing them individually; it is more importantly a way of transforming them collectively into a community of shared desire" (Ross, 275, 292).

17. Robinson's affiliation with the Della Cruscans was especially subject to attack: "Mrs. Robinson is most unfortunate in having adopted, as a model, the contortions

and dislocations of Della Crusca. If she had followed nature, seldom more justly or elegantly represented than in her own mind, free from the shackles of imitation, she would have produced sonnets nearer akin to the natural, pathetic, and passionate Sappho" (Review of *Sappho and Phaon, English Review* [December 1796: 583–84]; reprinted in RSP, 385).

18. Mason notes that "Hemans' ideal nation . . . was made up of private individuals of both sexes who related to one another in a communal, public sense: feminine, christian, domestic, chivalric and emotive" (Mason 2006, 31). Gary Kelly points out that this sovereignty is available in Hemans's work "only to people with certain education and cultural opportunities" (Kelly, 69). On Hemans's political work, see also Lootens 1994.

CHAPTER 2: TENNYSON'S TELEGRAPHIC POETICS

1. On the Adelaide Gallery, see Morus 1998, especially 70–98; my arguments here are indebted to this fine work. Altick's classic *The Shows of London*, 375–89, is also important.

2. We learn of Tennyson's attendance at the meeting from Francis Garden, who writes to Richard Monckton Milnes on 24 September 1833 of Tennyson "having stayed up at Cambridge to the meeting of the British Association" (TL, 1:92n).

3. Hallam Tennyson tells us that his father "took a lively interest in politics": "He was among the young supporters of the Anti-slavery Convention, and advocated the Measure for abolishing subscription to the Thirty-nine Articles, while admiring as statesmen Canning, Peel, and the Duke of Wellington. England was in a state of ferment with the hope or dread of the Reform Bill. Farms were fired, ricks were burnt. . . . Carlyle's account of Sterling best describes, as far as I can gather, the typical intellectual undergraduate of my father's set: who hated the narrow and ignorant Toryism to be found in country districts: who loathed parties and sects: who reverenced the great traditions and the great men of past ages, and eagerly sympathized with the misfortunes and disabilities of his fellow-men" (H. Tennyson, 1:41–42).

4. On Fox's debts to Coleridge, see Poston 1986. See also Armstrong 1993 (especially 25–40); Garnett 1910; and Mineka 1944, 259–71.

5. According to Mineka, Fox's political views in the period around the 1832 Reform were aligned with those of other political Radicals in calling for "(1) a further extension of suffrage, with the abolition of property qualifications, the adoption of the secret ballot, and the substitution of triennial parliaments for septennial; (2) the establishment of a national system of education free from pecuniary barriers and Church control, plus the repeal of all taxes upon the press; (3) reform of the civil and criminal law, including the virtual abolition of the death penalty; (4) reform of abuses in the Church and abolition of compulsory tithes; (5) reform of the condition of the poor through the revision of the Poor Laws and the abolition of all monopolies, especially the agricultural monopoly maintained through the Corn Laws; (6) the abolition of all slavery; (7) proscription of the military and naval practices of impressments and flogging, and a reduction in the size of the armed forces; [and] (8) abolition of sinecures and unmerited pensions" (Mineka, 261).

6. Compare Kant's view of perception: "When the senses present things outside me, the quality of the space in which these things are intuited is the merely subjective [feature] of my presentation of them (and because of this [feature] I cannot tell what such things may be as objects in themselves)" (Kant, 28–29).

7. Whewell continues: "Neither of these elements, by itself, can constitute substantial general knowledge. The impressions of sense, unconnected by some rational and speculative principle, can only end in a practical acquaintance with individual objects; the operations of the rational faculties, on the other hand, if allowed to go on without a constant reference to external things, can lead only to empty abstraction and barren ingenuity" (Whewell, 1:43).

8. Herbert Tucker sees the shift from "Armageddon" to "Timbuctoo" as a move from "the timeless sympathy of the individual heart with the universal soul" to "the historically conditioned give and take of myth, as made and remade in cultural transmission" (Tucker 1988, 53); see also Day 1983.

9. Hartley writes in 1775 that "words in passing over the ear must raise up trains of visible and other ideas by the power of association." Words related to the passions—"love, hatred, hope, fear, anger, &c."—work especially "to annex the ideas of the associated circumstances to them, and even the passions themselves, both from the infectiousness of our natures, and from the power of associated circumstances to raise the passions" (Hartley, 109).

10. Armstrong's 1972 edition of Hallam's essay prints *aristocratic* as *artistocratic*, perhaps an error from the first edition. Hallam complained of his review being execrably printed" (TL, 1:65); *artistocratic* remains suggestive, though, in its yoking of the aristocratic to the artistic, especially given Hallam's efforts to dissociate the two terms.

11. According to James Chandler, Hallam's "sensationalism would have to be understood in some kind of tension with, and as some kind of alternative to, [the] regnant bourgeois domain" (Chandler, 534).

12. Shaftesbury also argues that "virtue, according to Mr Locke, has no other measure, law, or rule, than fashion and custom: morality, justice, equity, depend only on law and will: and God indeed is a perfect free agent in his sense; that is, free to any thing, that is, however ill: for if he wills it, it will be made good; virtue may be vice, and vice virtue in its turn, if he pleases" (Shaftesbury, 346).

13. Poston analyzes the interconnection of Taylor's political and aesthetic views (see Poston 1978 and Poston 1980).

14. See Tucker 1988, which throughout makes the case for Tennyson's simultaneous engagement with and withdrawal from Romantic poetics.

15. According to Goodwin, Keble's definition of poetry might be simplified to the "troublesome and contradictory phrase" "expression . . . repressed" (Goodwin, 477). On the place of enthusiasm in romantic poetry and poetic theory, see Mee 2003; on post-Romantic enthusiasm see the work of Emma Mason (for example, Mason 2003). The standard history of Tractarianism and nineteenth-century poetry remains G. B. Tennyson's *Victorian Devotional Poetry;* see also Warren 1950, 46–65; Blair 2004a; and Blair and Mason 2006.

16. Mill clarifies in a footnote to his review of Tennyson's poetry that by "spiritual" he means "the converse of *sensuous,*" and not "*religious*" (Mill, 1:415).

17. Cat. no. 4251, P. 186, Tennyson Research Centre, Lincoln, UK. "Interleaved copy with corrections and notes in Tennyson's hand." Alfred Lord Tennyson, *The Princess* (London: MacMillan, 1891). These notes appear opposite page 108, handwritten. Hallam Tennyson reprints his father's comment (H. Tennyson, 1:251).

18. Tucker notes that "the occult force of electricity, handsomely harnessed into sound by the deft verb 'Dislinked,' arouses 'shrieks' and then 'laughter,' in that order, which gives in brief the whole order of the day" (Tucker 1988, 355–56).

19. See Beauchamp 2001, 6–8; and Clayton 2003, 58.

20. Clayton notes the variety of telegraph machines that were developed during the nineteenth century, some of which required visual scanning, others aural scanning. "The telegraph was the site of a prolonged debate over the comparative advantages of 'sound-reading' versus instruments that incorporated a recording apparatus for taking down messages in visible form" (Clayton, 52). I am concerned here not with the specific mechanical details of telegraphic communication but with the popular understanding of the telegraph: electrical communication by way of interspersed and regulated pulses.

21. As Anita B. Draper suggests, the seizures also make more clear the poem's complex argument about gender (see Draper 1979, especially 188).

22. For example, "[T]he telegraph signifies electric information that lacks a material body, and that seems identifiable with no body in particular" (Menke 2008, 90). Jeffrey Sconce argues that "the animating powers of electricity . . . gave the telegraph its distinctive property of simultaneity and its unique sense of disembodied presence" (Sconce, 28).

23. Matthew Reynolds likewise finds that "in the story of the Princess's revolt and reconciliation," we as readers "are encouraged . . . to find . . . a warning to Chartists, Saint-Simonians, or anyone else who would challenge the established social order from below" (Reynolds, 225).

24. Daniel Denecke suggests, compellingly, that the "sentimental effusion" of "Tears, Idle Tears" should be distinguished from genuine feeling such as that experienced by the princess at the poem's end (Denecke, 208).

25. Hill notes that the poem "trebled the circulation of *Punch*" and also that the poem "was republished, dramatized, and translated into German, French, Italian," as well as being "sung on street corners" (Hill, 153).

26. For analyses of "Break, Break, Break" that rely on biography with varying degrees of success, see Buckley 1960, 59–84; Nicolson 1962, 121–56; Ricks 1972, 118–74; H. Tennyson 1897, 1:116–81; and Tucker 1988, 177–90.

27. Robert W. Hill Jr. inserts a footnote after "voice" in line 11 to inform the reader that the hand and voice are those of Arthur Hallam (A. Tennyson 1971, 79). Ricks is more cautious, noting only that the poem "is on the death of Arthur Hallam" (ALT, 2:24).

28. On the "collective speech" of the Chartist movement, see Plotz 2000, 127–36.

CHAPTER 3: RHYTHMS OF SPASM

1. This is not always the case, of course. George Eliot, writing anonymously in the *Westminster Review*, finds in *Men and Women* "freshness, originality," and the feeling that "what we took for obscurity in [Browning] was superficiality in ourselves" (G. Eliot 1856a, 290, 291). On Browning's relation to the Spasmodics, see Harrison 1990, 44–68; and Weinstein 1968, 183–87.

2. See the recent *Victorian Poetry* special issue, titled *Spasmodic Poetry and Poetics* (Winter 2004), ed. Charles LaPorte and Jason R. Rudy. On gender and sexuality, see

Blair 2004b and Hughes 2004; on class and national identity, see Tucker 2004, Harrison 2004, and Boos 2004; on religious practice, see LaPorte 2004 and Mason 2004b; on the political, historical, and aesthetic contexts of the Spasmodic phenomenon, see also Cronin 1990 and 2002; and Buckley 1951.

3. See my discussion of Aytoun and the cultural work of poetic form in "On Cultural Neoformalism, Spasmodic Poetry, and the Victorian Ballad" (Rudy 2003). For Aytoun's political arguments, see especially "The Reform Measures of 1852," "The New Reform Bill," and "The Rights of Women" (Aytoun 1852, 1854c, and 1862).

4. For a thorough consideration of Dobell's connection to "The Church," as it was called by its members, see Mason 2004b.

5. All *Balder* quotations are cited by page and scene number.

6. See Blair 2004b.

7. See Hartley 1775, 25.

8. Physiology figures prominently in several studies of Victorian fiction; poetry, though more central to mid-Victorian thinking on physiological experience, figures less frequently in recent literary accounts of the period. Some recent prose studies include Dames 2007; Hardy 1985; Logan 1997; Stedman 2002; and Wood 1991.

9. See Shannon 1960, especially 155–56. My thanks to Herbert Tucker for pointing out the structural parallels between Dobell and Tennyson.

10. For the impact of Mill's science of human nature on Victorian thought, see Postlethwaite 1984, 25–39; and Snyder 2006.

11. I disagree here with Tucker's suggestion that Balder may not actually murder his daughter, but only contemplate the act (Tucker 2004, 439). Whatever the case, Dobell connects the idea of infanticide to an extreme poetic sensationalism.

12. On "unnatural [emotional] intensity" in Victorian dramatic monologues, see Langbaum 1963, especially 88–89.

13. Dobell seems to have experienced the world in much the same Spasmodic fashion that his verses attempt to embody. On traveling through the Welsh mountains by train, for example, he "sat speechless the whole way. All [his] brain made chaos, heaving over and over. Too great for tears or any quick emotions" (letter to his parents, 7 August 1850 [Jolly, 1:120]). Dobell was also ill throughout much of his life, suffering from what his father described in 1844 as a "spasmodic action of the heart" (Jolly, 1:99).

14. Victorian intellectuals agreed for the most part that passionate experience, though dangerous, was a necessary component of great art. Hallam, for example, writes glowingly in 1831 of the "poets of sensation," even while cautioning of the "danger" in "linger[ing] with fond attachment in the vicinity of sense" (Hallam, 87, 88). Mill, too, writes that the greatest of poets write "under the overruling influence of some one state of feeling"—and then warns against "stretching and straining; for strength, as Thomas Carlyle says, does not manifest itself in spasms" (Mill, 1:360, 353).

15. Jonathan Smith calls Lewes's approach to epistemology "controlled imagination" (Smith, 36); George Levine notes that Lewes remained wary that focusing on individual sensation may lead to solipsism (Levine, 182).

16. Levine argues that "[t]he question of how to universalize knowledge, lift it from *mere* contingency and singularity, pervades almost all nineteenth-century thought about how we know. Raw fact is not knowledge at all" (Levine, 68). Postlethwaite

writes that throughout the 1850s, the project for Lewes and his friend Herbert Spencer was to determine "the unity of composition and the multiplicity of adaptation; in man, the animal kingdom, organic creation, and, in a grand progressive synthesis, the cosmos itself" (Postlethwaite, 191). For Lewes's contributions to Victorian thought, see also Dale 1989, especially 59–84.

17. John M. Picker has recently suggested the importance to George Eliot of the German scientist Hermann von Helmholtz, who began work on acoustical physiology in 1856 (see Picker's *Victorian Soundscapes*, especially 84–99). Eliot's essays on poetry in the 1850s predate Helmholtz's important publications on the subject and show Eliot to have been thinking on the matter before she could have known of Helmholtz's work. More likely sources for her early thinking on sound, rhythm, and physiology include Alexander Bain, an acquaintance of both Lewes and Eliot, and the discourse on rhythm inspired by the Spasmodic controversy.

18. In fact, Patmore liked *Maud* and believed it to be metrically stable; see chapter 4.

19. There were cultural dangers for novel-readers as well, as Kate Flint has shown (1993).

20. "Here are mental spasms," writes Aytoun in *Norman Sinclair*, again denouncing the Spasmodic style, "compared with which the writhings of the cholera are languid—here is anatomy of soul more appalling than the demonstrations of Dante" (Aytoun 1861, 2:185).

21. In gesturing to universality, Dobell and his peers show their debts to the Romantic tradition: "[S]pasmodism was Romanticism in bells and whistles, hawking in the limelight of the Victorian market a gospel to which the poets of the early century had given unanimous, if less indiscreet, assent" (Tucker 2004, 429).

22. The details of "Firmilian" and Aytoun's involvement with the Spasmodics are best explained in Weinstein 1968, especially 119–52.

23. On the enthusiastic reception of *Festus*, see, for example, Richard Hengist Horne's 1844 *New Spirit of the Age*, especially 2:283–309.

24. Tennyson's copies of Dobell's *Balder* (no. 866; London: Smith, Elder, and Co., 1854) and Smith's *Poems* (no. 2056; London: Bogue, 1853) are housed at the Tennyson Research Centre in Lincoln, England. Both books are inscribed to Tennyson: Dobell's "with the author's admiration and regard," Smith's "with the author's compliments."

25. Linda K. Hughes connects the poem's "systolic-diastolic rhythms" to the speaker's unsteady consciousness (1987, 161; see also 166–67). For a full consideration of *Maud* as a Spasmodic poem, see Weinstein 1968, 172–83; see also Harrison 1990, 69–89.

26. See Blair 2006b, 205–24.

CHAPTER 4: PATMORE, HOPKINS, AND THE UNCERTAIN BODY OF VICTORIAN POETRY

1. Dennis Taylor suggests that "the New Prosody" as a term for describing the period between 1850 and 1900 dates from T. S. Omond's 1903 *English Metrists* (Taylor, 19). But Hopkins had used the term—privately—to describe his own system, sprung rhythm, in 1880: "The new prosody, Sprung Rhythm, is really quite a simple matter" (Hopkins 1955a, 39). More publicly, and also in 1880, Robert

Bridges notes in the introduction to his *Poems*, third series, that some of his poems "are written by the rules of a new prosody, which may very well exist by the side of the old"; Bridges then gives credit for this new system to Hopkins—"a friend, whose poems remain . . . in manuscript" (Hopkins 1955a, 310).

2. Linda K. Hughes shows that Patmore's revisions of *The Angel in the House* further cemented in place Honoria's metrical firmness: "[F]ar more in the final than in the first edition . . . the female becomes entombed, drained of life and vitality and encased in form" (Hughes 1991, 141).

3. Notable recent work on Patmore's *Essay* includes Prins 1999 and 2005; and D. Taylor 1988.

4. Attridge traces theories of isochrony through Sir Philip Sidney, Thomas Campion, Joshua Steele, and finally Patmore (Attridge 1982, 19–23).

5. John Maynard sees *The Angel* as more conservative than Patmore's other works: "By recovering [Patmore's] early career, virtually obliterated in the final poems, I could see . . . [his] more famous, certainly more notorious, *The Angel in the House* as essentially a conservative moment in his career, in which . . . he submitted to a self-censoring and self-repressive spirit that made that work conform to the more conservative standards of what historians have termed respectable Victorian sexual and gender morality" (Maynard 1996, 444).

6. Maynard is one of very few exceptions; *Victorian Discourses on Sexuality and Religion* offers nearly eighty pages of analysis (Maynard 1993, 193–270).

7. See especially D. Brown 1997 and Beer 1996. Jerome Bump helpfully reminds us that, for all his interest in the sciences, "Hopkins no more thought of his discipline [poetry] as a mirror of popular science than a scientist thinks of his as a mirror of popular poetry"; science was instead a means of "modeling and changing our conception of reality"—and, I would add, a means toward thinking differently about how poetry works (Bump, 89).

8. All quotations from Hopkins's poetry are cited by page and line number.

9. On "the relationship between Christianity and desire" in Hopkins's "Wreck," especially with respect to same-sex desire, see Roden 2002, 109–19; Armstrong writes that the "project of the poem is the attempt to justify the 'lash' of language by restoring and giving meaning to 'unshapeable' sound, just as it attempts to give meaning to the flux of the sea" (Armstrong 1993, 434).

10. See this volume's conclusion for a more thorough discussion of this moment in *Aurora Leigh*.

11. The finger returns in stanza 31: "lovely-felicitous Providence / Fínger of a ténder of, O of a féathery délicacy" (GMH, 127, lines 245–46).

12. Daniel Brown suggests that for Hopkins, "God's presence [is] a huge charge of energy that can be actualized at any moment" (Brown 2000, 154–55).

13. The ship was actually capsized by a "blinding snow" that hit the ship unexpectedly (GMH, 391). My thanks to Meredith Martin for pointing me to this poem.

14. Patmore refers to Gosse's essay in a letter to Bridges, 8 August 1877 (Hopkins 1955b, 42).

15. MacKenzie notes that, for the most part, the lines of "The Wreck of the Deutschland" follow a pattern of 2–3–4–3–5–5–4–6 stresses per line; the first line takes three stresses in the second part of the poem (GMH, 318).

CHAPTER 5: RAPTURE AND THE FLESH, SWINBURNE TO BLIND

1. For a history of nineteenth-century developments in electromagnetism, the most concise and cogent remains Harman 1982; see also Hunt 2003.

2. Alice Jenkins explores the ramifications of the "new spatial imagination" that comes, in part, from Faraday's and Maxwell's work (Jenkins, 1).

3. Three years later, he hypothesized that gravity might also be connected to the other forces: "Surely this force [gravity] must be capable of an experimental relation to Electricity, Magnetism and the other forces, so as to bind it up with them in reciprocal action and equivalent effect" (Faraday 1932–36, 5:150).

4. In *Making It Whole*, Diana Postlethwaite writes on the Victorian desire to see the various components of the world as interconnected; her work on George Eliot, George Henry Lewes, Auguste Comte, Herbert Spencer, and others supports the argument I make here about Swinburne and Blind.

5. I refer, of course, to M. H. Abrams's classic, *The Mirror and the Lamp*, and the metaphors Abrams uses to distinguish between an objective Neoclassicism (with its investment in mirrorlike imitation) and a subjective Romanticism (with its efforts to project, like a lamp, from the author to the reading public). Swinburne, I argue, moves to a third, extreme stage.

6. See also Catherine Maxwell's argument that "Swinburne's readers are meant to experience themselves as physical as well as intellectual beings as the verse communicates simultaneously to the mind and senses, predominantly through that psychologically-charged bodily element: the nerves" (Maxwell 2003, 88).

7. In addition to Prins 1999 and Maxwell 2003, see Armstrong 1993, 402–10; and Blair 2006b, 231–34.

8. James Richardson notes the "dissolution" in Swinburne's poetry "of the border between self and world" (Richardson, 125). Antony Harrison writes of the "desperation" among Swinburne's figures "to escape from the bonds of passion to the freedom of death and continuity with organic nature" (Harrison 1988, 35). Margot K. Louis discusses Swinburne's "sacrament of harmony," through which poetic personae are either "absorbed by" or "in communion with" the natural world (Louis, 50). Matthew Reynolds and Stephanie Kuduk Weiner each remind us of the important political implications in Swinburne's language of union and communality (Reynolds, 276; Kuduk Weiner, 167–69). And Catherine Maxwell has most recently written of *Tristram of Lyonesse* as "a secular gospel in which [Tristram and Iseult] incarnate or embody their author's ideals of love and his wider sense of the vital energies that reverberate through the universe and animate matter" (Maxwell 2006, 112).

9. On Swinburne's use of pathetic fallacy in *Tristram of Lyonesse* (1882), see Maxwell 2006, 112–21. According to Maxwell, though "[t]he pathetic fallacy generally suggests that the perceiver's passion or feeling is projected onto natural objects . . . Swinburne's poem repeatedly seems to say that feeling resides both in nature and its beholders and that they are thus co-involved and reinforce each other" (119).

10. On Swinburne's engagement with Wordsworth, see Harrison 1990, 177–204.

11. By coincidence, in this same letter to Watts, Swinburne notes that he is "most truly sorry . . . for the death of Sydney Dobell" despite never meeting Dobell in person (SL, 2:334).

12. On the connections between Swinburne, Darwin, Tyndall, and Victorian intellectual history, see Dawson 2007, especially 26–81.

13. Kirstie Blair has argued that Swinburne "in the late 1850s and 1860s . . . self-consciously portrayed himself as a spasmodic writer"; "If Swinburne had the acuteness to see through spasmodic poetry and to recognize its defects, he also saw that his own writing at times came dangerously close to resembling it" (Blair 2006a, 185, 186).

14. On Swinburne's theory of poetry and his thoughts on other nineteenth-century poets, see Connolly 1964, especially 64–80.

15. On Swinburne's politics, especially the Republican sympathies of *Songs before Sunrise*, see Rooksby 1997, 150–90; and Kuduk Weiner 2005, 133–80.

16. Speculation on Blind's relationship with Swinburne ranges widely, and most of it appears entirely unfounded: for example, the suggestion that Blind at one point "was throwing herself at [Swinburne]" (McGann 1972, 212).

17. Other recent Blind criticism includes Avery 2000 and LaPorte 2006. Isobel Armstrong writes that Blind "represents what [a gendered tradition in women's poetry from the nineteenth century] could do at its best: it could bring the resources of the affective state to social and political analysis and speculate on the constraints of the definition of feminine subjectivity in an almost innumerable variety of contexts, indirectly and directly" (Armstrong 1993, 377).

18. On Blind's personal history and her connections to radical politics, see Avery 2000 and Diedrick 1999.

19. Groth 1999 is an exception to this rule insofar as Groth situates Blind's poetry among that of other late-nineteenth-century women poets who integrated scientific discourses into their poetry and poetics.

20. Blind diverges from Darwinian theory in her insistence on teleological progress within both the universe and, more specifically, human development (hence her shift to an "Ascent of Man" in place of Darwin's "Descent"). "We must remember," Darwin writes in *The Descent of Man*, "that progress is no invariable rule. . . . Natural selection acts only in a tentative manner. Individuals and races may have acquired certain indisputable advantages, and yet have perished from failing in other characters" (Darwin, 1:177–78). My thanks to George Levine for suggesting to me this important—and no doubt intentional—distinction between Darwin and Blind.

21. On Blind's "*fin-de-siècle* positivism and post-Darwinian atheism," see LaPorte 2006, 433.

22. As Yopie Prins has shown, Meynell had close ties—both personal and poetic—to Patmore (see Prins 2005).

23. O'Shaughnessy "wing[s] his words by breathing into them the soul of music" (Blind 1874, 320).

24. On the Victorian ballad, see Friedman 1861 and Bratton 1975. See also my brief discussion of Victorian ballad culture (Rudy 2003).

CONCLUSION: SPIRITUAL AND MATERIAL POETICS

1. See also Peters 1999, 94; and Taves 1999, 172.

2. Roger Luckhurst's *Invention of Telepathy* offers the best history of the phenomenon and Myers's involvement with it (on Myers, see especially 107–12). See also Oppenheim 1985, 249–66; and Thurschwell 2001, 15–20.

3. For Tennyson, see chapter 2; for Dobell, see chapter 3.

4. See, respectively, Revelation 20, on which "Armageddon" is loosely based, and "The Word became flesh and made his dwelling among us" (John 1:14).

5. Both passages are underlined in pencil; the words set in italics here are marked heavily (Tennyson Research Centre, Lincoln; no. 2134).

6. According to Philip Elliott, "although never satisfied with the proofs spiritualism offer, [Tennyson] remained interested in it until his death" (Elliott, 98).

7. The British Society for Psychical Research was founded in 1882. Serious investigation into spiritualism as a scientific endeavor—tied especially to the emerging field of psychoanalysis—continued well into the twentieth century (and remains for some a study to this day); see Luckhurst, 252–78.

8. See for example letter #98 (ca. December 1819), "I strike the lyre / Who raises in my breast celestial fire" (Barrett Browning 1984, 1:87).

9. Barrett Browning was not without her doubts with respect to Swedenborg: "I can't receive everything," she writes to her friend Isa Blagden in 1853, "and there are points in his theology which don't in my mind, harmonize with the scriptures" (quoted in McAleer, 596).

10. On Barrett Browning's commitment to spiritualism, see Porter 1972, 28–71; and Lewis 1998, 136–42. On Browning's "Mr Sludge," see Armstrong 1964 and Porter 1972, 66–67.

11. Katherine H. Porter notes that "[t]he road from mesmerism to spiritualism was an easy one," given how mesmerism "acquainted people with a number of phenomena regarded as mysterious and abnormal" (Porter, 8).

12. According to Beverly Taylor, Barrett Browning's contemporary reviewers "indicate that it is on the basis of her spirituality that EBB transcends other writers" and that this spirituality derived in large part from Barrett Browning's well-publicized ill health, "her sickroom martyrdom" (Taylor, "Invalid Narratives," n.p.).

13. See Stone 1995, 84–93; Avery and Stott 2003, 82–83.

14. My thanks to Beverly Taylor for pointing me to this passage and suggesting its relevance to my argument.

15. On the physiology of Barrett Browning's poetry, see also Blair 2006b, 119–44; and Zonana 1996.

16. See Weinstein 1968, 187–90; Tucker 2004; and Blair 2006, 129–33. Barrett Browning writes to Horne of having been "much struck by 'Festus'"—Philip James Bailey's epic, which has been viewed by many as the first Spasmodic poem; its author, she judges, must be "a man of genius, & of no ordinary genius. . . . *He* is a man for heights & depths" (21 February 1844; Barrett Browning 1984, 8:216–17).

REFERENCES

Abernethy, John. 1817. *Physiological Lectures, Exhibiting a General View of Mr. Hunter's Physiology, and of His Researches in Comparative Anatomy*. London: Longman.

Abrams, M. H. 1953. *The Mirror and the Lamp: Romantic Theory and the Critical Tradition*. Oxford: Oxford University Press.

"Adelaide Gallery." 1835. *The Penny Magazine of the Society for the Diffusion of Useful Knowledge* 229 (31 October): 417–18.

Albright, Daniel. 1986. *Tennyson: The Muses' Tug-of-War*. Charlottesville: University Press of Virginia.

Aldini, John. 1803. *An Account of the Galvanic Experiments Performed by John Aldini on the Body of a Malefactor Executed at Newgate, Jan. 17, 1803*. London: Cuthell and Martin.

Allen, Grant. 1877. *Physiological Aesthetics*. London: Henry S. King and Co.

Altick, Richard D. 1978. *The Shows of London: A Panoramic History of Exhibitions, 1600–1862*. Cambridge, MA: Belknap.

[Archer, Charles Maybury]. 1848. *The London Anecdotes: The Electric Telegraph*. London: David Bogue.

Armstrong, Isobel. 1964. "Browning's *Mr. Sludge, 'The Medium.'*" *Victorian Poetry* 2:1–9.

———. 1982. *Language as Living Form in Nineteenth-Century Poetry*. Brighton, Sussex: Harvester.

———. 1993. *Victorian Poetry: Poetry, Poetics and Politics*. New York: Routledge.

Attridge, Derek. 1982. *The Rhythms of English Poetry*. London: Longman.

———. 1990. "Rhythm in English Poetry." *New Literary History* 21:1015–37.

Austin, Alfred. 1870. *The Poetry of the Period*. London: Richard Bentley.

Avery, Simon. 2000. "'Tantalising Glimpses': The Intersecting Lives of Eleanor Marx and Mathilde Blind." In *Eleanor Marx (1855–1898): Life, Work, Contacts*, edited by John Stokes, 173–87. Burlington, VT: Ashgate.

Avery, Simon, and Rebecca Stott. 2003. *Elizabeth Barrett Browning*. Harlow, UK: Pearson.

Aytoun, William Edmondstoune. 1852. "The Reform Measures of 1852." *Blackwood's* 71 (March): 369–86.

———. 1854a. "Firmilian: A Tragedy." *Blackwood's* 75 (May): 533–51.

———. 1854b. *Firmilian; or, The Student of Badajoz. A Spasmodic Tragedy* [by "T. Percy Jones"]. Edinburgh: Blackwood and Sons.

———. 1854c. "The New Reform Bill." *Blackwood's* 75 (March): 369–80.

———. 1855. "*Maud*, by Alfred Tennyson." *Blackwood's* 78 (September): 311–21.

———. 1857. "Mrs. Barrett Browning—*Aurora Leigh.*" *Blackwood's* 81 (January): 23–41.

———. 1861. *Norman Sinclair.* 3 vols. Edinburgh: Blackwood and Sons.

———. 1862. "The Rights of Women." *Blackwood's* 92 (August): 183–201.

———. 1867. "Ballad Poetry of Modern Europe." In *Memoir of William Edmondstoune Aytoun*, by Theodore Martin, 226–40. Edinburgh: Blackwood and Sons.

———. 1921. *Poems of William Edmondstoune Aytoun.* London: Oxford University Press.

———. n.d. *Lectures on Literature: Poetry.* MS. 4908. National Library of Scotland, Edinburgh.

"Aytoun's 'Bothwell.'" 1856. *Fraser's* 54:347–58.

Bain, Alexander. 1855. *The Senses and the Intellect.* London: John W. Parker and Son.

———. 1871. *English Composition and Rhetoric: A Manual* [1866]. New York: D. Appleton.

Barker-Benfield, G. J. 1992. *The Culture of Sensibility: Sex and Society in Eighteenth-Century Britain.* Chicago: University of Chicago Press.

Barrett Browning, Elizabeth. 1900. *The Complete Works of Elizabeth Barrett Browning.* 6 vols. New York: Thomas Y. Crowell and Co.

———. 1984–. *The Brownings' Correspondence.* 4 vols. Winfield, KS: Wedgestone.

Beach, Joseph Warren. 1936. *The Concept of Nature in Nineteenth-Century English Poetry.* New York: MacMillan.

Beauchamp, Ken. 2001. *History of the Telegraph.* London: Institute of Electrical Engineers.

Beer, Gillian. 1996. *Open Fields: Science in Cultural Encounter.* Oxford, UK: Clarendon.

Bird, James. 1828. *Dunwich: A Tale of the Splendid City; in Four Cantos.* London: Bladwin and Cradock.

Blair, Kirstie, ed. 2004a. *John Keble in Context.* London: Anthem.

———. 2004b. "Spasmodic Affections: Poetry, Pathology, and the Spasmodic Hero." *Victorian Poetry* 42 (Winter): 473–90.

———. 2006a. "Swinburne's Spasms: *Poems and Ballads* and the 'Spasmodic School.'" *Yearbook of English Studies* 36:180–96.

———. 2006b. *Victorian Poetry and the Culture of the Heart.* Oxford, UK: Clarendon.

———, and Emma Mason, eds. 2006. *Tractarian Poets.* Special issue of *Victorian Poetry* 44 (Spring).

Blind, Mathilde. 1870. "Shelley." *Westminster Review* 94 (July): 75–97.

———. 1874. "Music and Moonlight." *Examiner* (28 March): 320–21.

———. 1884. Review of *The Poetical Works of Frances Anne Kemble.* *Athenaeum* (12 January): 50–51.

———. 1886. *Shelley's View of Nature Contrasted with Darwin's.* London.

———. 1900. *The Poetical Works of Mathilde Blind.* Edited by Arthur Symons. London: T. Fisher Unwin.

———. 1904. *George Eliot* [1883]. Boston.

———. n.d. *The Commonplace Book of Mathilde Blind* [1892–96]. MS. Walpole e.1. Bodleian Library, Oxford University.

———. n.d. *Correspondence and Papers, 1860–1896.* Add. 61927–61930. British Library, London.

Bonds, Mark Evan. 2006. *Music as Thought: Listening to the Symphony in the Age of Beethoven.* Princeton: Princeton University Press.

Boos, Florence S. 2004. "'Spasm' and Class: W. E. Aytoun, George Gilfillan, Sydney Dobell, and Alexander Smith." *Victorian Poetry* 42 (Winter): 553–83.

Bratton, J. S. 1975. *The Victorian Popular Ballad.* Totowa, NJ: Rowman and Littlefield.

Bristow, Joseph. 1996. "Coventry Patmore and the Womanly Mission of the Mid-Victorian Poet." In *Sexualities in Victorian Britain*, edited by Andrew H. Miller and James Eli Adams, 118–39. Bloomington: Indiana University Press.

British Album, The. 1793. 1st American ed. Boston: Belknap and Hall.

Brontë, Charlotte. 2000. *Jane Eyre* [1847]. Peterborough, ON: Broadview.

Brontë, Emily. 1992. *The Complete Poems.* Edited by Janet Gezari. New York: Penguin.

Brown, Daniel. 1997. *Hopkins' Idealism: Philosophy, Physics, Poetry.* Oxford, UK: Clarendon.

———. 2000. "Victorian Poetry and Science." In *Cambridge Companion to Victorian Poetry*, edited by Joseph Bristow, 137–58. Cambridge: Cambridge University Press.

Buchanan, Robert. 1871. "The Fleshly School of Poetry: Mr. D. G. Rossetti." *Contemporary Review* 18:334–50.

Buckley, Jerome H. 1951. "The Spasmodic School." In *The Victorian Temper: A Study in Literary Culture*, 41–65. Cambridge, MA: Harvard University Press.

———. 1960. *Tennyson: The Growth of a Poet.* Boston: Houghton Mifflin.

Bump, Jerome. 1990. "Hopkins as Jesuit Poet" [1982]. In *Critical Essays on Gerard Manley Hopkins*, edited by Alison G. Sulloway, 61–91. Boston: G. K. Hall.

Burke, Edmund. 1968. *A Philosophical Enquiry into the Origin of Our Ideas of the Sublime and Beautiful* [1757]. Edited by James T. Boulton. Notre Dame: University of Notre Dame Press.

———. 1986. *Reflections on the Revolution in France* [1790]. Edited by Conor Cruise O'Brien. New York: Penguin.

Byrne, Paula. 2004. *Perdita: The Literary, Theatrical, Scandalous Life of Mary Robinson.* New York: Random House.

Byron, George Gordon. *The Complete Poetical Works.* Edited by Jerome J. McGann. 7 vols. Oxford, UK: Clarendon.

Cadbury, William. 1966. "The Structure of Feeling in a Poem by Patmore: Meter, Phonology, Form." *Victorian Poetry* 4:237–51.

Cahagnet, L. Alph. 1851. *The Celestial Telegraph; or, Secrets of the Life to Come, Revealed through Magnetism.* New York: J. S. Redfield.

Campbell, Lewis, and William Garnett. 1884. *The Life of James Clerk Maxwell.* London: Macmillan.

Campbell, Matthew. 1999. *Rhythm and Will in Victorian Poetry.* Cambridge: Cambridge University Press.

Carlyle, Thomas. 1980. *The Works of Thomas Carlyle.* Edited by H. D. Traill. 30 vols. New York: AMS Press.

Champneys, Basil. 1900. *Memoirs and Correspondence of Coventry Patmore.* 2 vols. London: George Bell and Sons.

Chandler, James. 1994. "Hallam, Tennyson, and the Poetry of Sensation: Aestheticist Allegories of a Counter-Public Sphere." *Studies in Romanticism* 33:527–37.

[Chorley, Henry]. 1855. Review of *Men and Women*, by Robert Browning. *Athenaeum:* 1327–28.

Christ, Carol T. 1984. *Victorian and Modern Poetics.* Chicago: University of Chicago Press.

Clapp-Itnyre, Alisa. 2000. "Marginalized Musical Interludes: Tennyson's Critique of Conventionality in *The Princess.*" *Victorian Poetry* 38 (Summer): 227–48.

Clayton, Jay. 2003. *Charles Dickens in Cyberspace: The Afterlife of the Nineteenth Century in Postmodern Culture.* Oxford: Oxford University Press.

Clough, Arthur Hugh. 1853. "Recent English Poetry." *North American Review* 77:1–30.

Cohen, Bernard. 1941. *Benjamin Franklin's Experiments.* Cambridge, MA: Harvard University Press.

Coleridge, Samuel Taylor. 1997. *Biographia Literaria* [1817]. London: J. M. Dent.

Connolly, Thomas E. 1964. *Swinburne's Theory of Poetry.* Albany: State University of New York Press.

Cranch, Christopher. 1887. *Ariel and Caliban, with Other Poems.* Boston: Houghton, Mifflin, and Co.

Cronin, Richard. 1990. "Alexander Smith and the Poetry of Displacement." *Victorian Poetry* 28:129–45.

———. 2002. "The Spasmodics." In *A Companion to Victorian Poetry*, edited by Richard Cronin, Alison Chapman, and Antony H. Harrison, 291–304. Malden, MA: Blackwell.

Curran, Stuart. 2002. "Mary Robinson and the New Lyric." *Women's Writing* 9:9–22.

Dale, Peter Allan. 1989. *In Pursuit of a Scientific Culture.* Madison: University of Wisconsin Press.

[Dallas, E. S.] 1852. *Poetics: An Essay on Poetry.* London: Smith, Elder, and Co.

Dames, Nicholas. 2007. *The Physiology of the Novel: Reading, Neural Science, and the Form of Victorian Fiction.* Oxford: Oxford University Press.

Darwin, Charles. 1981. *The Descent of Man, and Selection in Relation to Sex.* [1871]. 2 vols. in one. Princeton: Princeton University Press.

Dawson, Gowan. 2003. "Intrinsic Earthliness: Science, Materialism, and the Fleshly School of Poetry." *Victorian Poetry* 41 (Spring): 113–29.

———. 2007. *Darwin, Literature, and Victorian Respectability.* Cambridge: Cambridge University Press.

Day, Aidan. 1983. "The Spirit of Fable: Arthur Hallam and Romantic Values in Tennyson's 'Timbuctoo.'" *Tennyson Research Bulletin* 4:59–71.

Delbourgo, James. 2006. *A Most Amazing Scene of Wonders: Electricity and Enlightenment in Early America.* Cambridge, MA: Harvard University Press.

Denecke, Daniel. 2001. "The Motivation of Tennyson's Reader: Privacy and the Politics of Literary Ambiguity in *The Princess.*" *Victorian Studies* 43 (Winter): 201–27.

Diedrick, James. 1999. "Mathilde Blind." In *Dictionary of Literary Biography*, vol. 199, *Victorian Women Poets*, 28–39. Detroit: Gale Research.

———. 2002. "'My love is a force that will force you to care': Subversive Sexuality in Mathilde Blind's Dramatic Monologues." *Victorian Poetry* 40:359–86.

Dobell, Sydney. 1854. *Balder: Part the First.* London: Smith, Elder, and Co.

———. 1875. *The Poetical Works of Sydney Dobell.* 2 vols. London: Smith, Elder, and Co.

———. 1876. *Thoughts on Art, Philosophy and Religion.* London: Smith, Elder, and Co.

Doten, Lizzie. 1864. *Poems from the Inner Life* [1863]. Boston: William White.

Draper, Anita B. 1979. "The Artistic Contribution of the 'Weird Seizures' to *The Princess.*" *Victorian Poetry* 17:180–91.

Dyer, George. 1802. "Prefatory Essay: On Lyric Poetry." In *Poems*, vol. 1, i–xci. London: T. N. Longman and O. Rees.

Eagleton, Terry. 1978. "Tennyson: Politics and Sexuality in 'The Princess' and 'In Memoriam.'" In *1848, the Sociology of Literature*, edited by Francis Barker, 97–106. Colchester, UK: University of Essex.

Elfenbein, Andrew. 2006. "Cognitive Science and the History of Reading." *PMLA* 121:484–502.

[Eliot, George]. 1856a. Belles Lettres. *Westminster Review* 66 (January): 290–312.

———. 1856b. Belles Lettres. *Westminster Review* 66 (October): 566–82.

———. 1857a. Belles Lettres. *Westminster Review* 67 (January): 306–26.

———. 1857b. "Worldliness and Other-Worldliness: The Poet Young." *Westminster Review* 67 (January): 1–42.

Eliot, T. S. 1960. *Selected Essays.* New York: Harcourt, Brace and World.

Elliott, Philip. 1979. "Tennyson and Spiritualism." *Tennyson Research Bulletin* 3:89–100.

Ellis, Markman. 1996. *The Politics of Sensibility: Race, Gender and Commerce in the Sentimental Novel.* Cambridge: Cambridge University Press.

Ellison, Julie. 1999. *Cato's Tears and the Making of Anglo-American Emotion.* Chicago: University of Chicago Press.

"Evening with the Telegraph, An." 1851. *Chambers's Edinburgh Journal*, n.s. 15 (4 January): 1–4.

Faraday, Michael. 1932–36. *Faraday's Diary.* 7 vols. London: G. Bell and Sons.

———. 1965. *Experimental Researches in Electricity.* 3 vols. New York: Dover.

[Ferrier, James]. 1844. "Poems by Coventry Patmore." *Blackwood's* 56 (September): 331–42.

Flint, Kate. 1993. *The Woman Reader, 1837–1914.* Oxford, UK: Clarendon.

———. 1997. "Blood, Bodies, and the Lifted Veil." *Nineteenth-Century Literature* 51:455–73.

[Fox, William Johnson]. 1831. "Tennyson's Poems." *Westminster Review* 14 (January): 210–24.

Friedman, Albert B. 1961. *The Ballad Revival: Studies in the Influence of Popular on Sophisticated Poetry.* Chicago: University of Chicago Press.

Frith, Henry. [1888?] *Marvels of Electricity and Magnetism: Being a Popular Account of Modern Electrical and Magnetic Discoveries, Electrical Batteries and Machines, Galvanism, the Electric Telegraph, Electro-Plating, Magnets and Magnetism, the Mariner's Compass, the Electric Light, Animal and Atmospheric Electricity.* London: Ward, Lock and Co.

Frye, Northrop. 1986. "Towards Defining an Age of Sensibility." In *Poets of Sensibility and the Sublime*, edited by Harold Bloom, 11–18. New York: Chelsea House.

Fulford, Tim. 2002. "The Electrifying Mrs Robinson." *Women's Writing* 9:23–35.

Fulford, Tim, Debbie Lee, and Peter J. Kitson. 2004. *Literature, Science, and Exploration in the Romantic Era: Bodies of Knowledge.* Cambridge: Cambridge University Press.

Garnett, Richard. 1910. *The Life of W. J. Fox, Public Teacher and Social Reformer, 1786–1864*. London: J. Lane.

Gaskell, Elizabeth. 1997. *Ruth* [1853]. New York: Penguin.

Gifford, William. 1797. *The Baviad, and Mæviad*. London: J. Wright.

Gilmore, Paul. 2002a. "Aesthetic Power: Electric Words and the Example of Frederick Douglas." *American Transcendental Quarterly* 16:291–311.

———. 2002b. "The Telegraph in Black and White." *ELH* 69:805–33.

———. 2004. "Romantic Electricity, or the Materiality of Aesthetics." *American Literature* 76:467–94.

Goldfarb, Clare R., and Russell M. Goldfarb. 1978. *Spiritualism and Nineteenth-Century Letters*. Rutherford, NJ: Fairleigh Dickinson University Press.

Goodwin, Gregory H. 1987. "Keble and Newman: Tractarian Aesthetics and the Romantic Tradition." *Victorian Studies* 30:475–94.

Gosse, Edmund. 1877. "A Plea for Certain Exotic Forms of Verse." *Cornhill Magazine* 36:53–71.

———. 1905. *Coventry Patmore*. New York: Charles Scribner's Sons.

———. 1927. *The Life of Algernon Charles Swinburne*. Vol. 19 of Swinburne, *Complete Works*. New York: Gabriel Wells.

Gray, F. Elizabeth. 2006. "'Syren Strains': Victorian Women's Devotional Poetry and John Keble's *The Christian Year.*" *Victorian Poetry* 44 (Spring): 61–76.

Groth, Helen. 1999. "Victorian Women Poets and Scientific Narratives." In *Women's Poetry, Late Romantic to Late Victorian: Gender and Genre, 1830–1900*, edited by Isobel Armstrong and Virginia Blain, 325–51. New York: St. Martin's.

Hair, Donald S. 1991. *Tennyson's Language*. Toronto: University of Toronto Press.

Hallam, Arthur. 1972. "On Some of the Characteristics of Modern Poetry." Reprint, *Victorian Scrutinies: Reviews of Poetry, 1830–1870*, edited by Isobel Armstrong, 84–101. London: Athlone. Originally published, *Englishman's Magazine* 1 (August 1831): 616–28.

Hardy, Barbara. 1977. *The Advantage of Lyric: Essays on Feeling in Poetry*. Bloomington: Indiana University Press.

———. 1985. *Forms of Feeling in Victorian Fiction*. London: Peter Owen.

Hargreaves-Mawdsley, W. N. 1967. *The English Della Cruscans and Their Time, 1783–1828*. The Hague: Martinus Nijhoff.

Harman, P. M. 1982. *Energy, Force, and Matter: The Conceptual Developments of Nineteenth-Century Physics*. Cambridge: Cambridge University Press.

Harris, Thomas Lake. 1855. *An Epic of the Starry Heaven* [1854]. New York: Partridge and Brittan.

Harrison, Antony H. 1988. *Swinburne's Medievalism: A Study in Victorian Love Poetry*. Baton Rouge: Louisiana State University Press.

———. 1990. *Victorian Poets and Romantic Poems: Intertextuality and Ideology*. Charlottesville: University Press of Virginia, 1990.

———. 2004. "Victorian Culture Wars: Alexander Smith, Arthur Hugh Clough, and Matthew Arnold in 1853." *Victorian Poetry* 42 (Winter): 509–20.

Hartley, David. 1775. *Hartley's Theory of the Human Mind*. London: J. Johnson.

Hegel, Georg Wilhelm Friedrich. 1993. *Introductory Lectures on Aesthetics*. Translated by Bernard Bosanquet. New York: Penguin.

Heilbron, J. L. 1979. *Electricity in the 17th and 18th Centuries: A Study of Early Modern Physics*. Berkeley: University of California Press.

Hemans, Felicia. 1851. *The Complete Works of Mrs. Hemans*. 2 vols. New York: D. Appleton.

Hill, Jonathan E. 1990. "Thomas Hood." In *British Romantic Poets, 1789–1832: Second Series*, edited by John R. Greenfield, 144–56. Detroit: Thomson Gale.

Hoffmann, E. T. A. 1975. "Beethoven's Instrumental Music" [1810]. Translated by R. Murray Schafer. In *E. T. A. Hoffmann and Music*, edited by R. Murray Schafer, 81–89. Toronto: University of Toronto Press.

Hood, Thomas. 1920. *The Complete Poetical Works of Thomas Hood*. Edited by Walter Jerrold. London: Oxford University Press.

Hopkins, Gerard Manley. 1955a. *The Correspondence of Gerard Manley Hopkins and Richard Watson Dixon*. Edited by Claude Colleer Abbott. London: Oxford University Press.

———. 1955b. *The Correspondence of Gerard Manley Hopkins to Robert Bridges*. Edited by Claude Colleer Abbott. London: Oxford University Press.

———. 1956. *Further Letters of Gerard Manley Hopkins, Including His Correspondence with Coventry Patmore*. London: Oxford University Press.

———. 1959. *The Journals and Papers of Gerard Manley Hopkins*. London: Oxford University Press.

———. 1990. *The Poetical Works of Gerard Manley Hopkins*. Edited by Norman H. Mackenzie. Oxford, UK: Clarendon.

Horne, Richard Hengist, ed. 1844. *A New Spirit of the Age*. 2 vols. London: Smith, Elder and Co.

Hughes, Linda K. 1987. *The Manyfacèd Glass: Tennyson's Dramatic Monologues*. Athens: Ohio University Press.

———. 1991. "Entombing the Angel: Patmore's Revisions of *Angel in the House*." In *Victorian Authors and Their Works: Revision, Motivations and Modes*, edited by Judith Kennedy, 140–68. Athens: Ohio University Press.

———. 2004. "Alexander Smith and the Bisexual Poetics of *A Life-Drama*." *Victorian Poetry* 42 (Winter): 491–508.

———. 2005. *Graham R.: Rosamund Marriott Watson, Woman of Letters*. Athens: Ohio University Press.

Hume, David. 1999. *An Enquiry Concerning Human Understanding* [1748]. Edited by Tom L. Beauchamp. Oxford: Oxford University Press.

Hunt, Bruce J. 2003. "Electrical Theory and Practice in the Nineteenth Century." In *The Cambridge History of Science*, vol. 5, *The Modern Physical and Mathematical Sciences*, edited by Mary Jo Nye, 311–27. Cambridge: Cambridge University Press.

Jackson, Virginia, and Yopie Prins. 1999. "Lyrical Studies." *Victorian Literature and Culture* 27:521–30.

Janowitz, Anne. 1998. *Lyric and Labour in the Romantic Tradition*. Cambridge: Cambridge University Press.

Jeffrey, Francis. 1829. Review of *Records of Woman, with Other Poems* and *The Forest Sanctuary, with Other Poems*, by Felicia Hemans. *Edinburgh Review* 50 (October): 32–47.

Jenkins, Alice. 2007. *Space and the "March of Mind": Literature and the Physical Sciences in Britain, 1815–1850*. Oxford: Oxford University Press.

Johnston, W. J., ed. 1882. *Lightning Flashes and Electric Dashes: A Volume of Choice Telegraphic Literature, Humor, Fun, Wit and Wisdom* [1877]. New York: W. J. Johnston.

J[olly], E[mily], ed. 1878. *The Life and Letters of Sydney Dobell*. 2 vols. London: Smith, Elder, and Co.

Kant, Immanuel. 1987. *Critique of Judgment* [1790]. Translated by Werner S. Pluhar. Indianapolis: Hackett.

Keats, John. 2002. *Selected Letters*. Edited by Robert Gittings. Oxford: Oxford University Press.

Keble, John. 1912. *Keble's Lectures on Poetry, 1832–1841*. 2 vols. Translated by Edward Kershaw Francis. Oxford, UK: Clarendon.

Kelly, Gary. 2002. Introduction to *Felicia Hemans: Selected Poems, Prose, and Letters*, 15–85. Peterborough, ON: Broadview.

Killham, John. 1958. *Tennyson and* The Princess: *Reflections of an Age*. London: Athlone Press.

Kingsley, Charles. 1850. "Tennyson." Review of *In Memoriam, The Princess*, and *Poems*. *Fraser's* 42 (September): 245–55.

———. 1855. "Tennyson's *Maud*." *Fraser's* 52 (September): 264–73.

Kipling, Rudyard. 1994. *Collected Stories*. Edited by Robert Gottlieb. New York: Knopf.

Kittler, Friedrich. 1990. *Discourse Networks, 1800/1900* [1985]. Translated by Michael Metteer, with Chris Cullens. Stanford: Stanford University Press.

———. 1999. *Gramophone, Film, Typewriter* [1986]. Translated by Geoffrey Winthrop-Young and Michael Wutz. Stanford: Stanford University Press.

Kuduk Weiner, Stephanie. 2005. *Republican Politics and English Poetry, 1789–1874*. New York: Palgrave.

Labbe, Jacqueline M. 2000. *The Romantic Paradox: Love, Violence and the Uses of Romance, 1760–1830*. New York: St. Martin's.

Langbaum, Robert. 1963. *The Poetry of Experience: The Dramatic Monologue in Modern Literary Tradition*. New York: Norton.

LaPorte, Charles. 2004. "Spasmodic Poetics and Clough's Apostasies." *Victorian Poetry* 42 (Winter): 521–36.

———. 2006. "Atheist Prophecy: Mathilde Blind, Constance Naden, and the Victorian Poetess." *Victorian Literature and Culture* 34:427–41.

———, and Jason R. Rudy, eds. 2004. *Spasmodic Poetry and Poetics*. Special issue of *Victorian Poetry* 42 (Winter).

Leavis, F. R. 1966. "Gerard Manley Hopkins" [1932]. In *Hopkins: A Collection of Critical Essays*, edited by Geoffrey H. Hartman, 17–36. Englewood Cliffs, NJ: Prentice Hall.

Leighton, Angela. 1992. *Victorian Women Poets: Writing against the Heart*. Charlottesville: University Press of Virginia.

Levine, George. 2002. *Dying to Know: Scientific Epistemology and Narrative in Victorian England*. Chicago: University of Chicago Press.

Lewes, George Henry. 1853. "Poems of Alexander Smith." *Westminster Review* 59 (April): 522–34.

————. 1877. *Problems of Life and Mind*. Vol. 2, *The Physical Basis of Mind*. London: Trübner.

Lewis, Linda M. 1998. *Elizabeth Barrett Browning's Spiritual Progress: Face to Face with God*. Columbia: University of Missouri Press.

[Lister, Thomas Henry]. 1834. Review of *Philip van Artevelde*, by Henry Taylor. *Edinburgh Review* 60 (October): 1–24.

[Lockhart, J. G.] 1834. Review of *Philip van Artevelde*, by Henry Taylor. *Quarterly Review* 51:365–91.

Logan, Peter Melville. 1997. *Nerves and Narratives: A Cultural History of Hysteria in 19th-Century British Prose*. Berkeley: University of California Press.

Longinus. 1906. *On the Sublime*. Translated by A. O. Prickard. Oxford, UK: Clarendon.

Lootens, Tricia. 1994. "Hemans and Home: Victorianism, Feminine 'Internal Enemies,' and the Domestication of National Identity." *PMLA* 102:238–53.

————. 1996. *Lost Saints: Silence, Gender, and Victorian Literary Canonization*. Charlottesville: University Press of Virginia.

Louis, Margot K. 1990. *Swinburne and His Gods: The Roots and Growth of an Agnostic Poetry*. Montreal: McGill-Queen's University Press.

Luckhurst, Roger. 2002. *The Invention of Telepathy, 1870–1901*. Oxford: Oxford University Press.

Mackintosh, T[homas] S[immons]. 1846. *The "Electrical Theory" of the Universe; or, The Elements of Physical and Moral Philosophy*. 1st American ed., reprinted from the London edition of 1838. Boston: Josiah P. Mendum.

Mahon, Basil. 2003. *The Man Who Changed Everything: The Life of James Clerk Maxwell*. Chichester, UK: Wiley.

Markley, A. A. 2004. *Stateliest Measures: Tennyson and the Literature of Greece and Rome*. Toronto: University of Toronto Press.

Martin, Theodore. 1867. *Memoir of William Edmondstoune Aytoun*. Edinburgh: Blackwood and Sons.

Mason, Emma. 2003. "'Some God of Wild Enthusiast's Dreams': Emily Brontë's Religious Enthusiasm." *Victorian Literature and Culture* 31:263–77.

————. 2004a. "'Her Silence Speaks': Keble's Female Heirs." In *John Keble in Context*, edited by Kirstie Blair, 125–41. London: Anthem.

————. 2004b. "Rhythmic Numinousness: Sydney Dobell and 'The Church.'" *Victorian Poetry* 42 (Winter): 537–51.

————. 2006. *Women Poets of the Nineteenth Century*. Tavistock: Northcote.

Maudsley, Henry. 1870. *Body and Mind: An Inquiry into Their Connection and Mutual Influence, Specially in Reference to Mental Disorders*. London: Macmillan.

Maxwell, Catherine. 2003. "Swinburne: Style, Sympathy, and Sadomasochism." *Journal of Pre-Raphaelite Studies* 12:86–96.

————. 2006. *Swinburne*. Tavistock: Northcote.

Maynard, John. 1993. *Victorian Discourses on Sexuality and Religion*. Cambridge: Cambridge University Press.

————. 1996. "The Unknown Patmore." *Victorian Poetry* 34:443–55.

McAleer, Edward C. 1951. "New Letters from Mrs. Browning to Isa Blagden." *PMLA* 66:594–612.

McGann, Jerome. 1972. *Swinburne: An Experiment in Criticism.* Chicago: University of Chicago Press.

———. 1996. *The Poetics of Sensibility: A Revolution in Literary Style.* Oxford, UK: Clarendon.

McSweeney, Kerry. 1973. "Swinburne's 'By the North Sea.'" *Yearbook of English Studies* 3:222–31.

Mee, Jon. 2003. *Romanticism, Enthusiasm, and Regulation: Poetics and the Policing of Culture in the Romantic Period.* Oxford: Oxford University Press.

Menke, Richard. 2005. "Media in America, 1881: Garfield, Guiteau, Bell, Whitman." *Critical Inquiry* 31 (Spring): 638–64.

———. 2008. *Telegraphic Realism: Victorian Fiction and Other Information Systems.* Stanford: Stanford University Press.

Mermin, Dorothy. 1989. *Elizabeth Barrett Browning: The Origins of a New Poetry.* Chicago: University of Chicago Press.

Meynell, Alice. 1896. *The Rhythm of Life, and Other Essays* [1893]. London: John Lane.

Mill, John Stuart. 1981. *Collected Works.* Edited by John M. Robson and Jack Stillinger. 19 vols. Toronto: University of Toronto Press.

Mineka, Francis E. 1944. *The Dissidence of Dissent: The Monthly Repository, 1806–1838.* Chapel Hill: University of North Carolina Press.

More, Hannah. 1852. *The Works of Hannah More.* 2 vols. New York: Harper and Brothers.

Morrell, Jack, and Arnold Thackray. 1981. *Gentlemen of Science: Early Years of the British Association for the Advancement of Science.* Oxford, UK: Clarendon.

Morus, Iwan Rhys. 1998. *Frankenstein's Children: Electricity, Exhibition, and Experiment in Early-Nineteenth-Century London.* Princeton: Princeton University Press.

Mullan, John. 1988. *Sentiment and Sociability: The Language of Feeling in the Eighteenth Century.* Oxford, UK: Clarendon.

———. 1997. "Sensibility and Literary Criticism." In *Cambridge History of Literary Criticism*, vol. 4, *The Eighteenth Century*, edited by H. B. Nesbet and Claude Rawson, 419–33. Cambridge: Cambridge University Press.

Munro, John. 1891. *Heroes of the Telegraph.* London: Religious Tract Society.

Myers, Frederic William Henry. 1902. *Wordsworth.* New York: Harper and Brothers.

———. 1904. *Fragments of Prose and Poetry.* Edited by Eveleen Myers. New York: Longmans, Green, and Co.

Nicolson, Harold. 1962. *Tennyson.* Garden City, NY: Anchor Books.

Nixon, Jude V. 2002. "'Death blots black out': Thermodynamics and the Poetry of Gerard Manley Hopkins." *Victorian Poetry* 40 (Summer): 131–55.

Olsen, Charles. 1997. *Collected Prose.* Berkeley: University of California Press.

Omond, T[homas] S[teward]. 1903. *A Study of Metre.* London: Grant Richards.

Oppenheim, Janet. 1985. *The Other World: Spiritualism and Psychical Research in England, 1850–1914.* Cambridge: Cambridge University Press.

Otis, Laura. 2001. "The Other End of the Wire: Uncertainties of Organic and Telegraphic Communication." *Configurations* 9:181–206.

Pancaldi, Giuliano. 2003. *Volta: Science and Culture in the Age of Enlightenment.* Princeton: Princeton University Press.

Para, Marcello. 1992. *The Ambiguous Frog: The Galvani-Volta Controversy on Animal Electricity*. Translated by Jonathan Mandelbaum. Princeton: Princeton University Press.

Pascoe, Judith. 1997. *Romantic Theatricality: Gender, Poetry, and Spectatorship*. Ithaca, NY: Cornell University Press.

Patmore, Coventry. 1844. *Poems*. London: Edward Moxon.

———. 1848. Review of Tennyson's *Poems*, 4th ed., and *The Princess*. *North British Review* 9 (May): 23–39.

———. 1850. Review of *In Memoriam*, by Alfred Tennyson. *North British Review* 13 (August): 287–99.

———. 1855. "Tennyson's *Maud*." *Edinburgh Review* 102 (October): 498–519.

———. 1856. "New Poets." *Edinburgh Review* 104 (October): 337–62.

———. 1898. *Principle in Art*. Rev. ed. London: George Bell and Sons.

———. 1921. *Courage in Politics and Other Essays, 1885–1896*. London: Oxford University Press.

———. 1949. *The Poems of Coventry Patmore*. Edited by Frederick Page. London: Oxford University Press.

———. [1857] 1961. *Essay on English Metrical Law*. Washington, DC: Catholic University of America Press.

Peters, John Durham. 1999. *Speaking into the Air: A History of the Idea of Communication*. Chicago: University of Chicago Press.

Picker, John. 2003. *Victorian Soundscapes*. Oxford: Oxford University Press.

Pierson, Robert M. 1996. "Coventry Patmore's Ideas Concerning English Prosody and *The Unknown Eros* Read Accordingly." *Victorian Poetry* 34:493–518.

Pinch, Adela. 1996. *Strange Fits of Passion: Epistemologies of Emotion, Hume to Austen*. Stanford: Stanford University Press.

Plato. 1953. *The Dialogues of Plato*. 4th ed. 4 vols. Translated by Benjamin Jowett. Oxford, UK: Clarendon.

Plotz, John. 2000. *The Crowd: British Literature and Public Politics*. Berkeley: University of California Press.

"Poems of Alexander Smith, The." 1853. *Putnam's Monthly Magazine* 2 (July): 94–100.

Poliziano, Angelo. 2004. *Silvae*. Translated by Charles Fantazzi. Cambridge, MA: Harvard University Press.

Porter, Katherine H. 1972. *Through a Glass Darkly: Spiritualism in the Browning Circle* [1958]. New York: Octagon Books.

Postlethwaite, Diana. 1984. *Making It Whole: A Victorian Circle and the Shape of Their World*. Columbus: Ohio State University Press.

Poston, Lawrence. 1978. "Wordsworth among the Victorians: The Case of Sir Henry Taylor." *Studies in Romanticism* 17:293–305.

———. 1980. "*Philip van Artevelde*: The Poetry and Politics of Equipose." *Victorian Poetry* 18:383–91.

———. 1986. "Poetry as Pure Act: A Coleridgean Ideal in Early Victorian England." *Modern Philology* 84:162–84.

Priestley, Joseph. 1775. *History and Present State of Electricity*. 2 vols. [1767]. London: C. Bathurst and T. Lowndes.

Prins, Yopie. 1999. *Victorian Sappho*. Princeton: Princeton University Press.

———. 2000. "Victorian Meters." In *Cambridge Companion to Victorian Poetry*, edited by Joseph Bristow, 89–113. Cambridge: Cambridge University Press.

———. 2005. "Patmore's Law, Meynell's Rhythm." In *The Fin-de-Siècle Poem: English Literary Culture and the 1890s*, edited by Joseph Bristow, 261–84. Athens: Ohio University Press.

Review of *The Ascent of Man*, by Mathilde Blind. 1889. *Athenaeum* (20 July): 87–88.

Review of *Bothwell*, by W. E. Aytoun. 1856. *London Quarterly Review* 7:201–8.

Review of *England in Time of War*, by Sydney Dobell. 1856. *Saturday Review* 2:304–5.

Review of *Tales and Historic Scenes*, by Felicia Hemans. 1819. *Edinburgh Monthly Review* 2 (August): 194–209.

Reynolds, Matthew. 2001. *The Realms of Verse, 1830–1870: English Poetry in a Time of Nation-Building*. Oxford: Oxford University Press.

Richards, Eliza. 2004. *Gender and the Poetics of Reception in Poe's Circle*. Cambridge: Cambridge University Press.

Richardson, Alan. 2001. *British Romanticism and the Science of the Mind*. Cambridge: Cambridge University Press.

Richardson, James. 1988. *Vanishing Lives: Style and Self in Tennyson, D. G. Rossetti, Swinburne, and Yeats*. Charlottesville: University Press of Virginia.

Ricks, Christopher. 1972. *Tennyson*. New York: MacMillan.

Riede, David G. 1978. *Swinburne: A Study of Romantic Mythmaking*. Charlottesville: University Press of Virginia.

Riskin, Jessica. 2002. *Science in the Age of Sensibility: The Sentimental Empiricists of the French Enlightenment*. Chicago: University of Chicago Press.

Ritterbush, Philip C. 1964. *Overtures to Biology: The Speculations of Eighteenth-Century Naturalists*. New Haven, CT: Yale University Press.

Robinson, Mary. 1895. *Memoirs of Mary Robinson, "Perdita," from the Edition Edited by Her Daughter*. London: Gibbings and Co.

———. 2000. *Selected Poems*. Edited by Judith Pascoe. Peterborough, ON: Broadview.

Robson, Catherine. 2005. "Standing on the Burning Deck: Poetry, Performance, History." *PMLA* 120:148–62.

Roden, Frederick S. 2002. *Same-Sex Desire in Victorian Religious Culture*. New York: Palgrave.

Roe, Nicholas. 2001. "Introduction: Samuel Taylor Coleridge and the Sciences of Life." In *Samuel Taylor Coleridge and the Sciences of Life*, edited by Nicholas Roe, 1–21. Oxford: Oxford University Press.

Rooksby, Rikky. 1997. *A. C. Swinburne: A Poet's Life*. Aldershot, UK: Scholar Press.

Ross, Marlon B. 1989. *The Contours of Masculine Desire: Romanticism and the Rise of Women's Poetry*. Oxford: Oxford University Press.

Rudy, Jason R. 2003. "On Cultural Neoformalism, Spasmodic Poetry, and the Victorian Ballad." *Victorian Poetry* 41 (Winter): 590–96.

———. 2006. "Hemans' Passion." *Studies in Romanticism* 45 (Winter): 543–62.

Ruskin, John. 1912. *Complete Works of John Ruskin*. Edited by E. T. Cook and Alexander Wedderburn. 39 vols. London: George Allen.

Russell, G. W. 1877. "The Song of the Plug." In *Lightning Flashes and Electric Dashes*, edited by W. J. Johnston, 28. New York: W. J. Johnston.

Ruston, Sharon. 2005. *Shelley and Vitality*. New York: Palgrave.

Saintsbury, George. 1895. *Corrected Impressions: Essays on Victorian Writers*. New York: Dodd, Mead and Co.

Saville, Julia. 2000. *A Queer Chivalry: The Homoerotic Asceticism of Gerard Manley Hopkins*. Charlottesville: University Press of Virginia.

Scheinberg, Cynthia. 2002. *Women's Poetry and Religion in Victorian England: Jewish Identity and Christian Culture*. Cambridge: Cambridge University Press.

Schmidt, Leigh Eric. 2000. *Hearing Things: Religion, Illusion, and the American Enlightenment*. Cambridge, MA: Harvard University Press.

Sconce, Jeffrey. 2000. *Haunted Media: Electric Presence from Telegraphy to Television*. Durham, NC: Duke University Press.

Scott, Grant F. 1994. *The Sculpted Word: Keats, Ekphrasis, and the Visual Arts*. Hanover, NH: University Press of New England.

Sedgwick, Eve Kosofsky. 1985. *Between Men: English Literature and Male Homosocial Desire*. New York: Columbia University Press.

Shaftesbury, Anthony A. C. 2005. *Characteristics of Men, Manners, Opinions, Times, with a Collection of Letters*, vol. 1. Basil, 1790; facsimile reprint, Elibron Classics.

Shannon, Edgar F., Jr. 1960. "The History of a Poem: Tennyson's *Ode on the Death of the Duke of Wellington*." *Studies in Bibliography* 13:150–79.

Shelley, Percy Bysshe. 1965. *The Complete Works*. Edited by Roger Ingpen and Walter E. Peck. 10 vols. New York: Gordian Press.

Smee, Alfred. 1850. *Instinct and Reason: Deduced from Electro-biology*. London: Reeve, Benham, and Reeve.

Smith, Adam. 1984. *The Theory of Moral Sentiments* [1759]. Indianapolis: Liberty Fund.

Smith, Albert. 1846. "Tracts for the Trains." Pt. 1. *Illustrated London News* (21 March): 200.

Smith, Alexander. 1868. *Last Leaves: Sketches and Criticism*. Edinburgh: W. P. Nimmo.

Smith, Jonathan. 1994. *Fact and Feeling: Baconian Science and the Nineteenth-Century Literary Imagination*. Madison: University of Wisconsin Press.

Snyder, Laura J. 2006. *Reforming Philosophy: A Victorian Debate on Science and Society*. Chicago: University of Chicago Press.

Southey, Robert. 2000. *Wat Tyler* [1817]. In *Five Romantic Plays, 1768–1821*, edited by Paul Baines and Edward Burns, 71–99. Oxford: Oxford University Press.

Spencer, Herbert. 1868. "The Origin and Function of Music." *Fraser's* (October 1857); reprinted in Spencer, *Essays: Scientific, Political, and Speculative*, 210–38. London: Williams and Norgate.

Spillane, John D. 1981. *The Doctrine of the Nerves: Chapters in the History of Neurology*. Oxford: Oxford University Press.

Standage, Tom. 1998. *The Victorian Internet: The Remarkable Story of the Telegraph and the Nineteenth Century's On-line Pioneers*. New York: Walker and Co.

Stedman, Gesa. 2002. *Stemming the Torrent: Expression and Control in the Victorian Discourses on Emotions, 1830–1872*. Burlington, VT: Ashgate.

Sterling, John. 1842. Review of *Poems*, by Alfred Tennyson. *Quarterly Review* 70 (September): 385–416.

Stewart, Susan. 2002. *Poetry and the Fate of the Senses.* Chicago: University of Chicago Press.

Stiles, Anne, ed. 2007. *Neurology and Literature, 1860–1920.* New York: Palgrave.

Stone, Marjorie. 1995. *Elizabeth Barrett Browning.* New York: St. Martin's.

Stubbs, Katherine. 2003. "Telegraphy's Corporeal Fictions." In *New Media, 1740–1915,* edited by Lisa Gitelman and Geoffrey B. Pingree, 91–111. Cambridge, MA: MIT Press.

Swedenborg, Emanuel. 1844. *On the Intercourse of the Soul and the Body, Which Is Supposed to be Effected Either by Physical Influx, or by Spiritual Influx, or by Pre-established Harmony.* London: Newbery.

Swinburne, Algernon Charles. 1925–27. *The Complete Works of Algernon Charles Swinburne.* Edited by Sir Edmund Gosse and Thomas James Wise. "Bonchurch Edition." 20 vols. New York: Gabriel Wells.

———. 1959–62. *The Swinburne Letters.* Edited by Cecil Y. Lang. 6 vols. New Haven, CT: Yale University Press.

———. 1964. *New Writings by Swinburne, or Miscellanea Nova et Curiosa.* Edited by Cecil Y. Lang. Syracuse, NY: Syracuse University Press.

"Sydney Dobell's Poems on the War." 1856. *National Review* 3:442–48.

Taves, Ann. 1999. *Fits, Trances, and Visions: Experiencing Religion and Explaining Experience from Wesley to James.* Princeton: Princeton University Press.

Taylor, Beverly. 1992. "'School-Miss Alfred' and 'Materfamilias': Female Sexuality and Poetic Voice in *The Princess* and *Aurora Leigh.*" In *Gender and Discourse in Victorian Literature and Art,* edited by Antony H. Harrison and Beverly Taylor, 5–29. DeKalb: Northern Illinois University Press.

———. n.d. "Invalid Narratives." Unpublished chapter from a book in progress: *Elizabeth Barrett Browning: The Poetics of Engagement.* 58 pages.

Taylor, Dennis. 1988. *Hardy's Metres and Victorian Prosody.* Oxford, UK: Clarendon.

Taylor, Henry. 1834. *Philip van Artevelde: A Dramatic Romance.* 2nd ed. 2 vols. London: Edward Moxon.

Tennyson, Alfred. 1971. *Tennyson's Poetry.* Edited by Robert W. Hill Jr. New York: Norton.

———. 1981–87. *The Letters of Alfred, Lord Tennyson.* Edited by Cecil Y. Lang and Edgar F. Shannon. 3 vols. Cambridge, MA: Harvard University Press.

———. 1987. *The Poems of Tennyson.* 2nd ed. Edited by Christopher Ricks. 3 vols. Harlow, UK: Longman.

Tennyson, Charles. 1949. *Alfred Tennyson.* London: MacMillan.

Tennyson, G. B. 1981. *Victorian Devotional Poetry: The Tractarian Mode.* Cambridge, MA: Harvard University Press.

Tennyson, Hallam. 1897. *Alfred Lord Tennyson: A Memoir.* 2 vols. New York: Macmillan.

Thurschwell, Pamela. 2001. *Literature, Technology and Magical Thinking, 1880–1920.* Cambridge: Cambridge University Press.

Todd, Janet. 1986. *Sensibility: An Introduction.* London: Methuen.

Tsur, Reuven. 1998. *Poetic Rhythm: Structure and Performance; An Empirical Study in Cognitive Poetics.* Berne: Peter Lang.

Tucker, Herbert F. 1988. *Tennyson and the Doom of Romanticism.* Cambridge, MA: Harvard.

———. 2004. "Glandular Omnism and Beyond: The Victorian Spasmodic Epic." *Victorian Poetry* 42 (Winter): 429–50.

Tupper, Martin Farquhar. 1860. *Three Hundred Sonnets*. London: Arthur Hall, Virtue, and Co.

Tyndall, John. 1874. *Advancement of Science: The Inaugural Address*. New York: Asa K. Butts.

———. 1905. "The Constitution of Nature" [1865]. In *Fragments of Science*, 7–32. New York: P. F. Collier and Son.

Ure, Andrew. 1819. "An Account of Some Experiments Made on the Body of a Criminal Immediately after Execution, with Physiological and Practical Observations." *Quarterly Journal of Science, Literature and the Arts* 6:283–94.

Warren, Alba H., Jr. 1950. *English Poetic Theory, 1825–1865*. Princeton: Princeton University Press.

Weinstein, Mark A. 1968. *William Edmondstoune Aytoun and the Spasmodic Controversy*. New Haven, CT: Yale University Press.

Whewell, William. 1859. *History of the Inductive Sciences, from the Earliest to the Present Time*. 3rd ed. 2 vols. New York: D. Appleton.

White, Norman. 1992. *Hopkins: A Literary Biography*. Oxford, UK: Clarendon.

Whitman, Walt. 1982. *Complete Poetry and Collected Prose*. New York: Library of America.

Wilde, Oscar. 1989. *Complete Works of Oscar Wilde: Stories, Plays, Poems and Essays*. New York: Harper and Row.

Wilson, A. N. 2003. *The Victorians*. New York: Norton.

Wilson, Grant, and John Fiske, eds. 1888–89. *Appleton's Cyclopaedia of American Biography*. 6 vols. New York: D. Appleton and Co.

[Wilson, John]. 1832. "Tennyson's Poems." *Blackwood's* 31 (May): 721–41.

Winter, Alison. 1998. *Mesmerized: Powers of Mind in Victorian Britain*. Chicago: University of Chicago Press.

Wolfson, Susan. 2006. *Borderlines: The Shiftings of Gender in British Romanticism*. Stanford: Stanford University Press.

Wood, Jane. 1991. *Passion and Pathology in Victorian Fiction*. Oxford: Oxford University Press.

Woolf, Virginia. 1986. "Aurora Leigh" [1931]. In *The Second Common Reader*, 202–13. New York: Harcourt Brace Jovanovich.

Wordsworth, William. 1965. *Selected Poems and Prefaces*. Edited by Jack Stillinger. Boston: Houghton Mifflin.

Yeo, Richard. 1993. *Defining Science: William Whewell, Natural Knowledge, and Public Debate in Early Victorian Britain*. Cambridge: Cambridge University Press.

Zonana, Joyce. 1996. "The Embodied Muse: Elizabeth Barrett Browning's *Aurora Leigh* and Feminist Poetics." In *Victorian Women Poets: A Critical Reader*, edited by Angela Leighton, 53–74. Cambridge, MA: Blackwell.

INDEX

Abernethy, John, 22, 191n4
Adelaide Gallery of Practical Science, 44–46, 58, 74
affect, 5, 68–69, 79, 168; as figure for community, 19, 25, 32–33, 40, 48, 63, 66, 199n17; as mode of poetic communication, 7, 21, 24, 28, 31, 34, 36, 42, 46, 47, 51, 55, 74, 84, 93, 94, 168; as religious, 134
Aldini, John, 22
Allen, Grant, 146–47, 163, 165
Armstrong, Isobel, 11, 13, 52, 130, 134, 151, 197n9, 199n17
Arnold, Matthew, 80, 103
associative philosophy. *See* empiricism
Attridge, Derek, 10, 114, 125, 197n4
Austin, Alfred: *The Poetry of the Period*, 183
Avery, Simon, 199n18
Aytoun, William Edmondstoune, 79, 80–81, 82, 91, 99–106, 111, 112, 119, 122, 131, 145; on the ballad, 99–101, 104–5; as cultural conservative, 99–105; *Works: Bothwell*, 104; "Execution of Montrose," 100–101; *Firmilian*, 80, 102–4, 113; *Norman Sinclair*, 100, 102

Bailey, Philip James, 113; *Festus*, 105–6
Bain, Alexander, 10, 98, 138, 163, 190n12; *The Senses and the Intellect*, 82–83, 84, 86
ballad, 70, 91, 99–101, 104, 166, 199n24
Barrett Browning, Elizabeth, 5, 16, 113, 140, 165, 187; and materialism, 177–79; political idealism of, 181–83; and spasmody, 200n16; as spiritualist poet, 176–83, 200nn9–10. *Works: Aurora Leigh*, 11, 101–2, 131, 179–81;

Casa Guidi Windows, 182–83; *A New Spirit of the Age*, 74, 181–82; "A Vision of Poets," 177–79, 180
Bird, James, 147–48
Blair, Kirstie, 9, 14, 81, 108, 199n13
Blind, Mathilde, 5, 15–16, 110, 136, 140, 154–69, 179, 185; and evolutionary poetics, 156–62; and ideas on women, 161–66; and natural sympathy ("rapture"), 163–69; political upbringing of, 155, and Shelley, 155, 160, 164–66, 168; and spiritualism, 176. *Works: The Ascent of Man*, 15, 155–62; *Dramas in Miniature*, 161–66; "A Mother's Dream," 164, 176; "The Mirror of Diana," 167–68; "The Russian Student's Tale," 162–66
Bridges, Robert, 133, 135, 196n1, 197n14
British Association for the Advancement of Science, 46, 145
Brontë, Charlotte: *Jane Eyre*, 81
Brontë, Emily, 175–76
Browning, Elizabeth Barrett. *See* Barrett Browning, Elizabeth
Browning, Robert, 78, 90, 113, 177, 185; and Swinburne, 141
Buchanan, Robert, 8, 12, 144–45, 153. *See also* "Fleshly School of Poetry, The"
Burke, Edmund, 7, 69
Byron, George Gordon, 26, 55, 140, 151; conservative critique of, 54; electric metaphor in *Childe Harold's Pilgrimage*, 24–25; and Felicia Hemans, 39–41

Campbell, Matthew, 9, 130
Carlyle, Thomas, 76–77, 88, 99, 100